I0010414

Apache Roller 4.0
Beginner's Guide

A comprehensive, step-by-step guide on how to set up, customize, and market your blog using Apache Roller

Alfonso V. Romero

PUBLISHING

BIRMINGHAM - MUMBAI

Apache Roller 4.0
Beginner's Guide

Copyright © 2009 Packt Publishing

All rights reserved. No part of this book may be reproduced, stored in a retrieval system, or transmitted in any form or by any means, without the prior written permission of the publisher, except in the case of brief quotations embedded in critical articles or reviews.

Every effort has been made in the preparation of this book to ensure the accuracy of the information presented. However, the information contained in this book is sold without warranty, either express or implied. Neither the author, nor Packt Publishing, and its dealers and distributors will be held liable for any damages caused or alleged to be caused directly or indirectly by this book.

Packt Publishing has endeavored to provide trademark information about all of the companies and products mentioned in this book by the appropriate use of capitals. However, Packt Publishing cannot guarantee the accuracy of this information.

First published: December 2009

Production Reference: 1071209

Published by Packt Publishing Ltd.
32 Lincoln Road
Olton
Birmingham, B27 6PA, UK.

ISBN 978-1-847199-50-8

www.packtpub.com

Cover Image by Tina Negus (tina_manthorpe@sky.com)

Credits

Author
Alfonso V. Romero

Reviewers
Tarkan Karadayi
Ricardo Javier Romero

Acquisition Editor
James Lumsden

Development Editor
Swapna Verlekar

Technical Editors
Conrad Sardinha
Mazhar Shaikh

Copy Editor
Sanchari Mukherjee

Editorial Team Leader
Gagandeep Singh

Project Team Leader
Priya Mukherji

Project Coordinator
Zainab Bagasrawala

Indexer
Rekha Nair

Proofreader
Lynda Sliwoski

Production Coordinator
Shantanu Zagade

Cover Work
Shantanu Zagade

Foreword

Roller is not the most popular blog server out there, or the one with the most plugins and themes—that distinction goes to WordPress—but Roller can be the best choice in many situations. For an IT department seeking a Java-based blog server to run on their existing Java EE application server, Roller is the most complete open source option out there. It's also the best choice for developers looking to build full-fledged blogging features into an existing product. Roller's business-friendly Apache license means you can use Roller's code in your product even if your product is closed-source and commercial.

Alfonso's book fills a very important need for those of us who do find Roller the best choice. Roller has a basic installation guide, user guide, and template author guide. Roller also has user and developer mailing lists where you can ask questions and get some support from other Roller users. What this book provides, you won't find in the stock Roller documentation: illustrated, in-depth, and step-by-step instructions that explain how to setup, customize, and start blogging with Apache Roller.

Whether you're setting up an Apache Roller site for your own personal use or helping to set up a site for thousands of bloggers, this book is a great starting point for everybody involved.

David M. Johnson
Founder of Apache Roller
http://rollerweblogger.org/roller

About the Author

Alfonso V. Romero has been working with Linux and Open Source Software since 1999, when he started operating his first Web server (Apache) from a PC at home. Since then he's been working as a Computer consultant for LASECLAT & ProEco Laboratories in Mexico, along with several other clients, as a Java, C++, and web applications developer. He also works for Pearson Education in Mexico as a Computer Books Freelance Translator and Consultant. When he's not experimenting with new trends in Open Source and .NET applications, he enjoys spending some quality time with his beautiful wife, his three kids and his three dogs, or playing his old electric Ibanez guitar.

He's also a big fan of Stephen King, and one of his maximum aspirations is to write a fiction novel, but his passion for computers and information technology keeps him busy as a technical writer.

To my lovely wife Adelina, whose patience, love, encouragement, and support kept me working on this extreme project every time I just felt like bailing out... We finally made it through, baby! I love you very, very much! My heart will always be yours!

To my two daughters Adelina and Arlae, and to my son Alfonso Jr., because every time I got writer's block they always managed to cheer me up with a smile, a kiss or a hug... I love you infinitely, guys!

To my mother and father, for her unconditional support and for always showing me that patience, perseverance and stubbornness will always help you achieve whatever you're up to.

To all the staff at Packt Publishing for turning this dream into reality... Special thanks to: Kshipra, James, Swapna, and Zainab, who were always willing to answer my questions and coach me through the long journey of writing this book.

And last, but not least, to Dave Johnson, creator of Apache Roller, the best blog server I've ever worked with!

About the Reviewers

Tarkan Karadayi has been writing code since age 14. He has a Masters in Computer Science and is currently working as a Lead Developer.

> I would like to thank my wife Anna, my parents, and my three sons Taran, Kyle, and Ryan for their love and support.

Ricardo Javier Romero is an Electronic Systems Engineer with over thirteen years of software development experience, both as a developer and as a team leader, in many of the technologies that have surfaced over the past few years.

He has worked on military projects, and is currently a team leader for an oil and gas service company, focusing on .NET development in C#, C++, and MFC, as well as web development and database engines.

He has also translated two technical books into Spanish, and worked extensively in web development when the Internet was still in its infancy, using JavaScript, VBScript, and ASP.NET.

When he's not delving into his love for all things technical, he works on his screenwriting, filmmaking, and music.

Table of Contents

Preface

This hands-on and practical book introduces you to Apache Roller. Starting off with the configuration and installation of your own blog, you'll then quickly learn how to add interesting content to your blog, with the help of plenty of examples. You'll also learn how to change your blog's visual appearance with the help of Roller themes and templates and how to create a community of blogs for you and your colleagues or friends in your Apache Roller blog server. The book will also look at ways in which you can manage your community, and keep your site safe and secure, ensuring that it is a spam-free, enjoyable community for your users.

What this book covers

Chapter 1, *An Introduction to Weblogs*, gives you insight on weblogs and how they can be used to create a worldwide presence through the blogosphere. It also teaches you the difference between a blog and a CMS, the basics about newsfeeds and the important role they play for blogs, and how you can use them to spread information on the blogosphere.

Chapter 2, *Installing Roller on Windows*, teaches you how to install Apache Roller in a Windows environment, along with all the supporting software required—Apache web server, JDK SE 6, Tomcat servlet engine, and MySQL database server.

Chapter 3, *Installing Roller on Linux*, teaches you how to install Apache Roller in a Linux Ubuntu environment, along with all the supporting software required—Apache web server, JDK SE 6, Tomcat servlet engine, and MySQL database server.

Chapter 4, *How to Start Working with Roller*, teaches you the basics about blogging with Apache Roller, and how to manage the blogroll—an important element of every blog that shows up on the front page. You'll see how to create your first user and weblog, adjust basic settings of your server and weblog, create and edit weblog entries (posts), manage categories, use the Rich Text Editor included in Roller in order to enhance the appearance of your post, and maximize your front page's space by means of the Summary field.

Chapter 5, *Spicing Up Your Blog*, teaches you about all the different tools available on the Internet that can help you build a very attractive weblog for your visitors. You'll learn how to upload files to your blog and use the Rich Text Editor to insert images, sound files, and videos, change the file uploading size limit of your blog server in order to upload bigger files, and use Google Maps, YouTube, and SlideShare to embed maps, videos, and document presentations in your blog.

Chapter 6, *Roller Themes and Blog Promotion*, teaches you how to change your Roller weblog theme, download additional themes, and promote your weblog on all the popular bookmarking services. You'll learn how to choose a weblog theme from Roller's administration interface, download additional themes and install them in your Roller weblog server, create an account in No-IP.com—a dynamic DNS service provider—to run your Roller weblog from your own PC, open the web port (80) via port forwarding on your DSL modem/router firewall, and add a Digg It button to your weblog so that visitors can vote for your posts on the Digg.com social bookmarking website.

Chapter 7, *Working with Templates*, teaches you how to create and edit your first template in Roller, along with some basics about the Velocity template language, and how to create your first Roller theme from scratch. You'll also learn about Roller's model and data objects, and how to use these objects' properties, methods, and macros in a custom template to show data from your weblog.

Chapter 8, *Comments and Trackbacks*, will show you how to work with comments and trackbacks in your Apache Roller blog, using Roller's comment management tools to approve, disapprove, and delete comments. You'll also learn to moderate comments in Roller using comment management tools, avoid spam, and use all the anti-spam tools available in Roller, and how trackbacks can help you in interacting with other bloggers.

Chapter 9, *Advanced Topics*, will show you "some stuff" that will help in promoting your blog and creating your own weblog community. You will learn to manage group blogs, use aggregators and blog search engines, and configure Google webmaster tools to find out about visitors to your blog. You will also learn to use Google docs as a web client to publish entries, use podcasts in your weblog entries to attract visitors, and Planet Roller to aggregate external blogs along with your Roller blog.

Chapter 9 is not a part of the book, but you can download it from Packt's website. It is available at //www.packtpub.com/files/9508-Chapter-9-Advanced-Topics.pdf.

What you need for this book

Basically, you'll need a PC with Windows XP/Vista or Ubuntu Linux installed (you can use other Linux distributions, just be sure they have the GNOME desktop manager to follow all the exercises in this book), a text editor, and a web browser. In Windows, you can use Internet Explorer 7 or Mozilla Firefox 3 (or later versions); in Linux you can use Mozilla Firefox 3 or later.

The latest Apache Roller release is 4.0.1, and before installing it you'll need the following software:

- Apache web server 2.2.11 or later
- Java JDK 6 Update 1 or later
- Apache Tomcat 6.0.18 or later
- MySQL Community Server 5.1.33 or later
- JavaMail API 1.4.2 or later
- JavaBeans Activation Framework API 1.1.1 or later
- MySQL Connector/J 5.1.7 or later
- mod_jk Connector 1.2.28 or later

Who this book is for

If you are interested in establishing a blog, using Apache Roller and popular web applications to write attractive posts, and promoting your blog on all the major social bookmarking services, this book is for you. No previous experience on Tomcat, MySQL, the Apache web server, or Linux required.

Conventions

In this book, you will find several headings appearing frequently.

To give clear instructions of how to complete a procedure or task, we use:

Time for action – heading

1. Action 1
2. Action 2
3. Action 3

Instructions often need some extra explanation so that they make sense, so they are followed with:

What just happened?

This heading explains the working of tasks or instructions that you have just completed.

You will also find some other learning aids in the book, including:

Pop quiz – heading

These are short multiple choice questions intended to help you test your own understanding.

Have a go hero – heading

These set practical challenges and give you ideas for experimenting with what you have learned.

You will also find a number of styles of text that distinguish between different kinds of information. Here are some examples of these styles, and an explanation of their meaning.

Code words in text are shown as follows: "With the mod_jk connector, Apache and Tomcat will share the http://localhost address without conflicts."

A block of code is set as follows:

```
installation.type=auto
database.configurationType=jndi
database.jndi.name=jdbc/rollerdb
mail.configurationType=jndi
mail.jndi.name=mail/Session
```

When we wish to draw your attention to a particular part of a code block, the relevant lines or items are set in bold:

```
<param name="src" value=
"http://localhost/roller/main/resource/video/
  showvbox_controller.swf" />
<param name="bgcolor" value="#1a1a1a" />
```

New terms and **important words** are shown in bold. Words that you see on the screen, in menus or dialog boxes for example, appear in the text like this: "In the **Edit Entry** page, go to the **Content** field and click on the **Toggle HTML Source** button."

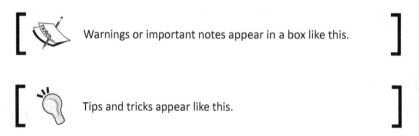

Warnings or important notes appear in a box like this.

Tips and tricks appear like this.

Reader feedback

Feedback from our readers is always welcome. Let us know what you think about this book—what you liked or may have disliked. Reader feedback is important for us to develop titles that you really get the most out of.

To send us general feedback, simply send an email to feedback@packtpub.com, and mention the book title via the subject of your message.

If there is a book that you need and would like to see us publish, please send us a note in the **SUGGEST A TITLE** form on www.packtpub.com or email suggest@packtpub.com.

If there is a topic that you have expertise in and you are interested in either writing or contributing to a book on, see our author guide on www.packtpub.com/authors.

Customer support

Now that you are the proud owner of a Packt book, we have a number of things to help you to get the most from your purchase.

Downloading the example code for the book

Visit http://www.packtpub.com/files/code/9508_Code.zip to directly download the example code.

The downloadable files contain instructions on how to use them.

Errata

Although we have taken every care to ensure the accuracy of our content, mistakes do happen. If you find a mistake in one of our books—maybe a mistake in the text or the code—we would be grateful if you would report this to us. By doing so, you can save other readers from frustration, and help us to improve subsequent versions of this book. If you find any errata, please report them by visiting http://www.packtpub.com/support, selecting your book, clicking on the **let us know** link, and entering the details of your errata. Once your errata are verified, your submission will be accepted and the errata added to any list of existing errata. Any existing errata can be viewed by selecting your title from http://www.packtpub.com/support.

Piracy

Piracy of copyright material on the Internet is an ongoing problem across all media. At Packt, we take the protection of our copyright and licenses very seriously. If you come across any illegal copies of our works, in any form, on the Internet, please provide us with the location address or web site name immediately so that we can pursue a remedy.

Please contact us at copyright@packtpub.com with a link to the suspected pirated material.

We appreciate your help in protecting our authors, and our ability to bring you valuable content.

Questions

You can contact us at questions@packtpub.com if you are having a problem with any aspect of the book, and we will do our best to address it.

1
An Introduction to Weblogs

*Welcome to the world of blogging with Apache Roller! In this first chapter of the book, you will learn some useful facts about blogs, and how you can use them to become a part of the **blogosphere**—a term used in the blogging world to describe all the blogs on the Internet as one giant community. We'll also see several examples about promoting your business or professional activities, how you can get in touch with customers (or potential customers) for your business, express your ideas, hobbies, feelings, and share your experiences with other bloggers. This chapter is designed to illustrate the world of blogs to absolute newcomers. It is intended to foster thoughts and ideas as to how you might use and gain advantage from blogs. Of course, it may be that you are well aware of the blogosphere, and are itching to get your feet wet with Apache Roller straightaway. If so, please feel free to skip ahead to the next chapter which shows you how to install Roller. If, however, you want to learn more about blogs, we shall:*

- Learn about the basic concepts of a blog, and what you can do with it
- See a comparison between blogs and Content Management Systems (CMS)
- Learn how newsfeeds can help to promote your blog

Are you ready? Let's begin.

Basic concepts about weblogs

Before we start with some examples and exercises, let's review some common terms used in the blogging arena:

Term	Definition	Tip
Weblog	A website that shows text entries, or posts in a chronological order.	The terms blog and weblog are interchangeable; you can use a weblog as a personal diary, as a journal to record your activities during working hours, to share photos from your last family vacation, and so on.
Post	An individual entry of a weblog.	In a post, you can include text, images, sounds and videos, links to other posts/websites, and so on. A post always includes the date and time of its creation.
Comment	A text-based response to a post.	Comments are very useful both for bloggers and blog visitors. They help to establish a two-way communication.
Newsfeed (or Feed)	A collection of the most recent posts and comments from a weblog in XML format (RSS or Atom feeds).	Newsfeeds can help you receive the latest information from any blog through RSS or Atom feeds. And you can offer these newsfeeds from your blog, too.
Newsfeed Reader	An application used to read one or more RSS or Atom feeds.	A feed reader gets you the latest information from one or more blogs, without even having to visit them!

These are just some of the terms we're going to use extensively in this chapter.

What can you do with a weblog?

Maybe we should rephrase the title of this section as "What can't you do with a weblog?", as the only limit is your imagination! We're about to take a ride along the cyber-universe of the blogosphere, where you'll see some interesting ways in which people use blogs.

Express your feelings to the world

One of the most popular uses of weblogs is to express people's thoughts and feelings. When you publish a post, it shows up in your weblog's front page. But if you know how to take advantage of websites such as Google, Technorati, Dzone, Digg, and Slashdot, among others, what you write can be read by hundreds, thousands, or even millions of people!

Time for action – a little visit to Technorati

In this little exercise, we're going to visit the Technorati website (`http://www.technorati.com`) and see how some people use their blogs to express their feelings and opinions about fiction writing.

It's very likely that your search results will differ from the ones shown in the following exercise, because Technorati updates its listings daily.

1. Open your web browser and go to `http://www.technorati.com`. Then, type **fiction writing** in the **search the blogosphere...** field and hit *Enter* or click on the magnifying glass icon. After a few seconds, Technorati will show you the latest posts related to your search. Your screen will look like the following screenshot:

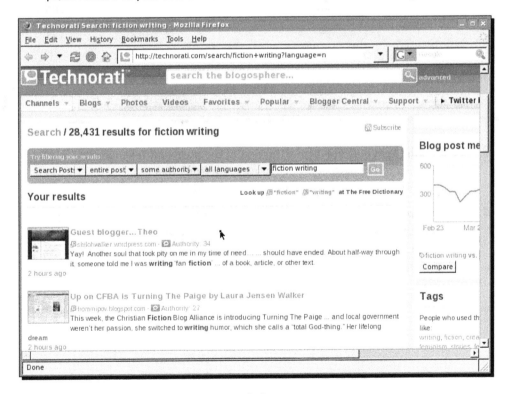

2. Move your mouse over the first post that appeared on the list (in the previous screenshot, the one named **Guest blogger... Theo**) and click on it. Technorati will show more information about the post, the blog, and the blogger, as shown in the following screenshot:

3. Click on the light blue link below the title of the post, and Technorati will take you to the blog where this post came from, that is `http://shilohwalker.wordpress.com`.

4. From there, you can continue browsing through the other posts in the blog, or you can return to Technorati and search for more blogs of the same subject, or change the search words to get information about other subjects.

What just happened?

Congratulations! You've just entered into the world of blogs and the blogosphere! Technorati is just one of several popular social bookmarking websites (or aggregators), where you can search for posts, which people like you publish on their websites. In the previous example, we saw that when you enter one or more search words, Technorati shows you a list of all the related posts and their corresponding blogs. There are millions of bloggers who use their own blogs to express their feelings and opinions. These blogs show up on Technorati, Digg, Dzone, del.icio.us, and many more social bookmarking websites, virtually covering every imaginable category or subject. With this book and Apache Roller, you're going to learn how to become one of them, and express your thoughts to the world through the blogosphere!

An **aggregator** is a website dedicated to collect information about other websites that share something in common. For example, Technorati aggregates blogs and classifies them into categories, as you saw in the previous example.

Get in touch with other people

Blogs let you express your feelings and thoughts, but that's not the only thing they can do. The real power invested in them is that, people can not only read your posts but can also interact with you, by means of the comments they leave! Your blog can help you start a two-way conversation; for example, let's say you write something about your favorite Italian dish. A couple of hours later, your post shows up on Technorati and someone reads it. As a result, the reader leaves a comment saying that it's his/her favorite dish, too. Now you can respond to that comment and maybe post something else about other Italian dishes. Suddenly, you realize there are several readers commenting about your posts and you decide to use your blog as an Italian food community! As you can see, a blog is not only static text; it's a dynamic tool that people can use every day to get in touch with other people who share their same interests.

Time for action – leaving comments on other people's weblogs

In this exercise, you'll visit my personal blog and leave a comment on one of its posts.

1. Open your web browser and go to `http://blog.ibacsoft.com`. There are several categories on this weblog such as **all**, **roller**, **general**, **java**, **linux**, and **games** as shown in the following screenshot (upper section of the screen):

2. Select the **roller** category to show only the posts related to it. Now scroll to the **How I ended up with Apache Roller as my main blog** post, and click on the **Read More** link, as in the following screenshot:

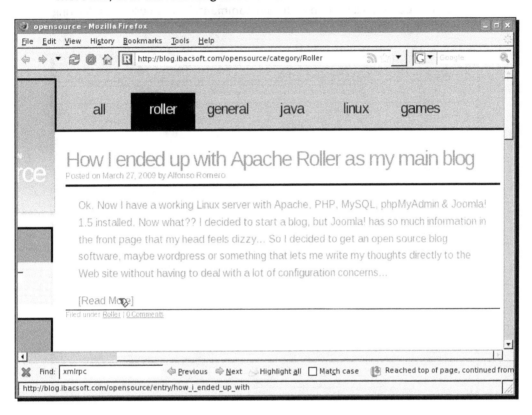

3. Next, scroll down to the **Comments** section and fill in the **Name, E-Mail**, and **URL** fields with your name, e-mail, and the URL of your website (if you have one) respectively. Select the **Notify me by email of new comments** checkbox and fill in the **Your Comment:** section with your comment. You can use the following screenshot as a guide:

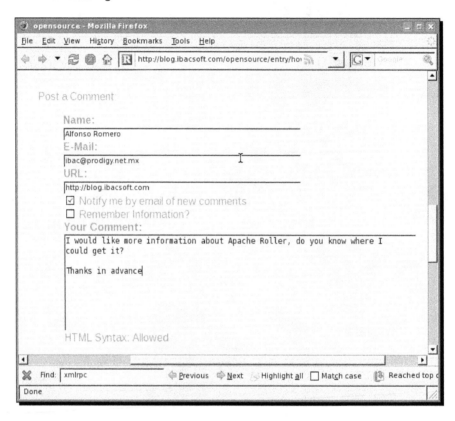

4. To send the comment, scroll down to the textbox below the **Please answer this simple math question** text and type the correct answer to validate your comment, as in the following screenshot:

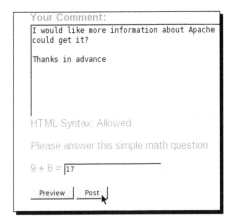

 Nowadays people use **validators** very frequently on websites where anyone can leave comments, as in the above example. There are several types of validators, but the basic operation is the same—they help us to avoid spam attacks caused by robots, as they can't answer to the validation question like an ordinary user would.

5. Click on the **Post** button to send your comment. If your answer is correct, Roller will take you back to the same post and will show your new comment below it, along with your name, the date and time you sent it, and the **Your comment has been accepted** message as shown in the next screenshot:

What just happened?

In the previous exercise, we saw how to leave a comment on a weblog. This is one of the most powerful uses of blogs—someone posts about a subject you're interested in, then you leave a comment on that post, and later the owner of that post answers you back with another comment. If you leave your e-mail, both can establish a two-way communication! With Apache Roller and this book, you'll learn how to make blogs and interact with other blog owners in the ever-expanding blogosphere universe.

Promote your business or professional activities

At the time of writing this book, a lot of companies are already using blogs to promote their products and services. There are employees from several companies who use internal blogs to communicate with other employees, and external blogs to communicate with clients, potential clients, and anyone who's interested in their professional activities, or even their hobbies. The beauty of it is that you can mix posts of your activities at work, along with posts of your hobbies and personal interests. Moreover, if someone has the same hobby as yours, he/she will be attracted to your blog. He/She will also see the other posts you have, including any promotional message about your professional activities, the company you work in, or your small business. The possibilities with this type of "free advertising" are endless.

Time for action – Microsoft employee blogs

In this exercise, we'll visit the Microsoft Community Blogs website, where you can see what Microsoft employees are writing in their blogs.

1. Type `http://www.microsoft.com/communities/blogs` in the address bar of your web browser. Next, the **Microsoft Community Blogs** page will appear:

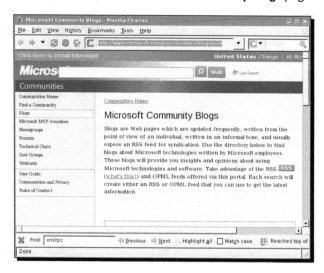

2. Scroll down the page until you see a search box and a list of blogs with recent posts:

3. Type **open source** in the **Keywords (Optional)** field inside **Search Microsoft Community Blogs** and click on the **Go** button. After a few seconds, you will see a list of all the blogs related to the search word(s) you typed:

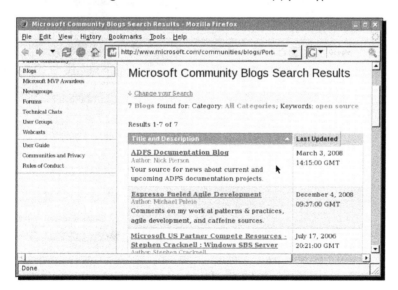

4. Scroll down the list until you find the **Port 25: Open Source Community at Microsoft** blog, as shown in the following screenshot:

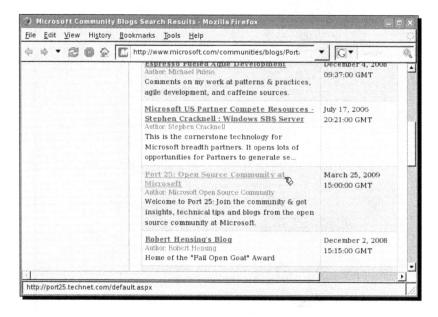

If you can't find it in the list, you can type the following URL: `http://port25.technet.com`. Next, the **Port 25** home page will appear, as shown in the next screenshot (it's very likely that your screen will have a different post on the front page, as this blog changes almost everyday):

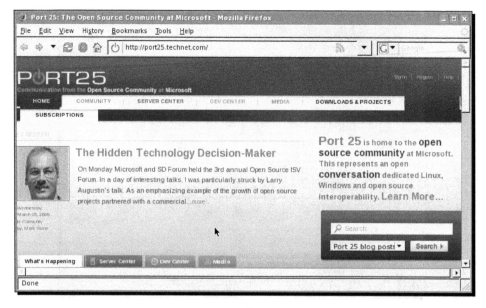

What just happened?

In this last exercise, you saw how Microsoft is making use of blogs so that its employees can communicate the latest news about Microsoft's posture on open source to the world. **Port 25** is a weblog dedicated to the open source community at Microsoft. Here you'll find discussions and posts on open source projects that Microsoft is collaborating with, or intends to collaborate with. However, Port 25 is just one little piece of the vast universe of employee blogs floating around. Some blogs are hosted on Microsoft websites, and others are hosted on employees' personal sites. All in all, you'll find a lot of interesting things about Microsoft and also about its employees' hobbies, personal experiences, and thoughts in general. This is a trend that's expanding through a lot of big companies nowadays.

Share experiences with other users

As we saw in previous exercises, blogs are a very powerful way to communicate with other people. That's the reason why big companies such as Microsoft let their employees use blogs to communicate within the company's premises (internal blogs) or with the rest of the world (external or personal blogs). For the open source community, blogs are the best tool to share their experiences and expertise on using open source software such as Linux, Apache Roller, WordPress, the Apache Web server, Tomcat, MySQL, PHP, and Java Web applications, and much more. For example, if you are working on an open source application, you can invite other fellow programmers and web designers through your blog to collaborate with you. With Apache Roller, you can create a multiuser weblog where several users can post messages (including yourself), and keep up-to-date on every aspect of the software you are developing. Then, you can release downloads so that other people can test your software and post comments on your blog about it. And all of this without even having to move away from your PC!

Who's using Apache Roller

I must say that one of the main reasons I decided to write a book about Apache Roller is the fact that the Apache Software Foundation converted Roller into an official Apache project in March 2007. Along with that, Roller is used by companies such as Sun, IBM, the N.C. State University, and the JRoller Java blogging community. Those facts definitely show that Roller is one of the best open source blogging solutions for personal use, and also for small or big communities, undoubtedly. In the next subsection, we'll see several examples of blogs and blog communities that use Apache Roller.

Rollerweblogger.org

This site hosts the Roller project announcements blog; it also hosts Dave Johnson's personal weblog. Dave is the original creator of Roller. If you go to `http://www.rollerweblogger.org`, you will see the latest news about Apache Roller development:

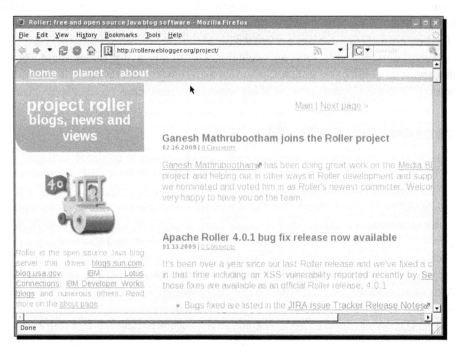

From here, you can follow the links to the `http://apache.roller.org` website, where you can download Apache Roller. There's also a link to Dave Johnson's personal weblog, and several links to the downloads, the Roller Wiki, the mailing lists, and an issue tracker for developers.

Blogs.sun.com

The `http://blogs.sun.com` site hosts several thousand blogs for Sun employees. In this site, you'll find everything about Sun and its employees, what projects are they working on, a video blog from Jonathan Schwartz, CEO of Sun Microsystems, Inc., and a lot of Java talk. You can even leave comments on some of the blogs. Imagine talking directly to the CEO of one of the most important companies in the computing industry! Who knows, maybe he could get you an exciting job!

Blog.usa.gov

This is the **U.S. government blog** site (`http://blog.usa.gov`). The bloggers are federal employees who work in the Office of Citizen Services and Communications at the U.S. General Services Administration. Here, you'll find useful information about services provided by the government of the United States.

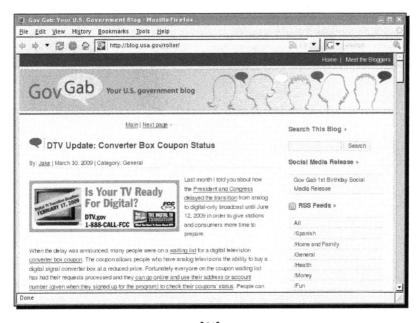

IBM developerWorks blogs

In this site (`http://www.ibm.com/developerworks/blogs/`), you'll find a lot of resources for software developers and IT professionals. You can also create an account and get involved in the community, sharing your IT knowledge. This would be a perfect place to create the next killer application, don't you think?

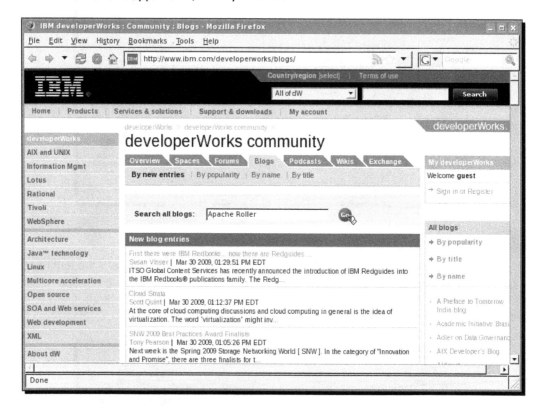

JRoller community

JRoller (`http://www.jroller.com`) is a community of webloggers who share their knowledge and expertise about Java-related technologies. If you're into Java programming, this is a good resource to learn all you can!

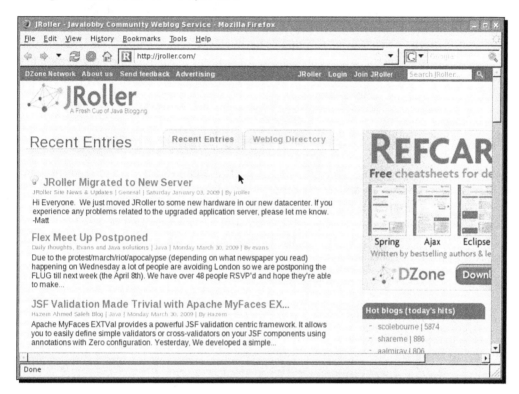

Weblogs versus Content Management Systems

When I started looking for open source software to create a blog, there were a lot of choices. I focused on several applications that were considered **Content Management Systems** (or **CMS**). At first glance, I thought it was just another name for blog applications, but when I downloaded and installed Joomla!®, it was clear that a CMS is more than a blog. In fact, if you want to use a CMS as a blog, it's very likely you'll need to download additional modules, because a CMS can do a lot of things besides blogging. For example, you can have an integrated forum, the news at the front page does not necessarily have a chronological order, some CMS systems have a chat and a photo gallery, and a lot of other things that were very confusing for me. All I wanted was, a blog where I could start writing stuff about computers, programming languages, and tutorials to share with other bloggers, and who knows, maybe one day start writing the next fiction bestseller!

A blog is not a CMS

In most cases, a blog is considered a CMS because it's used to manage content in a website. However, in my humble opinion, a *blog definitely is not a CMS*. With a CMS, you can do a lot more than post messages in a chronological order and receive comments. That beats one of the main purposes of a blog—to express yourself in a friendly environment, like a personal diary. Sure, you can use a CMS as a blog, but you'll have to learn how to manage its user interface and maybe add a few extra modules or plugins. With a weblog server like Apache Roller, you're ready to go! In later chapters, we'll talk about templates and how to modify the appearance of your blog's pages by adding video, audio, and images. You'll see how easy it is to manage your Apache Roller server.

Blogs and newsfeeds – the world is your audience

Thanks to newsfeeds, you can make your blog's posts available for people to read through Technorati, Digg, del.icio.us, and all the other social bookmarking sites or aggregators. Basically, you first need to register on the aggregator site, then configure your weblog to ping the social bookmarking site. After that, each time you post on your blog, it will ping Technorati, Digg, DZone, and so on, and the aggregator will pick up the latest content from your blog by means of your RSS feed.

The following diagram shows the full process with Technorati:

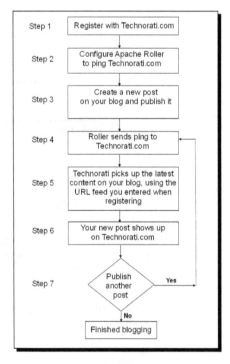

This is basically the same process for all social bookmarking sites and aggregators. So, as you can see, the URL feed (or newsfeed) of your blog helps you to promote your blog on the blogosphere!

What is a newsfeed

In short, a **newsfeed** (or **feed**) is a summary of the latest posts and comments of your blog in XML. The two formats used by Roller, and by almost every other weblog application and aggregator, are *RSS* and *Atom*. The following table shows these two formats—a brief description and an URL example of each one.

Feed Format	Definition	Example URL used by Roller
RSS	A collection of several related feed formats used to publish information (blog entries, audio, video, podcasts) in a standard format. The most recent standard is RSS 2.0.	`http://blog.ibacsoft.com/` `opensource/feed/entries/rss`
Atom	The Atom Syndication Format is a newer standard for newsfeeds, intended to replace RSS.	`http://blog.ibacsoft.com/` `opensource/feed/entries/atom`

At the time of this writing, both formats are widely used. Atom can be considered as the future of newsfeeds, but only time will prove it. In the meantime, we can use both of them.

How can a newsfeed help to promote your blog

When you subscribe to Technorati and Digg, every time you publish a post, your blog sends a ping, telling Technorati and Digg to check your most recent posts and to include them in their lists by means of an RSS or Atom feed. Then, visitors from Technorati and Digg go to your blog and, if they find it interesting, can subscribe to your RSS or Atom feeds. The following exercise will show you the process of subscribing to a newsfeed.

Time for action – subscribing to a newsfeed

In this exercise, you'll visit the Apache `rollerweblogger.org` site and subscribe to its Atom newsfeed. The web browser used in this exercise is Mozilla Firefox 3.0.4. You can download it for free from `http://www.mozilla.com`. You can use other web browsers such as Internet Explorer and Safari, but then the steps described in this exercise could be slightly different.

1. Open your web browser and go to `http://rollerweblogger.org`. Select the 🔲 button, located to the right of the address bar, as shown in the following screenshot:

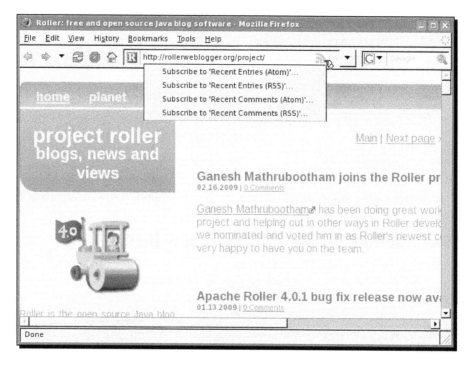

2. Select **Subscribe to 'Recent Entries (Atom)'** from the pop-up list. Next, you will see a **Subscribe to this feed using Live Bookmarks** message, along with a list of the most recent entries from the weblog:

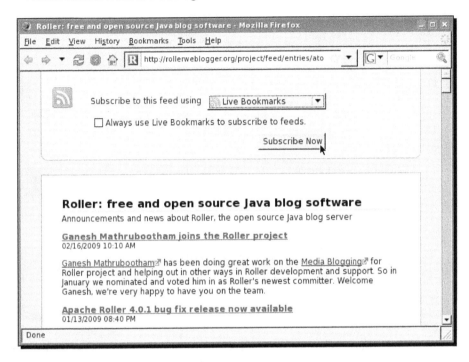

3. Click on the **Subscribe Now** button, and the **Add Live Bookmark** dialog will appear. Click on the **Add** button of this dialog box to finish the subscription process. The Atom feed will be added to your list of live bookmarks in Mozilla Firefox.

4. To verify that the subscription worked, click on the **Bookmarks** menu and select **Roller: free and open source java blog software** to see all the entries included in the Atom feed:

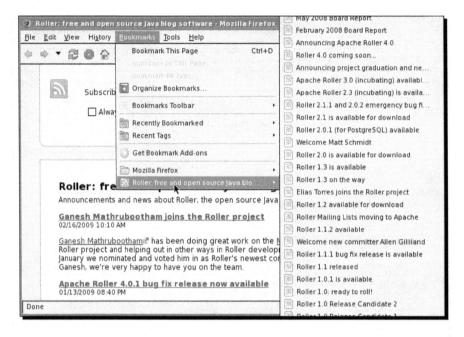

5. Select the **Announcing Apache Roller 4.0** entry, and Mozilla Firefox will take you to that post in the weblog, so that you can read the full entry:

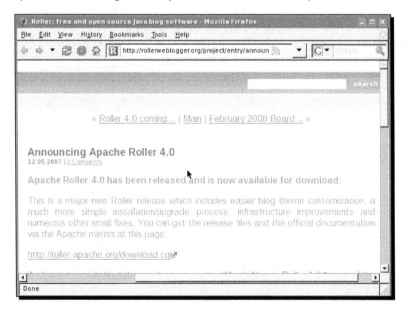

What just happened?

In the previous exercise, you learned how anyone can subscribe to a newsfeed, including newsfeeds from your blog. The process is the same for RSS and Atom newsfeeds. Mozilla Firefox is just one of the many available newsfeed readers. In fact, if you didn't notice in step 2 of the previous exercise, there are five options to choose from when subscribing to a newsfeed in Mozilla Firefox:

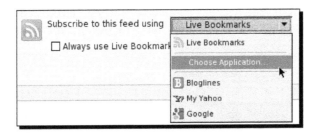

If you click on the **Live Bookmarks** pop-up listbox, you can select another newsfeed reader from the list such as **Bloglines**, **My Yahoo**, or **Google**, or even choose a different desktop application such as Ecto, MarsEdit, or Windows Live Writer depending on which operating system you are working on.

Thanks to newsfeeds and services such as Technorati, Digg, DZone, and del.icio.us, your blog can be followed by thousands, even millions of people!

Using newsfeed readers

In the previous exercise, you saw how anyone can subscribe to a newsfeed through the Mozilla Firefox newsfeed reader. Now, we'll see an example of a popular newsfeed reader that can be used both in Linux and Windows environments.

Time for action – using Bloglines

In this exercise, you'll create an account with **Bloglines**—a web-based newsfeed reader. You can use Bloglines from Mozilla Firefox, Internet Explorer, and all the other popular web browsers.

1. Open your web browser and go to `http://www.bloglines.com`. In the **Register For Your Free Account** green box, type your **EMAIL**, a **PASSWORD**, and **CONFIRM PASSWORD** as shown in the following screenshot:

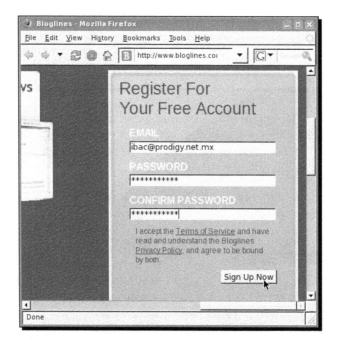

The Bloglines' main screen will appear next. In the right pane, there will be a message stating that you haven't confirmed your account yet. Go to your e-mail account (the one that you used to sign up in Bloglines) and look for the "Bloglines Validation Email". Follow the link inside that e-mail message to confirm your Bloglines account. A new web browser window will open up to tell you that your e-mail address was successfully validated. Now you can close that window and return to the Bloglines main screen.

2. Click on the **Reload current page** button on the toolbar, so that the previous message disappears. Your screen should look like this:

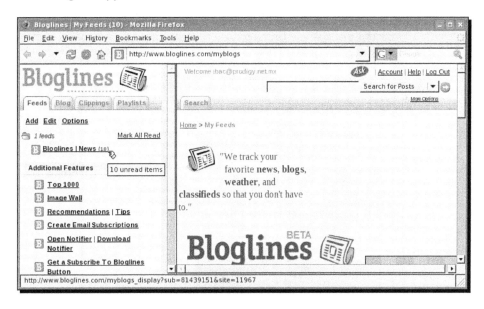

3. Select the **Bloglines | News** link on the left pane. The most recent posts about Bloglines will show up on the right pane, as shown in the following screenshot:

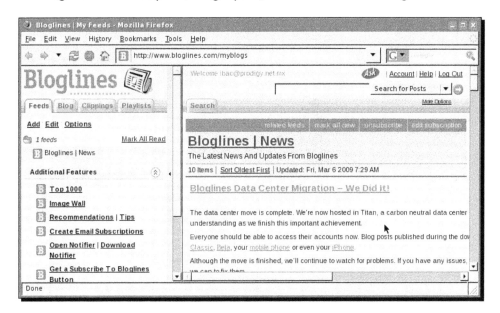

4. To add a new RSS/Atom feed, open a new web browser window and go to `http://www.technorati.com`. Right-click on the **Subscribe** link on the right part of the screen, and select **Copy Link Location** on the pop-up menu, as shown:

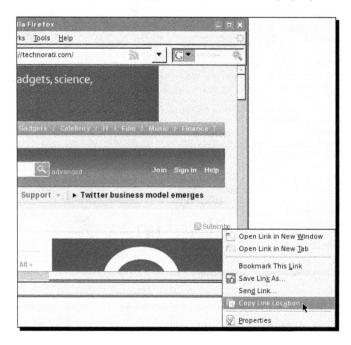

5. Close the Technorati web page window, go to the Bloglines web page that you previously opened and click on the **Add** link from the **Feeds** tab, in the left pane:

6. Right-click on the **Blog or Feed URL** text box in the right pane, and select **Paste** from the pop-up menu:

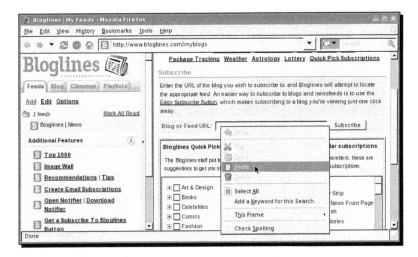

7. Now click on the **Subscribe** button to the right of the **Blog or Feed URL** textbox to subscribe to the Technorati newsfeed. The right pane will change to show the available feeds from the URL you entered. Scroll down the right pane until you see the **Subscribe** button, and click on it to finish the subscription process.

8. After a few seconds, the **Technorati Front Page** feed will appear on the left pane, below the **Bloglines | News** feed, showing the number of unread items:

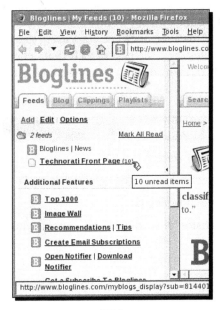

9. Click on the **Technorati Front Page** link, and the most recent posts from Technorati will show up in the right pane of Bloglines:

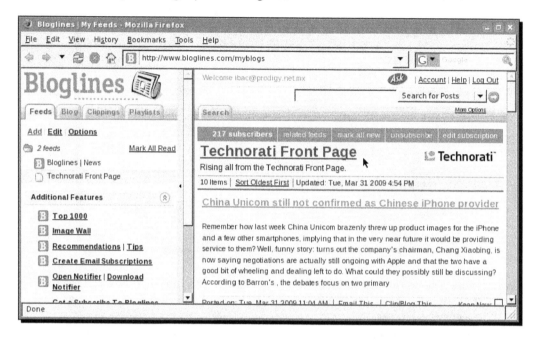

What just happened?

That pretty much covers the basic procedure for using a newsfeed reader. In Mozilla Firefox, you can select three web-based newsreaders—Bloglines, My Yahoo, and Google Reader. You need to register for a free account with any of these readers before you can start adding feeds from different sources. However, once you start using them, you'll see all the power that newsfeeds can bring to bloggers. The best of all is that, when you finish reading this book, your blog will be ready to take advantage of newsfeeds and feed readers, so that people from all over the world can see your posts!

Pop quiz – weblogs and newsfeeds

1. How would you define a weblog?

    a. A group of web pages.

    b. A collection of newsfeeds.

    c. A simple website for writing about anything you like.

2. In which of the following situations would you use a weblog?

    a. Promote your products online.

    b. Write a horror novel.

    c. Meet people.

    d. All of the above.

3. How would you find out if your blog shows up on Technorati?

    a. Looking into the comments section of your blog, to see if anyone has made a comment.

    b. Searching in the Technorati website.

    c. Creating a subscription to the Technorati Front Page feed, and checking all recent posts to see if there's one from your blog.

4. What would be the best way to promote your blog?

    a. Registering with Technorati, Digg, and all the popular aggregators or social bookmarking sites.

    b. Sending e-mails to all your friends and colleagues, to tell them you have a new blog!

    c. Both a and b.

5. Can you use a newsfeed to communicate with other bloggers?

    a. No, because you can't establish a two-way communication.

    b. Yes, because in a way you read posts from another blogger, and then you can go to his/her blog and leave comments.

Have a go hero – doing more with the thing

Now that you have an account in Bloglines, use it to start your own newsfeeds collection. You can begin with a Google search for your favorite hobbies, local news, and so on. Try subscribing to several newsfeeds from different blogs or social bookmarking sites such as Digg, DZone, or anything of your interest. Explore all of the settings available in Bloglines (that is, open posts in the same window or in a new one, display entire posts or just a summary, and so on) until you feel comfortable using it.

Try to create accounts on the other two web-based feed readers (Google Reader and My Yahoo), and compare features between them and Bloglines.

Summary

In this chapter, we learned about weblogs, and how they can be used to create a world presence through the blogosphere. We saw the basic difference between a blog and a CMS, and why a blogging system like Roller can't be considered a full-fledged CMS. The chapter also covered the basics about newsfeeds and the important role they play for blogs. You worked with the Mozilla Firefox integrated newsfeed reader and Bloglines—a popular web-based feed reader. We also saw several live websites that use Apache Roller as their blog server.

Specifically, we covered:

- The basic concepts about weblogs.
- What you can do with a weblog—express your feelings to the world, get in touch with other people, promote your business or professional activities, share experiences with other users, and who is using Apache Roller.
- A brief comparison between a blog and a CMS. What can you do with a CMS, and the reason why a blog can't be considered a fully-fledged CMS.
- What are newsfeeds and how are they used in conjunction with blogs to spread information on the blogosphere.

This is just an introduction to the world of blogs and the blogosphere. In the next two chapters, you will learn to install Apache Roller, along with the software required to run it on Windows and Linux environments.

So, get ready and grab your hard hat, because you're about to start constructing your very own Apache Roller blog server!

2
Installing Roller on Windows

In this chapter, you'll learn to download and install Apache Roller, along with all the software applications (Apache web server, Java JDK, Tomcat servlet engine, MySQL database server, and `mod_jk` *connector) required to run this powerful weblog server on a Windows environment.*

In the previous chapter, we saw an overview of blogs and how Apache Roller could get you into the ever-expanding world of the blogosphere. Now, I'll teach you how to put Apache Roller to work. At the same time, you'll learn some basic stuff about using the Apache web server, the Tomcat servlet engine, and the MySQL database server—three of the most popular open source applications in the world!

In short, we shall:

◆ Install the Apache web server, the Java JDK, the Tomcat servlet engine, and the MySQL database server

◆ Test and configure the software installed, to make sure it's ready for Apache Roller

◆ Download and install Apache Roller

◆ Test your Apache Roller installation

◆ Install and configure the `mod_jk` connector for Apache and Tomcat integration

Now, let the show begin.

Checking your environment

Before installing the open source software, check your Windows environment to see if you already have any of these components installed—Apache, Tomcat, Java SE Development Kit, or MySQL. Feel free to skip the installation instructions for any of these components that you may already have installed in your PC.

Installing Apache, Java, Tomcat, and MySQL

Finally, it's time to start working! In the next exercises, you will download and install all the software components required to run Apache Roller on a Windows PC.

Apache web server

The Apache web server (or HTTP server) is the most popular open source web server for Linux and Windows. Trust me, I've been using it since the year 2000 and have never had a performance problem, not even on slow hardware and low memory systems. Now it's your turn to try it on your PC. I am sure you won't be disappointed!

Time for action – installing the Apache web server

In this exercise, you'll go to the Apache HTTP server site to download the latest stable version and install it on your Windows PC.

1. Open your web browser and go to `http://httpd.apache.org/download.cgi`. Scroll down through the web page until you locate the **Apache HTTP Server 2.2.x** section. In this section, there are several links to choose from. Click on the link for the **Win32 Binary without crypto (no mod_ssl) (MSI Installer)** file, as shown in the following screenshot:

 At the time of this writing, the most recent version of the Apache 2.2 series is *2.2.11*. It's perfectly okay if you download a newer version—just be sure it's from the *2.2.x* series.

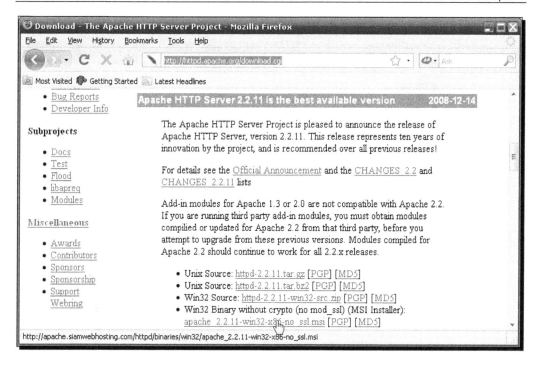

2. Next, your web browser will ask if you want to download and save the file. Click on the **Save File** button to download the file. When finished, double-click on the downloaded file in the **Downloads** dialog box, and then click on the **OK** button to start installing the Apache Web server.

3. Click on the **Run** button in the **Open File – Security Warning** dialog:

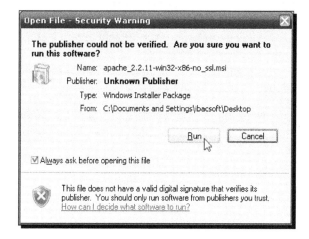

4. Click on the **Next** button in the **Welcome to the Installation Wizard for Apache HTTP Server** dialog. Then, click on the **I accept the terms in the license agreement** radio button from the **Installation Wizard** dialog, and click on **Next** to continue.

5. The next dialog will show information about the Apache HTTP server. Read it if you like, and then click on **Next**.

6. The **Server Information** dialog box will appear. This is where you need to enter some information about your server. Type `localhost` in the **Network Domain** and **Server Name** fields, and type a valid e-mail address in the **Administrator's Email Address** field. Leave the next option as it is (**for All Users**) and click on **Next** to continue:

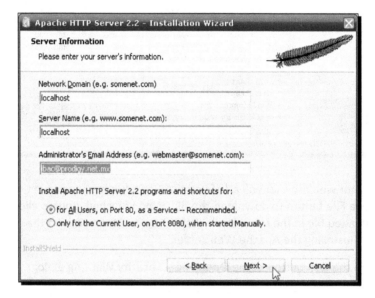

7. On the **Setup Type** dialog, make sure the **Typical** option is selected and click on **Next** to continue. In the **Destination Folder** dialog, leave the default option and click on **Next**. Now the wizard will be ready to start the installation. Click on the **Install** button to continue.

8. After a few seconds (or minutes, depending on your PC's hardware) the **Installation Wizard Completed** dialog will appear. Click on the **Finish** button to close the Apache installation wizard.

9. To test if your installation was successful, open your web browser and type `http://localhost` on the address bar. You should see a web page with the **It works!** message, as shown in the following screenshot:

What just happened?

Well, now you have the Apache web server installed and running on your Windows PC! The installation process was pretty simple—you just needed to provide the wizard with some basic information and click on a few buttons. In step 9, to test your Apache installation, you used `http://localhost` as the URL address for the Apache web server installed in your PC. **Localhost** is the standard hostname used when you're accessing a web server installed on the same machine where you use a web browser.

Although Windows is not as secure as Linux, when using a regular home PC as a web server, you can definitely run an Apache Roller blog server to publish your own blogs from there. However, you should take several security measures to prevent hackers from wrecking your precious information. A good antivirus is also a requirement, along with an equally good firewall. However, don't worry because when you finish reading this book, you'll be ready to show your blog to the Internet world and, you will use a real Internet URL like everybody else. For now, let's focus on Roller's installation.

The Java SE Development Kit

The next step in our Apache Roller installation path is the **Java Development Kit (JDK)**. However, have no fear; we're not going to see any Java programming in here. It's just that the Tomcat servlet engine (or Java Application server) needs a JDK to run. That's one of the greatest things about Java—you can use the same application on different operating systems, without any additional modifications to the code! Take Tomcat for example, you can download the same files both on Windows and Linux, and because of the JDK, they run seamlessly on both operating systems! That's enough techie-talk for now. Let's get to work before you fall asleep with all that boring theory!

Time for action – installing a JDK

There are several versions of the Java Development Kit. In this exercise we're going to install the Java SE Development Kit 6, the most up-to-date version of the JDK at the time of this writing.

1. If you have an open web browser window from the previous exercise, go to `http://java.sun.com/javase/downloads/index.jsp` and look for the most recent Java SE Development Kit (JDK) version:

2. Click on the **Download** button to start downloading the JDK 6 to your computer. You'll need to provide some information about your operating system, as shown in the following screenshot:

As with the Apache installation exercise, it doesn't matter if you download *JDK 6 Update 13* or a more recent update; just be sure it's the *JDK SE 6* version.

3. Select **Windows** in the **Platform** drop-down list. Select **I agree to the Java SE Development Kit 6 License Agreement** and click on **Continue**.

4. Scroll down to the **Available Files** section on the next web page, and click on the **jdk-6u13-windows-i586-p.exe** link:

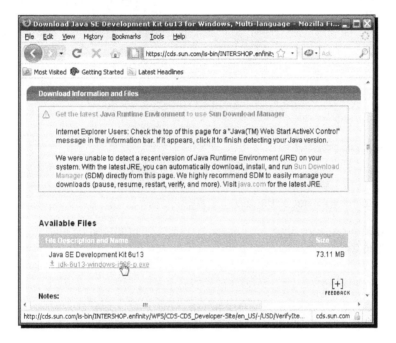

5. Click on the **Save** button in the **Opening jdk-6u13-windows-i586-p.exe** dialog to start the downloading process. When finished, go to the directory where you downloaded the JDK file and double-click on it to start the installation process.

6. Click on the **Run** button in the **Open File – Security Warning** dialog. After a few seconds, the **JDK License Agreement** window will appear. Click on the **Accept** button to continue.

7. Leave the default settings in the **Custom Setup** dialog and click on **Next** to continue. The Java SDK Install Wizard will begin to install the Java SDK on your computer. Wait until the **Destination Folder** shows up, stick with the default destination folder option and click on **Next** to continue. The JDK Install Wizard will continue the installation process.

8. Click on the **Finish** button when the installation wizard shows the **JDK Successfully Installed** screen.

9. To test your Java installation, open a **Command Prompt** window and type `java -version` at the system prompt. You should receive the following output:

```
Command Prompt                                                    _ □ ×
Microsoft Windows XP [Version 5.1.2600]
(C) Copyright 1985-2001 Microsoft Corp.

C:\Documents and Settings\ibacsoft>java -version
java version "1.6.0_13"
Java(TM) SE Runtime Environment (build 1.6.0_13-b03)
Java HotSpot(TM) Client VM (build 11.3-b02, mixed mode, sharing)

C:\Documents and Settings\ibacsoft>_
```

10. Type `exit` in the command prompt to close this window.

What just happened?

Is Java easy to install on Windows, or not? As you can see from the previous exercise, the JDK installation process is pretty straightforward, and you don't need to change any default option. It's ready to work out of the box!

With the JDK, you can learn basic Java programming without needing anything else, just the Notepad text editor and the Java compiler *javac*. So, once you get comfortable working with Apache Roller and your blog, maybe you can learn Java and make contributions to the Roller project, how about that?

Let's see further! We've installed Apache and the JDK. Now guess what? It's "Tomcat time"!

Tomcat servlet engine

Now it's Tomcat's turn on the stage. This open source servlet engine, also known as a *Java Application Server*, is the heart that drives Apache Roller. Tomcat needs the JDK to run on Windows, Linux, or any other operating system with Java support. Moreover, the big advantage of using Java applications is that you don't need to rewrite code, so that they can work on different operating systems. This applies to Apache Roller also, because the same files are used both in Windows and Linux. However, for now, let's focus on the Tomcat installation.

Time for action – installing Tomcat

Tomcat is an open source project from the Apache Software Foundation, the same guys that are behind Apache Roller. Isn't that great? In a few seconds, you're going to have in your hands one of the most popular and powerful Java servlet engines around, used by a lot of big industries and organizations worldwide. Ready for some action? Let's begin.

1. Open your web browser and go to `http://tomcat.apache.org`. Look for the **Download** section and click on the **Tomcat 6.x** link:

2. Scroll down the **Tomcat 6 Downloads** web page, until you locate the **Binary Distributions** section, and click on the **Windows Service Installer** link:

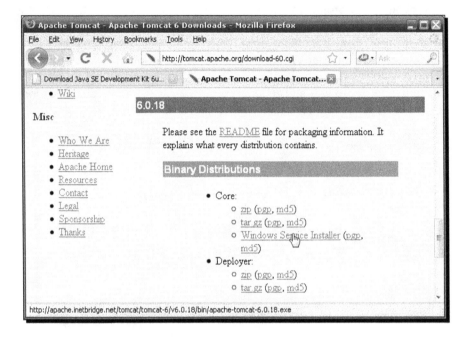

3. Click on the **Save File** button in the **Open apache-tomcat** dialog box and wait for the file to download. When finished, go to the directory where you downloaded the file and double-click on it to start the installation process, and click on the **Run** button in the **Open File** dialog box that will show up. The **Apache Tomcat Setup Wizard** will appear afterwards. Click on **Next** to continue.

4. Click on the **I Agree** button in the **License Agreement** dialog box. The **Choose Components** dialog will appear next. Leave the default options selected and click on **Next** to continue.

5. In the **Choose Install Location** dialog box, leave the default folder installation option and click on **Next** to continue.

6. Next you will see the **Configuration** dialog box. Leave the default **HTTP/1.1 Connector Port** number (**8080**). Fill in the **User Name** and **Password** fields with a username and a password for your Tomcat administrator. You can use **admin** as the username, just make sure to choose a strong password, as shown in the following screenshot:

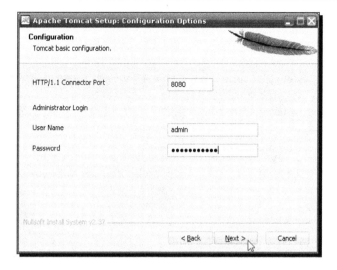

7. Now, the **Java Virtual Machine** dialog box will appear. You can leave the default option, as the Tomcat setup wizard detects your JDK installation automatically. Click on **Install** to begin installing Tomcat on your computer.

8. At the end of the installation process, you will see the **Completing the Apache Tomcat Setup Wizard** dialog box. Uncheck the **Show Readme** box and click on the **Finish** button.

9. The Apache Service Manager will try to run Tomcat. To test your installation, open your web browser and type `http://localhost:8080` in the address bar. You should see the following *Welcome to Tomcat* web page:

10. You can close your web browser now.

What just happened?

This was the third installation exercise on our way to *blogger's* land. Tomcat's installation as a service in Windows is a piece of cake. You don't need to tweak any of the default settings to start using it right away; that's the beauty of it. Although there's another way to install Tomcat on Windows using the standard `zip` file, it's better to install it as a service, because it means that when you shutdown and restart your computer, Tomcat will start up automatically.

We already have a web server, a Java environment, and a servlet engine. Now it's time to install the MySQL Database server—the data-handling component for Apache Roller.

MySQL database server

The MySQL database server is a powerful open source application, capable of running the most data-intensive applications for small, medium, and big companies worldwide. So, along with the other three components that we've already installed (Apache, Java, and Tomcat), you don't have anything to worry about MySQL, because you're in good hands.

Time for action – installing MySQL

I've been using MySQL for as long as I can remember using web applications, PHP, and Java. I still can't believe it is open source, which means it's free! Well, at least the Community Server. There is also an Enterprise Server where you receive support and a lot of goodies from the MySQL team for a certain price, but as we're already experts at installing things on Windows, let's try the Community MySQL Edition.

1. Open your web browser and go to the MySQL downloads web page on `http://dev.mysql.com/downloads/`. Then, scroll down until you locate the **MySQL Community Server Download** link, and click on it:

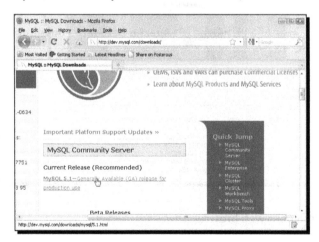

2. You'll be taken to the **MySQL 5.1 Downloads** page. Scroll down until you locate the **Windows downloads** section, and click on the **Windows Essentials (x86) Pick a mirror** link:

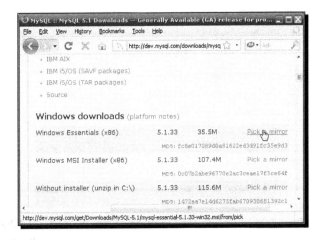

3. On the **Select a Mirror** web page, select the **No thanks, just take me to the downloads!** link:

4. Scroll down the **Select a Mirror** web page until you find a mirror near your location, and click on the **HTTP** link (the following screenshot shows mirrors in the United States):

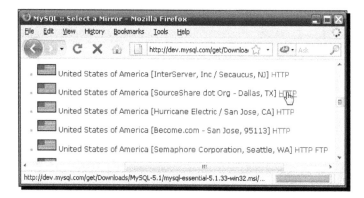

5. Click on the **Save File** button in the **Opening mysql-essential-5.1.XX-win32.msi** dialog box and wait for the file to download through your web browser. Double-click on the downloaded file when the download process is complete.

6. The **Open File – Security Warning** dialog box will appear next. Click on the **Run** button to open the **MySQL Server 5.1 Setup Wizard**:

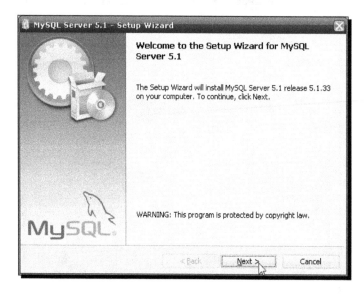

7. Click on the **Next** button to continue. In the **Setup Type** screen of the installation wizard, make sure the **Typical** setup option is selected and click on **Next**. The **Ready to Install the Program** dialog will show the **Current Settings** for the MySQL installation. Just click on **Install** to continue.

8. After a few seconds (or minutes, depending on your computer speed), the MySQL Wizard will show you a **MySQL Enterprise** window. Click on **Next** twice to complete the installation process. At the end, you'll see a **Wizard Completed** dialog box, as shown in the following screenshot:

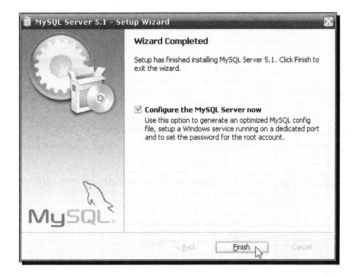

9. Make sure the **Configure the MySQL Server now** box is selected, and click on the **Finish** button to close the **MySQL Installation Wizard**. The **MySQL Server Instance Configuration Wizard** will show up afterwards.

10. Click on **Next** to continue. Choose the **Detailed Configuration** option and then click on **Next**:

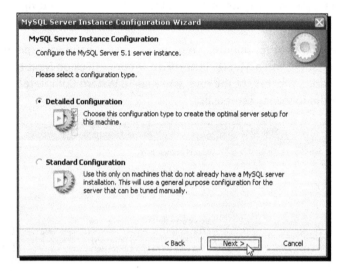

11. Select the **Developer Machine** option in the next dialog box, and click on **Next** to continue.

12. Select the **Multifunctional Database** option in the next dialog box, and click on **Next** to continue.

13. Leave the default settings for the InnoDB data file, and click on **Next** to continue:

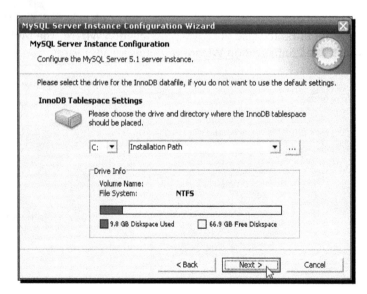

14. Select the **Decision Support (DSS)/OLAP** option in the next dialog, and click on **Next** to continue.

15. Make sure the **Enable TCP/IP Networking** option is selected. Leave the **Port Number** as **3306**, and select the **Enable Strict Mode** option too. Click on **Next** when you're ready:

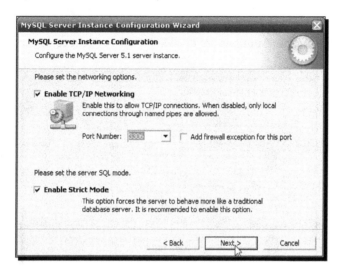

16. Select the **Best Support for Multilingualism** option and click on **Next** to continue.

17. Select the **Install As Windows Service** option on the next dialog. Make sure the **Launch the MySQL Server automatically** box is selected. Select the **Include Bin Directory in Windows PATH** option, and click on **Next** to continue:

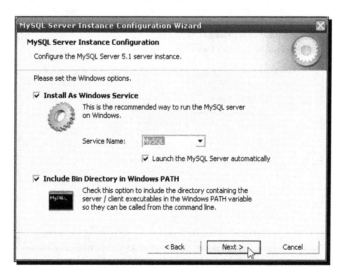

18. In the next dialog, make sure the **Modify Security Settings** option is selected. Enter a password in the **New root password:** and **Confirm:** fields.

 Don't forget this password, because without it you won't be able to access the MySQL client to create databases later.

Make sure the **Enable root access from remote machines** and the **Create an Anonymous Account** options are disabled. Click on **Next** to continue:

19. The **MySQL Server Instance Configuration Wizard** is now ready to prepare and write the configuration file to disk, start the MySQL service and apply the security settings:

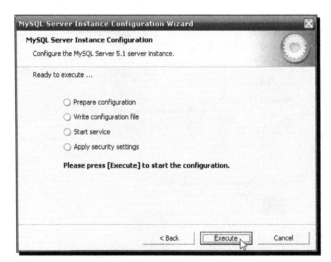

20. Press the **Execute** button to continue. The Wizard will show you when it has completed every stage of the configuration process. When the wizard completes its task, just press the **Finish** button to close it.

21. To test the MySQL installation, open a **Command Prompt** window and type `mysql -u root -p`, followed by *Enter*. The MySQL monitor will prompt for a password. Enter the password you used at the time of installation and hit *Enter*. The monitor then responds with a welcome message, as shown in the following screenshot:

22. Type `exit` to close the MySQL monitor and close the **Command Prompt** window.

What just happened?

Now you have all the open source software required to install Apache Roller on your Windows machine. This last exercise showed you that MySQL server is a bit more complicated to install than Apache, Java, and Tomcat. That's because there are a lot of settings to consider when using this powerful database server.

In step 10 of the previous exercise (use the screenshot shown in step 10 as a reference), you had two choices—**Detailed Configuration** and **Standard Configuration**. If you select the standard configuration, the installation process will be shorter. However, for Apache Roller, there are some special settings that we need to adjust on MySQL server and the standard configuration doesn't include them. There are some other settings, that although not necessarily involved with the Apache Roller installation process, will indeed help to improve your machine's performance, and consequently, your Apache Roller blog server's performance.

For example, in step 11 you have the following options about memory usage:

◆ Developer Machine: This option is for testing applications such as Apache Roller, because MySQL server uses just the minimal memory space it requires to work, without burdening the host computer. If you're going to run a personal blog on your home PC (where you use several applications, such as a word processor, spreadsheets, games, and so on), this is the recommended option.

◆ Server Machine: This option is for running Apache Roller on a dedicated web server machine. You can have a personal blog or several multiuser blogs, it all depends on your machine's hardware.

◆ Dedicated MySQL Server Machine: If you run a big company, you could assign a dedicated machine to act as a database server with MySQL, and use another machine for the Apache web server and the Tomcat servlet engine. This way you could host thousands of blogs with Apache Roller!

Steps 12, 13, and 14 of the installation process are not directly related to the Apache Roller installation requirement, that's why we just left the default options selected, and moved along.

Steps 15 and 16 are very important for a successful Apache Roller installation. You need to enable TCP/IP networking so that Roller can connect with the MySQL server through a TCP/IP port, and the default character set must be UTF-8.

Step 17 is for installing MySQL server as a Windows service; that means MySQL server will startup and shutdown automatically each time you start/restart your PC. This step also lets you add the MySQL server and client executables to the Windows PATH variable, so you can use the MySQL monitor program to create or delete databases, as we will see later when installing Apache Roller.

The last configuration step is where you enter a password for the MySQL root user. This is the administrator user who has the power to create, delete, or modify any database handled by MySQL. So be careful with the password, because anyone could delete your entire blog! I definitely recommend you change the root user password frequently, to enhance the overall security of your blog server.

That pretty much covers all you'll need to know about MySQL to run your own Apache Roller blog server. Finally, we've came to the point you've been waiting for since you started reading this book.

Downloading and installing Apache Roller

At last! You will finally get your hands on Roller's installation process! I hope you enjoyed the previous sections, and now you'll get the chance to put it all together.

Files required for Apache Roller

The first thing to do before deploying Apache Roller on your computer is getting all the required files—the JavaMail API and the **Java Application Framework (JAF)** for Roller's e-mail notification features, and the JDBC driver for connecting to the roller MySQL database.

The JavaMail API

With the JavaMail API, you can build mail and messaging applications. Roller uses this API to send e-mails from your blog, so that you and your readers can receive notifications when they leave a comment.

Time for action – downloading the JavaMail API

All you need to do is download a ZIP file from the Sun website, unzip it, and copy the `mail.jar` file to the `lib` folder in Tomcat, from where Roller can use it along with all the other common library files needed.

1. Open your web browser and type `http://java.sun.com/products/javamail/downloads/index.html`. Scroll down through the page until you find the **Download JavaMail 1.4.2** link:

2. Click on the **Download** button to go to the download page. Select the **I agree to the JavaMail 1.4.2 License Agreement** box and click on the **Continue** button:

3. On the next download page, click the `javamail-1.4.2.zip` link to open the **Opening javamail-1.4.2.zip** dialog. Select the **Save File** radio button and click on the **OK** button to start the download process.

4. Once the download completes, go to the directory where you downloaded the `javamail-1.4.2.zip` file.

5. Unzip the `javamail-1.4.2.zip` file and locate the `mail.jar` file inside the `javamail-1.4.2` folder. Right-click on the `mail.jar` file and select **Copy** from the pop-up menu:

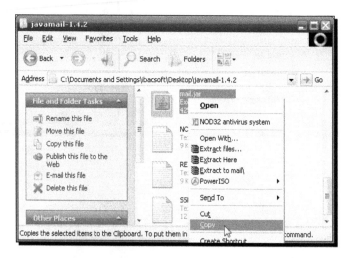

6. Now open Windows Explorer and navigate to Tomcat's `lib` folder (`C:\Program Files\Apache Software Foundation\Tomcat 6.0\lib`). Right-click inside the folder and select **Paste** from the pop-up menu:

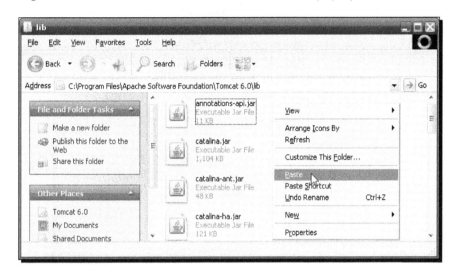

7. You can close Windows Explorer and your web browser now.

What just happened?

All right! You've just added mail capacity to your Tomcat installation! Although you'll never need to deal directly with `mail.jar` from your Roller blog, it's necessary to install this file before attempting to install Roller because it contains all the Java code required to send e-mail messages. There's one more file that the Roller needs to send e-mails, and we'll see how to download and install it in the next exercise.

The JavaBeans Activation Framework API

The **JavaBeans Activation Framework** (**JAF**) API allows Java developers to use standard services for working with arbitrary pieces of data in a uniform way. Roller uses the JavaMail and JAF APIs to send e-mail notifications. You need to put the `mail.jar` and `activation.jar` files on Tomcat's `lib` folder, so Roller can use them. We already saw how to download and copy `mail.jar` to your Tomcat's `lib` folder. Now let's see how to do the same with `activation.jar`.

Time for action – downloading the JAF API

In this exercise, we're going to download the JAF API from the Sun website. The steps are almost identical to the JavaMail exercise, so you can use it as a reference.

1. Open your web browser and go to `http://java.sun.com/javase/ technologies/desktop/javabeans/jaf/downloads/index.html`. Scroll down through the page until you find the **Download JavaBeans Activation Framework 1.1.1 release Download** link, and click on it:

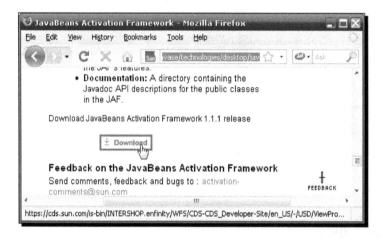

2. Select **I agree to the Software License Agreement** and click on **Continue**:

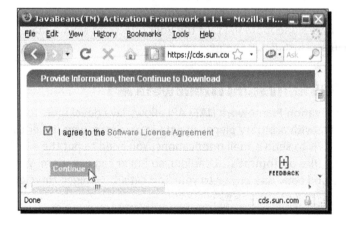

3. Click on the **jaf-1_1_1.zip** link to open the **Opening jaf-1_1_1.zip** dialog. Select the **Save File** radio button and click on the **OK** button:

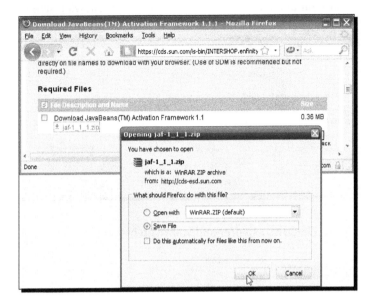

4. Once the download is complete, go to the directory where you downloaded the `jaf-1_1_1.zip` file.

5. Unzip the `jaf-1_1_1.zip` file and locate the `activation.jar` file inside the `jaf-1_1_1` folder. Right-click on the `activation.jar` file and select **Copy** from the pop-up menu:

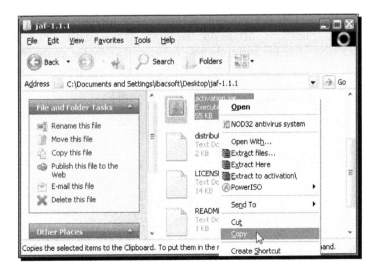

6. Use Windows Explorer to navigate to Tomcat's `lib` directory and paste the `activation.jar` file in there. Your Tomcat's `lib` folder should now include the **activation.jar** and **mail.jar** files, as shown in the following screenshot:

7. You can close Windows Explorer and your web browser now.

What just happened?

Now that you have the `mail.jar` and `activation.jar` files inside Tomcat's `lib` folder, Roller will be able to send e-mail notifications when someone leaves comments on your blog. The good part is that you don't need to know how to manipulate the Java code inside `mail.jar` or `activation.jar`, Roller takes care of that automatically, and you just have to blog, blog, and blog!

The MySQL JDBC driver

MySQL `Connector/J 5.1` is the official JDBC driver used for connecting to MySQL databases from Java applications such as Apache Roller. In this next exercise, you'll download the `Connector/J 5.1 jar` file and copy it to Tomcat's `lib` folder, so that Roller can communicate with the `rollerdb` database that you'll create in a later section.

Time for action – installing MySQL connector/J 5.1

You can download the `Connector/J 5.1` JDBC driver from MySQL Developer Zone. Just follow the simple steps:

1. Open your web browser and go to `http://dev.mysql.com/downloads/connector/j/5.1.html`. Scroll down until you locate the **Source and Binaries (zip) Download** link:

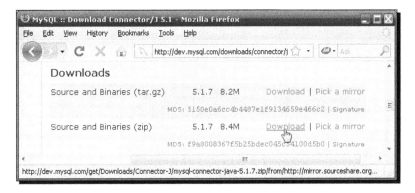

2. Click on this link to start the download. Select the **Save File** radio button in the **Opening mysql-connector-java-5.1.7.zip** dialog and click on the **OK** button.

3. Once the file has been downloaded, navigate to the directory where you downloaded the file.

4. Unzip the file and double-click on the `mysql-connector-java-5.1.7` folder. Look for the `mysql-connector-java-5.1.7.jar` file, right-click on it and select **Copy**:

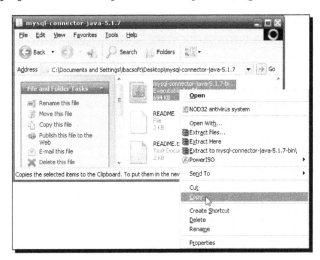

5. Now go to Tomcat's `lib` folder (`C:\Program Files\Apache Software Foundation\Tomcat 6.0\lib`), right-click on an empty space in Windows Explorer's right panel and select **Paste** from the pop-up menu to paste the `mysql-connector-java-5.1.7.jar` file:

6. You can close Windows Explorer and your web browser now.

What just happened?

In the previous exercise, you downloaded *MySQL* `Connector/J 5.1`—a JDBC driver that Apache Roller uses to communicate with the MySQL database that holds all the information related to blogs, users, comments, and configuration parameters. This file contains all the Java code needed to communicate with the MySQL database server, and Roller does it for you automatically. Now let's see how to install Roller on Tomcat.

Deploying Roller files to Tomcat

OK, it's time to finally deploy Apache Roller to the Tomcat servlet engine, and start the configuration process! "But what does *deploy* mean?" you may ask. In case of a Java web application, like Roller, it means you have to download the Roller ZIP file from the official website, then unzip it and copy the `roller` folder inside the Tomcat `webapps` folder, so that you can access it from a web browser. We'll see how to do that in the next exercise.

Time for action – downloading and deploying Roller

In this exercise, we'll go to the Roller download website, grab the latest Roller ZIP file and copy it to Tomcat's `webapps` folder.

1. Go to the Apache Roller downloads web page (`http://roller.apache.org/downloads.html`) and click on the **Roller 4.0.1 ("best available")** link from the **General Availability (GA) Releases** section:

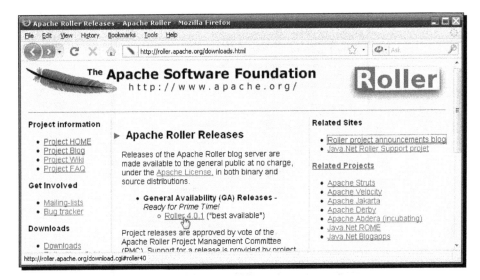

2. Scroll down to the **Roller 4.0.1** section of the next page, and click on the `apache-roller-4.0.1.zip` link:

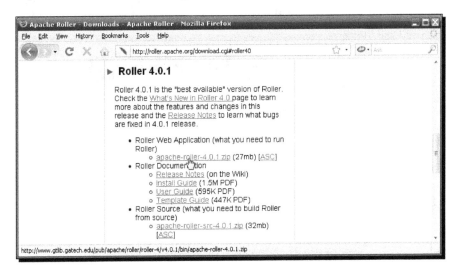

3. Select the **Save File** radio button from the **Opening apache-roller-4.0.1.zip** dialog and click on **OK** to start the download process. The file will take several seconds to download (or minutes, depending on your Internet connection speed).

4. Go to the directory where you downloaded the `apache-roller-4.0.1.zip` file.

5. Unzip the file and double-click on the `apache-roller-4.0.1` folder that you've just unzipped. Then double-click on the `webapp` folder, right-click on the `roller` folder and select **Copy** from the pop-up menu:

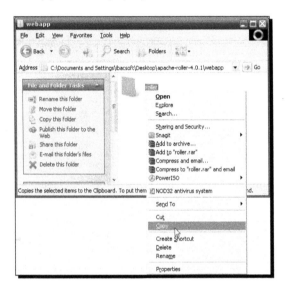

6. Use Windows Explorer to navigate to the Tomcat `webapps` folder (`C:\Program Files\Apache Software Foundation\Tomcat 6.0\webapps`), right-click on a blank area in the Windows Explorer right panel and select **Paste** from the pop-up menu:

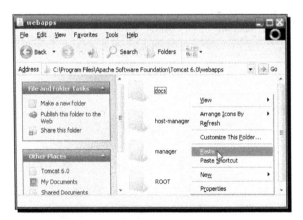

7. Wait until the copying process finishes. There should now be a `roller` folder inside Tomcat's `webapps` folder, as shown in the following screenshot:

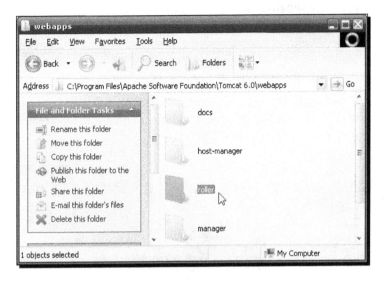

8. Now you can close Windows Explorer.

What just happened?

In this last exercise, you downloaded and copied the Apache `Roller` folder to Tomcat's `webapps` folder. Now that you have all the Roller files and folders inside Tomcat, you need to create a database where Roller can save all the information related to your blog.

Creating the Roller database

The next step is to create a MySQL database for Roller. You'll need root access to the MySQL server installed in your Windows PC, so now's the time to go back to the MySQL installation section and recover the username and password you assigned to your MySQL root user.

Time for action – creating a MySQL database for Roller

In this exercise, you'll use the MySQL monitor to create a database for your Apache Roller blog site.

1. Open a command prompt window (**Start | All Programs | Accessories | Command Prompt**) and type `mysql -u root -p`.

2. The MySQL monitor will ask you to **Enter Password**. This is the password you used when installing MySQL Server. Type it and press *Enter*. If the password is correct, the following screen shall appear:

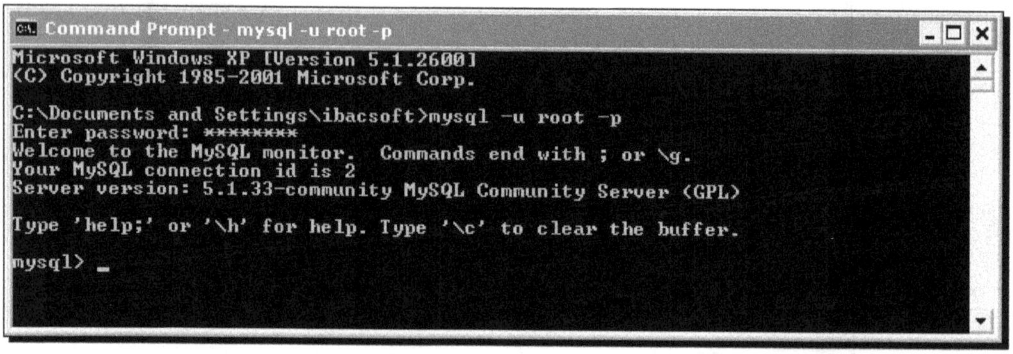

3. Now type the following lines after the `mysql>` prompt (remember to replace *password* with a secure password) and press *Enter* after each line:

```
create database rollerdb;
grant all on rollerdb.* to roller_user@'%' identified by
'password';
grant all on rollerdb.* to roller_user@localhost identified by
'password';
```

4. When finished, your screen should look like this:

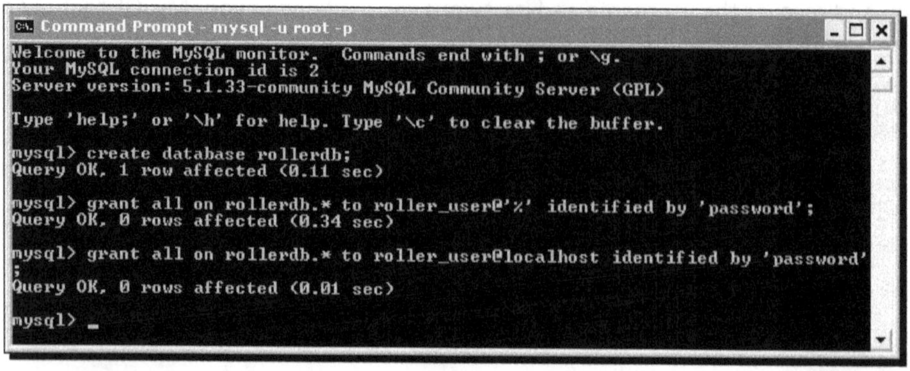

5. Notice the **Query OK, 0 rows affected (X.XX sec)** line after each line you typed. It means there were no errors with the commands you entered. Now type exit and press *Enter* to exit the MySQL monitor, then type exit to close the **Command Prompt** window.

What just happened?

In this last exercise, you used the MySQL monitor to create the rollerdb database, and then created a database user named roller_user. You then assigned permissions to roller_user, so it can create, modify, and delete tables inside the rollerdb database. Note that the password you used for the rollerdb database isn't the same as your MySQL root user's password. Remember that the "root" user has access to all the MySQL server configuration, and the user named roller_user only has access to your rollerdb database.

Roller properties and context files

OK, you downloaded and copied the Apache Roller files to Tomcat, and then you created the rollerdb MySQL database. Now it's time to create the roller-custom.properties file. Inside this file there are all the parameters you can use to fine-tune Apache Roller's behavior during the installation process. After that you'll need to create a file named Context. xml for Roller. This file is called a **Context Configuration** file, and it's used to describe all the resources (in this case—the JDBC database driver, the JavaMail API, and the JavaBeans Framework API) used inside a context (the Apache Roller blog server).

However, that's enough smart-talk for now, let's see how to create the roller-custom. properties file first.

The roller-custom.properties file

In the next exercise, you'll create the roller-custom.properties file and save it in Roller's WEB-INF/lib folder, where Roller can read it.

Time for action – creating roller-custom.properties

In this exercise, you'll create a `roller-custom.properties` file with the basic parameters and I'll show you where it has to be saved.

1. Open the Notepad editor (**Start | All Programs | Accessories | Notepad**) and write the following lines:

```
installation.type=auto
database.configurationType=jndi
database.jndi.name=jdbc/rollerdb
mail.configurationType=jndi
mail.jndi.name=mail/Session
```

2. Select **File | Save** from the Notepad menu bar. In the **Save As** dialog box, navigate to the `C:\Program Files\Apache Software Foundation\ Tomcat 6.0\webapps\roller\WEB-INF\classes` folder, type `roller-custom.properties` in the **File name** listbox, select **All Files** in the **Save as type** listbox and click on the **Save** button:

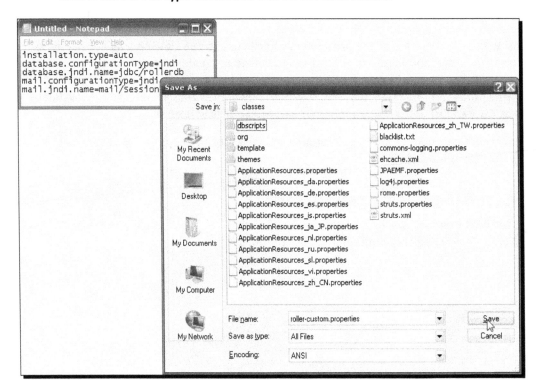

3. You can close Notepad now.

What just happened?

The `roller-custom.properties` file you've just created is used by Roller to look for the database and mail configuration; in this case, the name of the resources it has to look for in the `Context.xml` file that you'll create in the next exercise.

The Context.xml file

The context configuration file (`Context.xml`) is used by Roller to read the configuration parameters for the JDBC driver and the mail properties, so that it can communicate with the `rollerdb` database to perform all the required chores for running the blog server, and with the JavaMail API to send e-mail notifications. Now let's see how to create that file.

Time for action – creating Context.xml

In this exercise, you'll learn how to create a `Context.xml` file with all the parameters required for the `MySQL Connector/J` driver, the `activation.jar`, and the `mail.jar` files that you downloaded before.

> You're going to need a valid e-mail address for Roller's e-mail notification features. I chose to use a Gmail account for this exercise, because it lets you send e-mail from your Roller blog server without any problems. So, I definitely recommend you to create a Gmail account for your Roller blog server, if you haven't got one already. That way, you'll just need to change the e-mail address and password used in the next exercise, and leave all the other parameters intact.

1. Open Notepad and type or copy the following lines:

```
<Context path="/roller"
    docBase="c:\Program Files\Apache Software Foundation\Tomcat
    6.0\webapps\roller" debug="0">

  <Resource name="jdbc/rollerdb" auth="Container"
    type="javax.sql.DataSource"
      driverClassName="com.mysql.jdbc.Driver"
      url="jdbc:mysql://localhost:3306/rollerdb?
      autoReconnect=true&amp;useUnicode=true&amp;
      characterEncoding=utf-&amp;mysqlEncoding=utf8"
    username="roller_user"
    password="password"
    maxActive="20" maxIdle="3" removeAbandoned="true"
    maxWait="3000" />

  <Resource name="mail/Session"
            auth="Container"
            type="javax.mail.Session"
```

```
                    username="alromeromx@gmail.com"
                    password="password"
                    mail.debug="false"
                    mail.user="alromeromx@gmail.com"
                    mail.password="password"
                    mail.smtp.from="alromeromx@gmail.com"
                    mail.transport.protocol="smtp"
                    mail.smtp.port="465"
                    mail.smtp.host="smtp.gmail.com"
                    mail.smtp.auth="true"
                    mail.smtp.starttls.enable="true"
                    mail.smtp.socketFactory.port="465"
                    mail.smtp.socketFactory.
                    class="javax.net.ssl.SSLSocketFactory"
                    mail.smtp.socketFactory.fallback="false" />
</Context>
```

2. Change the parameters in bold to reflect your own values for the database user password, the e-mail username, password, and SMTP server you're going to use for e-mail notifications (if you're going to use a Gmail account, use the same server).

3. Select **File | Save** from the Notepad menu bar. In the **Save As** dialog box, navigate to the `C:\Program Files\Apache Software Foundation\Tomcat 6.0\ webapps\roller\META-INF` folder, type `Context.xml` in the **File name** listbox, select **All Files** in the **Save as type** listbox and click on the **Save** button:

4. You can close Notepad now.

What just happened?

The `Context.xml` file has all the parameters Roller needs to communicate with the `rollerdb` database, and to send e-mail notifications when visitors to your blog leave comments. Now you just need to modify some security settings, and then you can start testing your Roller installation!

Changing keys in security.xml

The `security.xml` file contains some security keys you need to change because anyone can get access to Roller's documentation and, if you leave the default values, hackers could infiltrate your blog server.

Time for action – changing key values in security.xml

This is a simple process, you just need to change four key values in the `security.xml` file, inside Roller's `WEB-INF` folder.

1. Use Windows Explorer to navigate to Roller's `WEB-INF` folder (`C:\Program Files\Apache Software Foundation\Tomcat 6.0\webapps\roller\WEB-INF`), and open the `security.xml` file with Notepad, WordPad, or some other text editor.

2. Scroll down through the file until you locate the following lines:

```
<bean id="anonymousAuthenticationProvider"
      class="org.acegisecurity.providers.anonymous.
            AnonymousAuthenticationProvider">
<property name="key" value="anonymous"/>
</bean>
```

3. Replace the value in bold text (**anonymous**) with any other value of your choice. Use only letters and numbers.

4. Now locate the following lines:

```
<bean id="anonymousProcessingFilter"
      class="org.acegisecurity.
            providers.anonymous.AnonymousProcessingFilter">
<property name="key" value="anonymous"/>
```

5. Replace the value in bold text (**anonymous**) with the same exact value you used in step 3. These two values must be identical.

6. Now keep scrolling down through the file until you locate the following lines:

```
<bean id="rememberMeServices"
    class="org.acegisecurity.ui.rememberme.
    TokenBasedRememberMeServices">
 <property name="userDetailsService"
    ref="jdbcAuthenticationDao"/>
 <property name="key" value="rollerlovesacegi"/>
    <property name="parameter" value="rememberMe"/>
</bean>
    <bean id="rememberMeAuthenticationProvider"
        class="org.acegisecurity.providers.
        rememberme.RememberMeAuthenticationProvider">
      <property name="key" value="rollerlovesacegi"/>
    </bean>
```

7. Replace the values in bold text (**rollerlovesacegi**) with another value of your liking, but don't use the same one as in steps 3 and 4. Again, use letters and numbers only. You have to use the same value in the two **rollerlovesacegi** entries.

8. Save the file and exit the text editor.

What just happened?

The key values you modified in the previous exercise will prevent hackers from breaking Roller's security and tampering with your site. As anyone can have access to Roller's installation files and documentation, you need to change these key values so that no one besides you has the chance of reading them from your installation files. As the security.xml file can't be accessed from outside your server, no one will know what values you're using, unless you tell them!

Testing your Roller installation

At last! You made it through the whole installation process! I hope it was as entertaining and valuable an experience for you as it was for me—the first time I installed Roller. Now let's test all the work you've done in the previous sections of this chapter.

Time for action – testing Roller

Now that you have everything installed and are waiting for your commands, let's start the testing process.

1. First, let's check that your Tomcat server is up and running. Select **Start | All Programs | Apache Tomcat 6.0 | Configure Tomcat** to open the **Apache Tomcat 6 Properties** dialog box. Click on the **General** tab and make sure the **Startup type** option is on **Automatic**. Also, check the **Service Status** option to see if it says **Started**. If it says **Stopped**, click on the **Start** button and wait until Tomcat starts, then click on the **OK** button to close the dialog:

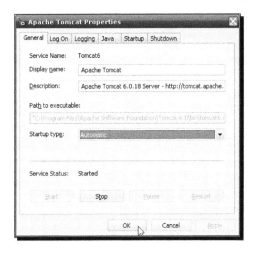

2. Open your web browser and go to `http://localhost:8080/roller`. You should see the following screen:

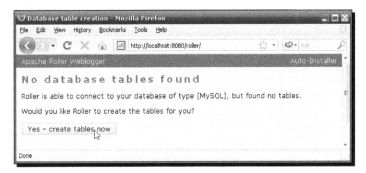

3. This screen indicates that Roller can connect to the JDBC driver you configured before, and so the installation can proceed. Click on the **Yes - create tables now** button to continue.

4. Wait until the **Tables created successfully** page appears, as shown in the following screenshot:

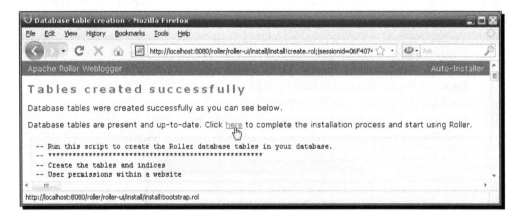

5. Click on the **here** link to complete the installation process. When Roller finishes installing all the required data, the following screenshot shall appear:

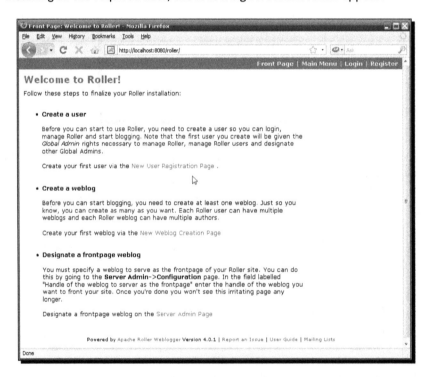

6. Now you can be sure that Roller is properly installed on your Windows PC!

What just happened?

You've just tested your Roller installation. Now you're ready for the real fun part—beginning to use your Roller blog server! However, before starting with the fun stuff, we need to do a little modification so that Tomcat and the Apache web server can work together with a connector named `mod_jk`; that way visitors won't have to use the `:8080` special notation in the URL address of your blog.

The mod_jk connector for Apache and Tomcat

This little tiny piece of code is the bridge that helps Apache and Tomcat collaborate together to help you host the most powerful web applications from your own PC! Maybe you're wondering, "But why do I need that module?" Well, if you have noticed the screenshot of step 5 from the previous exercise, to access your Roller homepage you need to type `http://localhost:8080/roller`. The `:8080` part is necessary to access Tomcat, because the Apache web server uses `http://localhost` to serve web pages. With the `mod_jk` connector, Apache and Tomcat will share the `http://localhost` address without conflicts, and you will access your Roller homepage with `http://localhost/roller`.

Time for action – installing the mod_jk connector

This is the last piece of open source software you'll need, to run Apache Roller on your Windows PC. Using the `mod_jk` connector is considered an advanced topic, but don't worry; I'll guide you through all the steps involved.

1. Open your web browser and go to `http://tomcat.apache.org/download-connectors.cgi`. Scroll down through the page until you locate the **Tomcat Connectors JK 1.2** section:

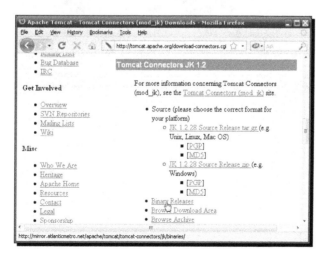

2. Click on the **Binary Releases** link. On the mirror web page, locate the `Win32` folder and click on it:

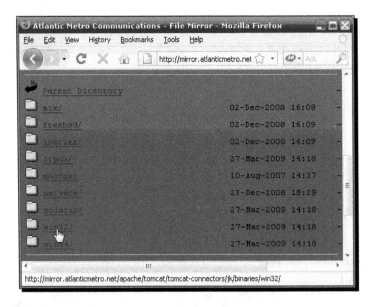

3. Now locate the `jk-1.2.28` folder and click on its link:

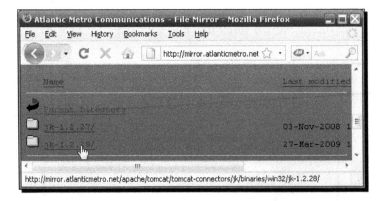

4. On the next web page, look for the `mod_jk-1.2.28-httpd-2.2.3.so` link and click on it to start downloading the connector:

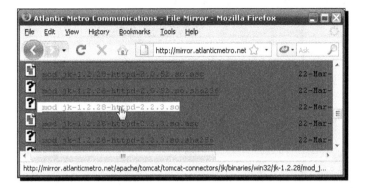

5. The **Opening mod_jk** dialog box will appear next. Click on the **OK** button to save the `mod_jk` file on disk.

6. Now navigate to the directory where you downloaded the `mod_jk` file, select it and then click on **Edit | Copy To Folder**:

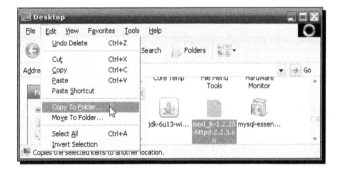

7. The **Copy Items** dialog box will appear next. Now navigate to the Apache `modules` folder (`C:\Program Files\Apache Software Foundation\Apache 2.2\ modules`) and click on the **Copy** button:

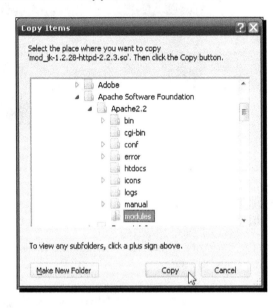

8. The `mod_jk` file will be copied to the Apache `modules` folder. Use Windows Explorer to navigate to this folder and rename the `mod_jk-1.2.28-httpd-2.2.3.so` file to `mod_jk.so`, as shown in the following screenshot:

9. Next, open the Notepad editor (**Start|All Programs|Accessories|Notepad**) and type the following lines into the blank area:

```
# Define 1 real worker using ajp13
worker.list=worker1
# Set properties for worker1 (ajp13)
worker.worker1.type=ajp13
worker.worker1.host=localhost
worker.worker1.port=8009
```

10. Name the file `workers.properties` (**File | Save**) and save it into the Apache `conf` folder:

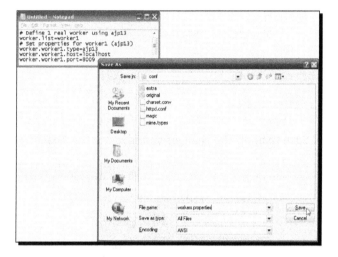

11. The next step is to open the Apache configuration file, `httpd.conf`, with Notepad and add some lines to it. Open Windows Explorer (**Start|My Computer**), go to the `C:\Program Files\Apache Software Foundation\Apache2.2\conf` folder and double-click on the `httpd.conf` file to open it:

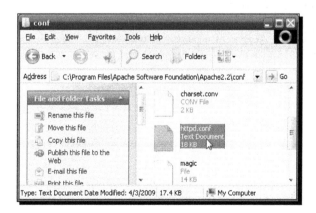

12. Scroll down through the file until you locate the last **LoadModule** directive. Put the following lines after this directive:

```
# Load mod_jk module
LoadModule jk_module modules/mod_jk.so
# Where to find workers.properties
JkWorkersFile "c:/Program Files/Apache Software
Foundation/Apache2.2/conf/workers.properties"
# Where to put jk shared memory
JkShmFile "c:/Program Files/Apache Software Foundation/Apache2.2/
logs/mod_jk.shm"
# Where to put jk logs
JkLogFile "c:/Program Files/Apache Software Foundation/Apache2.2/
logs/mod_jk.log"
# Set the jk log level [debug/error/info]
JkLogLevel info
# Select the timestamp log format
JkLogStampFormat "[%a %b %d %H:%M:%S %Y] "
# Send everything for context /roller to worker named worker1
JkMount /roller worker1
JkMount /roller/* worker1
```

13. Select **File | Save** to apply the changes you made to the Apache configuration file:

14. Close the `httpd.conf` file. Select **Start | All Programs | Apache Tomcat 6.0 | Configure Tomcat** to open the Tomcat Monitor:

15. Click on the **Stop** button to stop the Tomcat service. The **Apache Service Manager dialog** will show up and after a few seconds it will disappear. The **Service Status** label on the **Apache Tomcat Properties** dialog will show the **Stopped** message and the **Start** button will be enabled. Click on this button to restart Tomcat. The **Service Status** label will show the **Started** message again. You can close the **Apache Tomcat Properties** dialog now.

16. To restart Apache, select **Start | All Programs | Apache HTTP Server 2.2 | Control Apache Server | Stop**, wait for a few seconds until Apache stops, and select **Start | All Programs | Apache HTTP Server 2.2 | Control Apache Server | Start**. Wait for a few seconds until Apache starts, then open a web browser window and go to `http://localhost/roller`. The following screen shall appear:

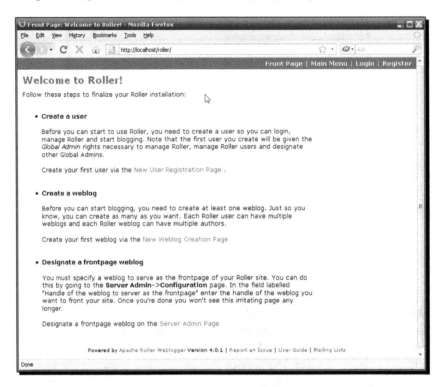

17. You can close your web browser now.

What just happened?

This was the last step needed to complete Apache Roller's installation process on your Windows PC. The `mod_jk` connector helps you to operate Apache Roller seamlessly with your website, without having to type the annoying `:8080` port number. Now you can go to Chapter 4, *How to start working with Roller*, and start with the really fun part of this book!

Pop quiz – installing Roller on Windows

1. The Apache Web server lets you:

    a. Create and manage your `rollerdb` database.

    b. Show your Apache Roller blog to the Internet world.

    c. Change the security parameters of your Roller installation.

2. How can you create a database in MySQL?

    a. Using the `mod_jk` module to integrate Tomcat and Apache.

    b. Installing the Java SDK and Tomcat.

    c. Opening a Command Prompt window and using the MySQL monitor.

3. Apache Tomcat is:

    a. A web server.

    b. A Java Application server.

    c. A database manager.

4. Deploying Roller means:

    a. Modifying its source code to add bells and whistles.

    b. Integrating Apache with Tomcat through the `jk_mod` connector.

    c. To download Roller files from the official website, unzip them and copy the `roller` folder, including all files in it, to Tomcat's `webapps` folder so you can access your Roller blog from a web browser.

Have a go hero – doing more with the thing

Well, you have succeeded at installing Roller on your Windows PC. Congratulations! Now, what if you wanted to use another name for your blog, instead of *roller*? With the examples in this chapter, you can access your blog with the `http://localhost/roller` URL, right? Well, what if you wanted to use `http://localhost/blogging`, `http://localhost/sports`, or just `http://localhost`?

What about having two different Apache Roller instances? Let's say your name is Rick and you want to create a blog for you, `http://localhost/rick` for example. You already have `http://localhost/roller` installed. Just follow the same instructions to create an extra installation using rick (or your real name, if you're not Rick!).

You can go back to the *Downloading and Installing Roller* section if you need help. Just remember some important things:

- Don't copy the `roller` folder directly on Tomcat's `webapps` folder, because you've already got one in there! You need to rename it first to `rick` and then copy it to `webapps`.

- You also need to create a different database, so use `rickdb` for `rollerdb` and `rick_user` for `roller_user` anywhere they appear in the `roller-custom.properties` and `Context.xml` files, and when creating the database with the MySQL monitor.

- In the `Context.xml` you'll need to change the `Context path` from `/roller` to `/rick`.

- Remember also to change the `docBase` line in `Context.xml`, from `\roller` to `\rick`.

- You can use the same Gmail account you used for your first Roller installation, unless you really want to use two blogs. In that case, you'll need to create another Gmail account, and change the user and password.

- After that, you need to add some properties to the `roller-custom.properties` file:

  ```
  uploads.dir=${user.home}/rick_data/uploads
  search.index.dir=${user.home}/rick_data/search-index
  log4j.appender.roller.File=${catalina.base}/logs/rick.log
  ```

  The first line defines the folder where Roller stores files you upload, such as images and other media you plan to use in your blog postings. We didn't use that property before because the default folder is `roller_data`. However, now, as you are going to have another Roller installation under the `rick` name, it's necessary to define a separate upload directory named `rick_data`. Be sure to always use a different upload directory for each installation of Roller in your server.

  The second line is necessary because you're using the `rick_data` folder as the upload directory, and the third line defines a separate log file for the *rick* blog, so you can track errors and other information about visits, and so on. I recommend you to always use the same name as your blog; in this case, `rick.log`.

- Oh, and I almost forgot! You need to add the following lines to the `httpd.conf` file, below the ones you added in step 9 from the `mod_jk` *Connector for Apache and Tomcat* section:

  ```
  JKMount /rick worker1
  JKMount /rick/* worker1
  ```

- This is so that you can use the URL without the annoying `:8080` port number.

Well, that's all you need to know to install another instance of Roller, besides what you've read in this chapter, so if you're up to the challenge, go for it! You'll not regret it! If you get stuck somewhere along the process, I'm always an e-mail away!

Summary

In this chapter, you learned how to install Apache Roller on a Windows environment, along with all the supporting software required—Apache Web server, JDK SE 6, Tomcat servlet engine, and MySQL database server.

Specifically, we covered:

- ◆ How to download, install, and test the Apache web server
- ◆ How to download, install, and test the Java SE Development Kit
- ◆ How to download, install, and test the Tomcat servlet engine (also known as Java Application server)
- ◆ How to download, install, and test the MySQL Server, Community Edition
- ◆ How to download, install, and test Apache Roller to make sure it's correctly installed on your Windows PC

We also discussed the basic Apache Roller properties you need to include in the `roller-custom.properties` file, along with the resources in the `Context.xml` file, so Roller can communicate with the MySQL database and send e-mail notifications when visitors to your blog leave comments.

Now that you have a functional Roller installation in your PC, you can go to Chapter 4 and start working with your Apache Roller blog. Or, if you feel really intrepid, get a Linux box and read Chapter 3, *Installing Roller on Linux*, to install Apache Roller on it; that way you'll get the opportunity to compare Roller's performance on a production environment in your own home!

3
Installing Roller on Linux

In this chapter, you'll learn to download and install Apache Roller, along with all the software applications (Apache web server, Java JDK, Tomcat servlet engine, MySQL database server, and mod_jk *connector) required to run this powerful weblog server on a Linux environment.*

In Chapter 1, Introduction to Weblogs, we saw an overview of blogs and how Apache Roller could get you into the ever-expanding world of the blogosphere. Now, I'll teach you how to put Apache Roller to work. At the same time, you'll learn some basic stuff about using the Apache web server, the Tomcat servlet engine, and the MySQL database server—three of the most popular open source applications in the world.

In short, we shall:

♦ Install the Apache web server, the Java JDK, the Tomcat servlet engine, and the MySQL database server

♦ Test and configure the software installed to make sure it's ready for Apache Roller

♦ Download and install Apache Roller

♦ Test your Apache Roller installation

♦ Install and configure the mod_jk connector for Apache and Tomcat integration

And now, let the show begin.

Checking your environment

Before installing the open source software, it's convenient to check your Linux environment to see if you already have any of these components installed—Apache, Tomcat, Java SE Development Kit, or MySQL. As there are so many Linux distributions around, the installation process for Apache, the Java JDK, MySQL, and Tomcat depends on what packages you selected when installing Linux. For example, I am running my official Apache Roller blog on a Slackware Linux PC, but you can use any distribution of your choice. According to DistroWatch (http://distrowatch.com/dwres.php?resource=major), the most popular ones at the time of writing this book are Ubuntu, openSUSE, Fedora, Debian, Mandriva, Mint, PCLinuxOS, Slackware, Gentoo, and CentOS. Each distribution has its pros and cons. If you're new to Linux, I definitely recommend you to go for Linux Ubuntu. In fact, I used Ubuntu when writing this chapter's material, so you can just go and grab a copy from the Ubuntu official site and follow all the exercises. What's more, you can download the Ubuntu Desktop Live CD (I used version 9.04) from http://www.ubuntu.com/getubuntu/download. Then create a CD following the instructions from the Ubuntu website, and install it in your PC's hard drive without any hassles, as a standalone Linux system, or you can even share your hard drive with a Windows system.

On the other hand, if you already have Linux installed, feel free to skip the installation instructions for any of these components that you may already have installed in your PC.

Installing Apache, Java, Tomcat, and MySQL

Finally, it's time to start working. In the following exercises, you will download and install all the software components required to run Apache Roller on a Linux PC. There are a lot of similarities between Windows and Linux installations, but there are a lot of differences also. As strange as that may sound, don't worry, I'll guide you all the way through.

Apache web server

The Apache web server (or HTTP server) is the most popular open source web server for Linux and Windows. Trust me, I've been using it since the year 2000 and have never had a performance problem, not even on slow hardware and low memory systems. Now it's your turn to try it on your PC. I'm sure you won't be disappointed.

 In case you didn't know, a Linux distribution, or "**distro**", is a collection of software applications included with the Linux operating system, and each distro is oriented towards a specific class of users. For example, the Ubuntu Linux distribution is oriented towards users of the Windows operating systems, and the Slackware Linux distro is oriented towards system administrators or more experienced users with a Unix background.

Time for action – installing the Apache web server

In this exercise, I'll show you how to install the Apache web server (httpd) in a PC with Ubuntu Linux. On some distros such as Slackware, you can choose to install Apache when installing Linux on your PC. Other distros may have similar installation steps as follows, but I recommend you to check the official website for your Linux distro to be sure what to do exactly.

 If you want to be sure you're installing the most recent apache2 package on Ubuntu, you need to open a terminal window and type sudo apt-get update followed by sudo apt-get upgrade.

1. On your Ubuntu GNOME desktop, select **System | Administration | Synaptic Package Manager**. Scroll down the left panel below the toolbar of the manager dialog until you find the **World Wide Web** section. Click on that section to select it, and then look for the **apache2** package on the right panel. Right-click on that package and select **Mark for Installation**:

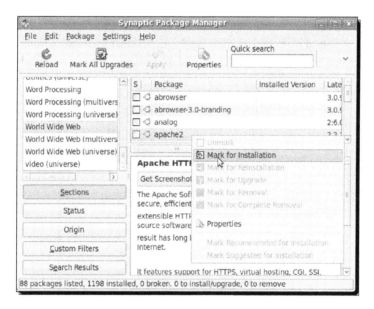

2. The **Mark additional required changes?** dialog will appear next. Click on the **Mark** button to continue:

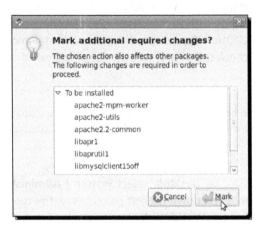

3. Now click on the **Apply** button in the **Synaptic Package Manager** dialog. The **Summary** dialog will appear, asking if you want to apply the changes you selected. You can click on the **To be installed** element in the white area to see all the packages that are going to be installed. Click on **Apply** to start installing the Apache web server in your PC:

4. The Synaptic Package Manager will begin to download and install all the packages needed for the Apache web server. When finished, the following screen will appear:

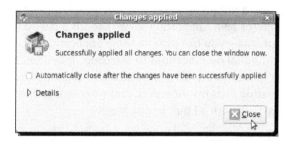

5. Click on the **Close** button and then close the **Synaptic Package Manager** dialog.

6. To test if your installation was successful, open Mozilla Firefox and type `http://localhost` on the address bar. You should see a web page with the **It works!** message, as shown in the following screenshot:

What just happened?

Well, now you have the Apache web server installed and running in your Linux PC. The installation process was pretty simple. With Ubuntu's Synaptic Package Manager, it's even quicker than the Windows installation. In step 6, to test your Apache installation, you used `http://localhost` as the URL address for the Apache web server installed in your PC. **Localhost** is the standard hostname used when you're accessing a web server installed on the same machine where you use a web browser.

And because Linux is the best environment for running a web server in your home PC, you can definitely run an Apache Roller blog server to publish your own blogs from there. However, you should take several security measures to prevent hackers from wrecking your precious information. A good antivirus is very convenient, along with an equally good firewall. However, don't worry because when you finish reading this book, you'll be ready to show your blog to the Internet world and you will use a real Internet URL like everybody else. For now, let's focus on Roller's installation.

The Java SE Development Kit

The next step in our Apache Roller installation path is the **Java Development Kit** (JDK). However, have no fear; we're not going to see any Java programming here. It's just that the Tomcat servlet engine (or Java Application server) needs a JDK to run. That's one of the greatest things about Java—you can use the same application on different operating systems, without any additional modifications to the code. Take Tomcat for example; you can download the same files both on Windows and Linux, and because of the JDK, they run seamlessly on both operating systems. However, that's enough techie-talk for now. Let's get to work before you fall asleep with all that boring theory.

Time for action – installing a JDK

There are several versions of the Java Development Kit. In this exercise, we're going to install the Java SE Development Kit 6, the most up-to-date version of the JDK at the time of this writing.

1. Open the Synaptic Package Manager again (**System | Administration | Synaptic Package Manager**) and select the **Development (multiverse)** section on the left pane. Then locate the **sun-java6-jdk** package on the right pane, right-click on it and select the **Mark for Installation** option.

2. Click on the **Mark** button from the **Mark additional required changes?** dialog, and then click on the **Apply** button in the **Synaptic Package Manager** dialog:

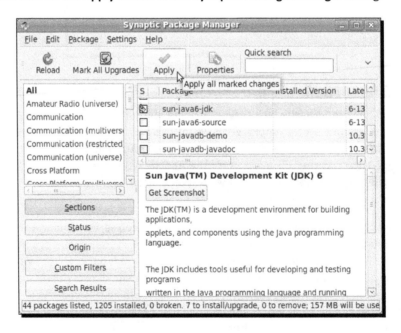

3. Click on the **Apply** button from the **Summary** dialog to apply the changes you selected. The **Synaptic Package Manager** will start to download the Sun Java JDK 6 package.

4. When the downloading process is complete, the **Operating System Distributor License for Java** will appear. Click on the **Do you agree with the DLJ license terms?** box to enable it and then click on the **Forward** button to continue.

5. The **Synaptic Package Manager** will continue to install the Sun Java JDK 6 package:

6. If you have the **Automatically close after the changes have been successfully applied** box selected, the **Applying Changes dialog** will close automatically and you will return to the **Synaptic Package Manager** main screen. You can close it now.

7. To test your Sun Java JDK 6 installation, open a terminal window (**Applications | Accessories | Terminal**) and type `java -version` at the system prompt. You should receive the following output:

8. Type `exit` on the terminal to close this window.

What just happened?

Is Java easy to install on Linux, or not? As you can see from the previous exercise, the JDK installation process is pretty straightforward on Linux Ubuntu, thanks to the Synaptic Package Manager, and you don't need to change any default option. It's ready to work out of the box.

With the JDK you can learn basic Java programming without needing anything else, just a text editor and the Java compiler *javac*. So, once you get comfortable working with Apache Roller and your blog, maybe you can learn Java and make contributions to the Roller project, how about that?

We've installed Apache and the JDK. Now guess what? It's "Tomcat time".

Tomcat servlet engine

Now it's Tomcat's turn on the stage. This open source servlet engine, also known as a **Java Application server**, is the heart that drives Apache Roller. Tomcat needs the JDK to run on Windows, Linux, or any other operating system with Java support. Moreover, the big advantage of using Java applications is that you don't need to rewrite code so they can work on different operating systems. This also applies to Apache Roller, because the same files are used both in Windows and Linux. However, for now, let's focus on Tomcat's installation.

 A **servlet** is a piece of code that lets you add dynamic content to a website, using the Java programming language.

Time for action – installing Tomcat

Tomcat is an open source project from the Apache Software Foundation, the same guys that are behind Apache Roller. Isn't that great? In a few seconds, you're going to have in your hands one of the most popular and powerful Java servlet engines around, used by a lot of big industries and organizations worldwide. Ready for some action? Let's begin.

1. Open Mozilla Firefox and go to `http://tomcat.apache.org`. Look for the **Download** section and click on the **Tomcat 6.x** link:

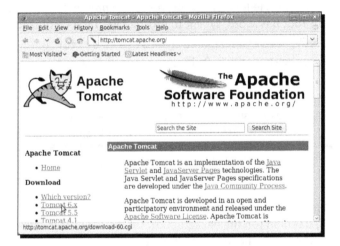

2. Scroll down the **Tomcat 6 Downloads** web page until you locate the **Binary Distributions** section, and click on the **tar.gz** link from the **Core** category:

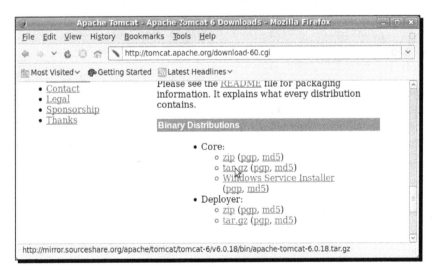

The Tomcat version downloaded in this example is 6.0.18, but maybe you'll download a more recent version. Don't forget to change the 6.0.18 number in the following lines of code to the corresponding version you downloaded.

3. Select the **Save File** option in the **Open apache-tomcat** dialog box, click on the **OK** button and wait for the file to download through Mozilla Firefox Download Manager. When finished, open a Terminal window (**Applications | Accessories | Terminal**) and type the following lines, pressing *Enter* after each line (if Ubuntu asks for your root password, type it to proceed with the command execution):

```
sudo tar xvfz Desktop/apache-tomcat-6.0.18.tar.gz
sudo mv apache-tomcat-6.0.18 /usr/local/tomcat
```

In the next step, you're going to need a package called autoconf. To install it, type sudo apt-get install autoconf on the Terminal window before proceeding to step 4. You can also install it from the Synaptic Package Manager.

4. Now you have to compile and install a little program called jsvc to run Tomcat as a daemon (on the background). On the same Terminal window you used before, type the following lines, pressing *Enter* after each line:

```
cd /usr/local/tomcat/bin
sudo tar xvfz jsvc.tar.gz
cd jsvc-src
sudo autoconf
sudo ./configure --with-java=/usr/lib/jvm/java-6-sun
sudo make
sudo cp jsvc ..
```

5. The next thing to do is create a special group called tomcat, along with a special user also called tomcat, to run the Tomcat servlet engine in a safe way, and give that group and user the ownership of the Tomcat folder (/usr/local/tomcat). Type the following lines on a Terminal window, pressing *Enter* after each line:

```
sudo groupadd tomcat
sudo useradd -g tomcat -c "Tomcat User" -d /usr/local/tomcat tomcat -p tomcat
sudo chown -R tomcat:tomcat /usr/local/tomcat
```

6. Now you need to copy and modify a startup script, `Tomcat.sh`, so that Tomcat can start/stop automatically every time you startup/shutdown your Linux box. Type the following lines on a Terminal window, pressing *Enter* after each line:

```
sudo cp /usr/local/tomcat/bin/jsvc-src/native/Tomcat.sh
                                        /etc/init.d/tomcat
sudo gedit /etc/init.d/tomcat
```

7. On the text editor, modify the following lines in bold text, so the script can work on your Linux machine:

```
JAVA_HOME=/usr/lib/jvm/java-6-sun
CATALINA_HOME=/usr/local/tomcat
DAEMON_HOME=/usr/local/tomcat/bin
TOMCAT_USER=tomcat
TMP_DIR=/var/tmp
CATALINA_OPTS=
CLASSPATH=\
$JAVA_HOME/lib/tools.jar:\
$DAEMON_HOME/bin/commons-daemon.jar:\
$CATALINA_HOME/bin/bootstrap.jar

case "$1" in
  start)
    #
    # Start Tomcat
    #
    $DAEMON_HOME/jsvc \
    -user $TOMCAT_USER \
    -home $JAVA_HOME \
    -Dcatalina.home=$CATALINA_HOME \
    -Djava.io.tmpdir=$TMP_DIR \
    -outfile $CATALINA_HOME/logs/catalina.out \
    -errfile '&1' \
    $CATALINA_OPTS \
    -cp $CLASSPATH \
    org.apache.catalina.startup.Bootstrap
    #
    # To get a verbose JVM
    #-verbose \
    # To get a debug of jsvc.
    #-debug \
    ;;
  stop)
    #
    # Stop Tomcat
```

```
       #
       PID=`cat /var/run/jsvc.pid`
       kill $PID
       ;;
  *)
       echo "Usage tomcat.sh start/stop"
       exit 1;;
esac
```

8. Once you've done all the modifications required for the `tomcat` startup/shutdown script, save the file (**File | Save**) and close the text editor:

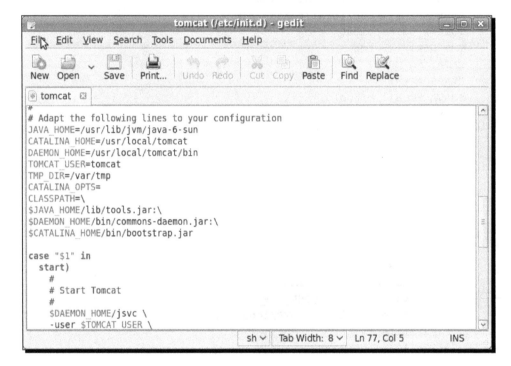

9. Now, to test your Tomcat installation, open a Terminal window and type the following lines to make the startup/shutdown script executable and to test it:

```
sudo chmod 755 /etc/init.d/tomcat
sudo /etc/init.d/tomcat start
```

10. Open Mozilla Firefox and type `http://localhost:8080` on the address bar. You should see the following **Welcome to Tomcat** web page:

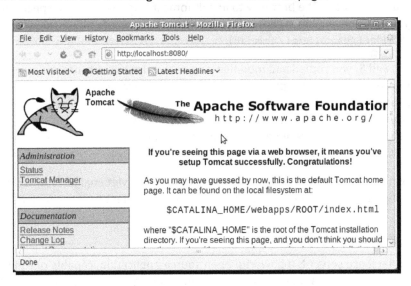

11. The last step is linking the startup/shutdown script to the startup/shutdown folders of your Linux system. In Ubuntu and other Debian-based systems, type the following lines in a Terminal window, pressing *Enter* after each line:

```
sudo ln -s /etc/init.d/tomcat /etc/rc1.d/K99tomcat
sudo ln -s /etc/init.d/tomcat /etc/rc2.d/S99tomcat
```

12. You can close the Terminal window now. Every time you startup/shutdown your Linux machine, the Tomcat script will startup/shutdown automatically, too.

What just happened?

This was the third installation exercise on our way to *blogger's land*. Installing Tomcat on Linux is a little bit more complicated than installing it on Windows, because Linux has some security restrictions that we have to take into account when installing software. The `sudo` command helps us to take care of the administrative chores in Linux Ubuntu, as we saw in steps 3 to 11 of the previous exercise.

In step 4, we used the `jsvc` program to run Tomcat as a daemon. This has the same effect as a service in Windows that is to run Tomcat as an independent process in the background, without having to start it up/shut it down manually, every time we startup or shutdown the Linux PC.

In step 5 you created a user and a group named `tomcat`. On Linux systems, there are several users and groups for doing daily chores, such as backing up the system, installing software, or working as a regular user. The best way to install Tomcat is to assign it to a special group and user, and they are the only ones allowed to write, read, or execute files inside the Tomcat installation folder (`/usr/local/tomcat`).

In steps 6, 7, and 8, you copied and modified a special script to startup/shutdown Tomcat on your Linux machine. This script has to be inside a special folder, `/etc/init.d`, where other software components such as the MySQL server and the Apache web server have their own startup/shutdown scripts, and with the symbolic links you created in step 11, Linux can startup or shutdown Tomcat whenever needed (for example, when you startup or shutdown your Linux PC), without you having to worry about it.

We already have a web server, a Java environment, and a servlet engine. Now it's time to install the MySQL database server, the data-handling component for Apache Roller.

MySQL database server

The MySQL database server is a powerful open source application, capable of running the most data-intensive applications for small, medium, and big companies worldwide. So, along with the other three components that we've already installed (Apache, Java, and Tomcat), you don't have anything to worry about with MySQL, because you're in good hands.

Time for action – installing MySQL

I've been using MySQL for as long as I can remember using web applications, PHP, and Java. I still can't believe it is open source, which means it's free, well, at least the Community Server. There is also an Enterprise Server where you receive support and a lot of goodies from the MySQL team for a certain price, but as we're already experts at installing things on Linux, let's go and try the Community MySQL Edition.

1. Open the **Synaptic Package Manager** and type `mysql` in the **Quick search** button. Scroll down the right panel until you locate the `mysql-server` and `mysql-client` packages. Right-click on the `mysql-server` package and select the **Mark for installation** option, then click on the **Mark** button in the **Mark additional required changes?** dialog. Right-click on the `mysql-client` package and select the **Mark for installation** option as well. Then click on the **Apply** button in the **Synaptic Package Manager** main screen:

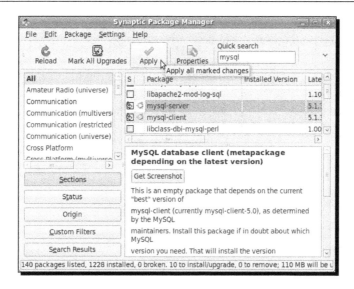

2. Click on the **Apply** button in the **Summary** dialog, and wait for the Synaptic Package Manager to download the required packages (approximately seven minutes on a 512 KBps DSL connection).

3. Once the downloading process completes, the **Configuring mysql-server-5.0** dialog will appear, asking for the "root" password. Enter a password in the **New password for the MySQL "root" user:** field. Don't forget that password, because you won't be able to access the MySQL client to create databases later without it. Click on the **Forward** button to continue:

4. Repeat the password on the following dialog, and click on **Forward** to continue. The Synaptic Package Manager will continue installing the MySQL server packages. If you have the **Automatically close after the changes have been successfully applied** box selected, the **Applying Changes dialog** will close automatically and you will return to the **Synaptic Package Manager** main screen. You can close it now.

5. To test the MySQL installation, open a Terminal window (**Applications | Accessories | Terminal**) and type `mysql -u root -p`, followed by *Enter*. Then type the password you assigned to the "root" user. The MySQL monitor will respond with a welcome message, as shown in the following screenshot:

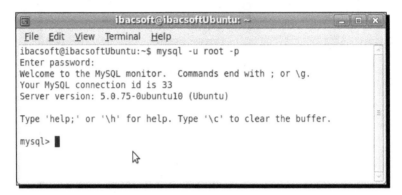

```
ibacsoft@ibacsoftUbuntu: ~
File  Edit  View  Terminal  Help
ibacsoft@ibacsoftUbuntu:~$ mysql -u root -p
Enter password:
Welcome to the MySQL monitor.  Commands end with ; or \g.
Your MySQL connection id is 33
Server version: 5.0.75-0ubuntu10 (Ubuntu)

Type 'help;' or '\h' for help. Type '\c' to clear the buffer.

mysql>
```

6. Type `exit` to close the MySQL monitor and close the Terminal window.

What just happened?

Now you have all the open source software required to install Apache Roller in your Linux box. As with the Apache web server and the Java JDK, you can see that the Synaptic Package Manager simplifies the installation process in Linux Ubuntu for some open source components. As I mentioned earlier, there are several ways to install the MySQL server on a Linux environment, but I wanted to show you how easy it is to configure a PC with Linux Ubuntu to run your favorite open source software.

That pretty much covers all you'll need to know about MySQL to run your own Apache Roller blog server. And finally, we've come to the point you've been waiting for since you started to read this book.

Downloading and installing Apache Roller

At last, you will finally get your hands on Roller's installation process. I hope you enjoyed the previous sections, and now you'll get the chance to put it all together.

Files required for Apache Roller

The first thing to do before deploying Apache Roller on your computer is to get all the required files—the JavaMail API and the **Java Application Framework (JAF)** for Roller's e-mail notification features, and the JDBC driver for connecting to the roller MySQL database.

The JavaMail API

With the JavaMail API, you can build mail and messaging applications. Roller uses this API to send e-mails from your blog, so that you and your readers can receive notifications when they leave a comment.

Time for action – downloading the JavaMail API

All you need to do is download a ZIP file from the Sun website, unzip it, and copy the `mail.jar` file to the `lib` folder in Tomcat, from where Roller can use it along with all the other common library files needed.

1. Open Mozilla Firefox and type `http://java.sun.com/products/javamail/downloads/index.html`. Scroll down through the page until you find the **Download JavaMail 1.4.2** link:

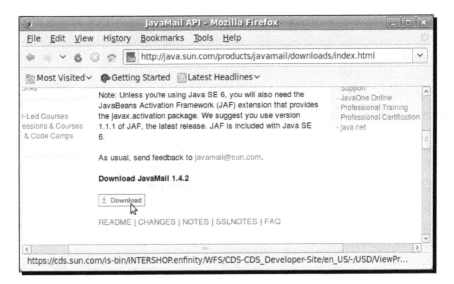

2. Click on the **Download** button to go to the download page. Select **I agree to the JavaMail 1.4.2 License Agreement** and click on the **Continue** button:

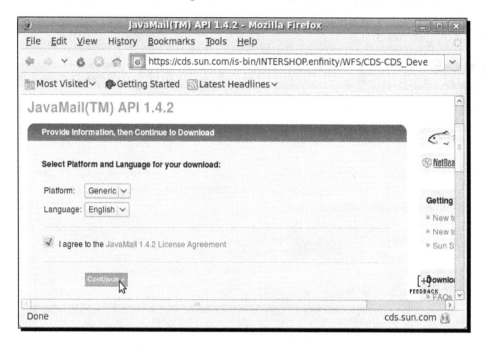

3. On the next download page, select the **javamail-1.4.2.zip** link to open the **Opening javamail-1.4.2.zip** dialog. Select the **Save File** radio button and click on the **OK** button to start the download process.

4. Once the download completes, use the Mozilla Firefox Download Manager to open the folder containing the **javamail-1.4.2.zip** file (right-click on the file name and select **Open Containing Folder** from the pop-up menu):

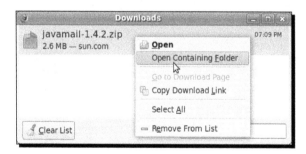

5. Right-click on the `javamail-1.4.2.zip` file and select **Extract here** from the pop-up menu to extract its contents into the `javamail-1.4.2` folder. Then double-click on that folder and locate the `mail.jar` file:

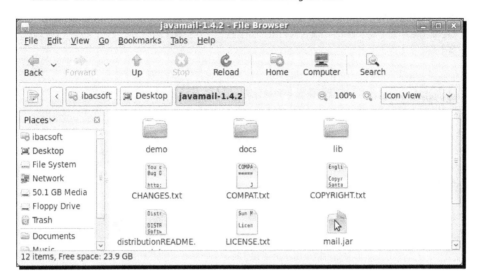

 The `sudo` command will ask for the *super user password* of your Linux machine. Make sure you have "root" access to the Linux PC where you plan to install Apache Roller, or ask your System Administrator how to copy the `mail.jar` file into your system.

6. Now close the **File Browser** dialog, open a Terminal window (**Applications | Accessories | Terminal**), type the following lines to copy the `mail.jar` file into Tomcat's `lib` folder, and make the `tomcat` user and group owners of that file (don't forget to press *Enter* after each line):

```
sudo cp Destkop/javamail-1.4.2/mail.jar /usr/local/tomcat/lib
sudo chown tomcat:tomcat /usr/local/tomcat/lib/mail.jar
```

7. Type `exit` to close the Terminal window.

What just happened?

All right. You've just added mail capacity to your Tomcat installation. Although you'll never need to deal directly with `mail.jar` from your Roller blog, it's necessary to install this file before attempting to install Roller, because it contains all the Java code required to send e-mail messages. There's one more file Roller needs to send e-mails, and we'll see how to download and install it in the next exercise.

The JavaBeans Activation Framework API

The JAF API allows Java developers to use standard services for working with arbitrary pieces of data in a uniform way. Roller uses the JavaMail and JAF APIs to send e-mail notifications. You need to put the `mail.jar` and `activation.jar` files on Tomcat's `lib` folder, so that Roller can use them. We already saw how to download and copy `mail.jar` to your Tomcat's `lib` folder. Now let's see how to do the same with `activation.jar`.

Time for action – downloading the JAF API

In this exercise, we're going to download the JAF API from the Sun website. The steps are almost identical to the JavaMail exercise, so you can use it as a reference.

1. Open Mozilla Firefox and go to `http://java.sun.com/javase/technologies/desktop/javabeans/jaf/downloads/index.html`. Scroll down through the page until you find the **Download JavaBeans Activation Framework Download** link, and click on it:

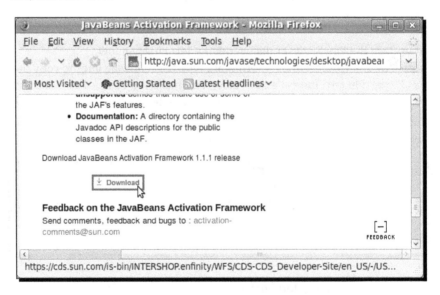

2. Select the **I agree to the Software License Agreement** box and click on **Continue**:

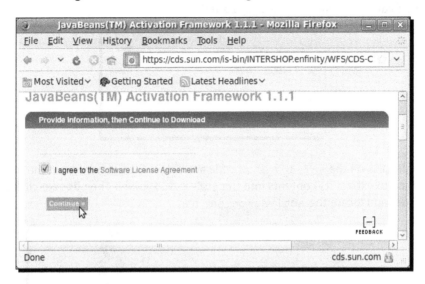

3. Click on the **jaf-1_1_1.zip** link to open the **Opening jaf-1_1_1.zip** dialog. Select the **Save File** radio button and click on the **OK** button:

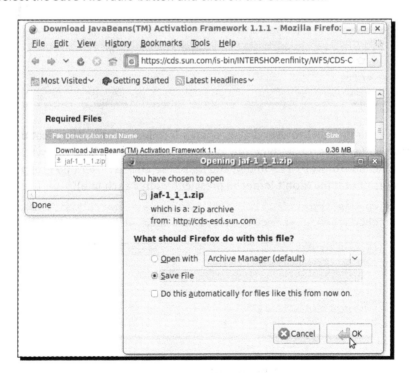

4. Once the download is complete, use the Mozilla Firefox Download Manager to open the folder containing the **jaf-1_1_1.zip** file:

5. Right-click on the `jaf-1_1_1.zip` file and select **Extract here** from the pop-up menu to extract its contents into the `jaf-1.1.1` folder. Then double-click on that folder and locate the `activation.jar` file:

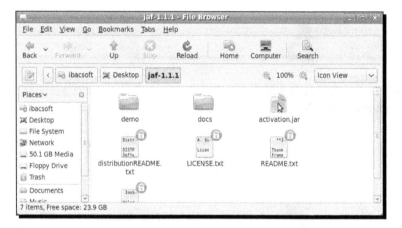

6. Now close the **File Browser** dialog, open a Terminal window (**Applications | Accessories | Terminal**), type the following lines to copy the `activation.jar` file into Tomcat's `lib` folder, and make the `tomcat` user and group owners of that file (don't forget to press *Enter* after each line):

```
sudo cp Desktop/jaf-1.1.1/activation.jar /usr/local/tomcat/lib
sudo chown tomcat:tomcat /usr/local/tomcat/lib/activation.jar
```

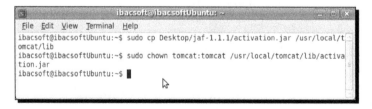

7. Type `exit` to close the Terminal window.

What just happened?

Now that you have the `mail.jar` and `activation.jar` files inside Tomcat's `lib` folder, Roller will be able to send e-mail notifications when someone leaves comments on your blog. The good part is that you don't need to know how to manipulate the Java code inside `mail.jar` or `activation.jar`, Roller takes care of that automatically, and you just have to blog, blog, and blog.

The MySQL JDBC driver

MySQL `Connector/J 5.1` is the official JDBC driver used for connecting to MySQL databases from Java applications, like Apache Roller. In this next exercise, you'll download the `Connector/J 5.1 jar` file and copy it to Tomcat's `lib` folder, so Roller can communicate with the `rollerdb` database that you'll create in a later section.

Time for action – downloading and installing MySQL connector/J 5.1

You can download the `Connector/J 5.1` JDBC driver from MySQL Developer Zone. Just follow the simple steps:

1. Open Mozilla Firefox and go to `http://dev.mysql.com/downloads/connector/j/5.1.html`. Scroll down the page until you locate the **Source and Binaries (tar.gz) Pick a mirror** link:

2. Click on this link to go to the **Select a Mirror** web page. Scroll down the page until you locate the **No thanks, just take me to the downloads!** link, and click on it:

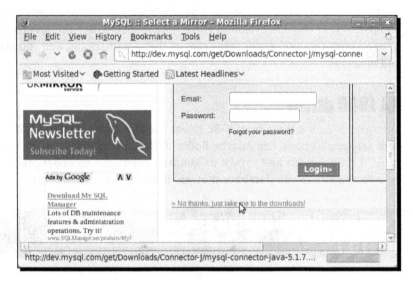

3. Scroll down the next web page until you find a mirror near your location, and click on the **HTTP** link (the following screenshot shows mirrors in the United States):

4. Click on the **Save File** button in the **Opening mysql-connector-java-5.1.7.tar.gz** dialog box, press the **OK** button and wait for the file to download through the Mozilla Firefox Download Manager. Right-click on the downloaded file and select **Open containing folder** from the pop-up menu when the download process is complete:

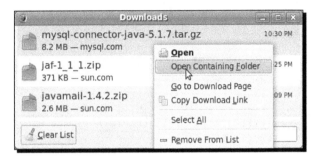

5. Right-click on the `mysql-connector-java-5.1.7.tar.gz` file and select **Extract here** from the pop-up menu to extract its contents into the `mysql-connector-java-5.1.7` folder. Then double-click on that folder and locate the `mysql-connector-java-5.1.7-bin.jar` file:

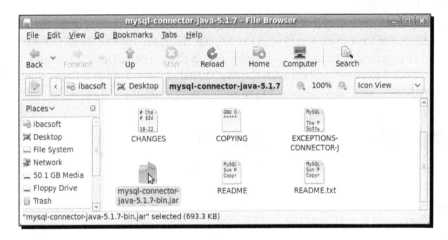

The `sudo` command will ask for the *super user password* of your Linux machine. Make sure you have *root access* to the Linux PC where you plan to install Apache Roller, or ask your System Administrator about how to copy the `mysql-connector-java-5.1.7-bin.jar` file into your system.

6. Now close the **File Browser** dialog, open a Terminal window (**Applications | Accessories | Terminal**), type the following lines to copy the `mysql-connector-java-5.1.7-bin.jar` file into Tomcat's `lib` folder, and make the `tomcat` user and group, owners of that file (don't forget to press *Enter* after each line):

```
sudo cp Desktop/mysql-connector-java-5.1.7/mysql-connector-java-
5.1.7-bin.jar /usr/local/tomcat/lib
sudo chown tomcat:tomcat /usr/local/tomcat/lib/mysql-connector-
java-5.1.7-bin.jar
```

7. Type `exit` to close the Terminal window.

What just happened?

In the previous exercise, you downloaded MySQL `Connector/J 5.1`, a JDBC driver that Apache Roller uses to communicate with the MySQL database that holds all the information related to blogs, users, comments, and configuration parameters. This file contains all the Java code needed to communicate with the MySQL database server, and Roller does it for you automatically. Now let's see how to install Roller on Tomcat.

Deploying Roller files to Tomcat

OK, it's time to finally deploy Apache Roller to the Tomcat servlet engine, and start the configuration process. "But what does *deploy* mean?" you may ask. In case of a Java web application, like Roller, it means you have to download the Roller ZIP file from the official website, then unzip it, and copy the `roller` folder inside Tomcat's `webapps` folder, so that you can access it from a web browser. We'll see how to do that in the next exercise.

Time for action – downloading and deploying Roller

In this exercise, we'll go to the Roller download website, grab the latest Roller `zip` file, and copy it to Tomcat's `webapps` folder.

1. Go to the Apache Roller downloads web page (`http://roller.apache.org/downloads.html`) and click on the **Roller 4.0.1 ("best available")** link from the **General Availability (GA) Releases** section:

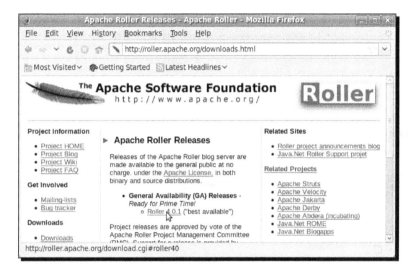

2. Scroll down to the **Roller 4.0.1** section of the next page, and click on the **apache-roller-4.0.1.zip** link:

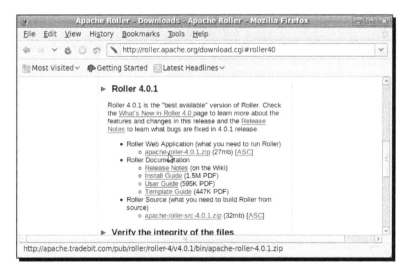

3. Select the **Save File** radio button from the **Opening apache-roller-4.0.1.zip** dialog and click on **OK** to start the download process. The file will take several seconds to download (or minutes, depending on your Internet connection speed).

4. Right-click on the `apache-roller-4.0.1.zip` file you've just downloaded and select **Open Containing Folder** from the pop-up menu:

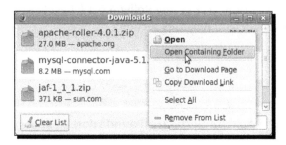

5. Right-click on the `apache-roller-4.0.1.zip` file and select **Extract here** from the pop-up menu:

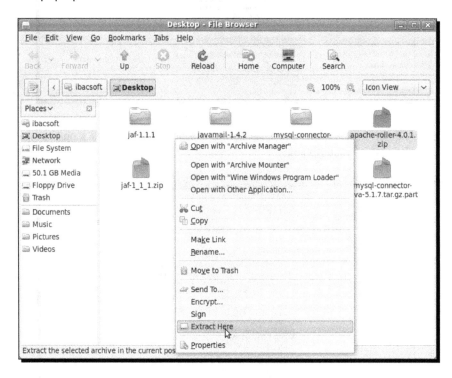

6. The extracted files will be inside the `apache-roller-4.0.1` folder. Now open a Terminal window (**Applications | Accessories | Terminal**) and type `sudo cp -R Desktop/apache-roller-4.0.1/webapp/ roller /usr/local/tomcat/webapps` to copy the `roller` folder into Tomcat's `webapps` folder (don't forget to press *Enter* after each line):

7. Type `exit` to close the Terminal window. Now, to verify that Roller was extracted correctly, open the Nautilus File Browser (**Places | Computer**) to navigate to Tomcat's `webapps` folder. Double-click on the **Filesystem** icon, then double-click on the `usr`, `local`, `tomcat`, and `webapps` folders. There should now be a `roller` folder inside Tomcat's `webapps` folder, as shown in the following screenshot:

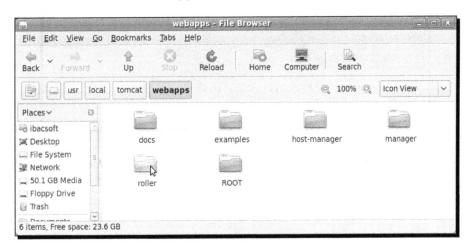

8. Now you can close the Nautilus File Browser.

What just happened?

In this last exercise, you downloaded and copied Apache Roller's files to Tomcat's `webapps` folder. Now that you have all the Roller files and folders inside Tomcat, you need to create a database where Roller can save all the information related to your blog.

Creating the Roller database

The next step is to create a MySQL database for Roller. You'll need root access to the MySQL server installed in your Linux PC, so now's the time to go back to the MySQL installation section, and recover the username and password you assigned to your MySQL root user.

Time for action – creating a MySQL database for Roller

In this exercise, you'll use the MySQL monitor to create a database for your Apache Roller blog site.

1. Open a Terminal window (**Applications | Accessories | Terminal**) and type

    ```
    mysql -u root -p.
    ```

2. The MySQL monitor will ask you for the "root" user password. This is the password you used when installing MySQL server. Type it and press *Enter*. If the password is correct, the following screen shall appear:

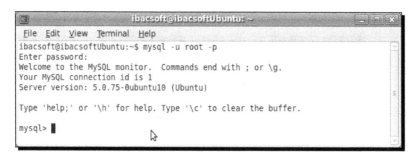

3. Now type the following lines after the `mysql>` prompt (remember to replace *password* with a secure password) and press *Enter* after each line:

    ```
    create database rollerdb;
    grant all on rollerdb.* to roller_user@'%' identified by
      'password';
    grant all on rollerdb.* to roller_user@localhost identified by
      'password';
    ```

4. When finished, your screen should look like this:

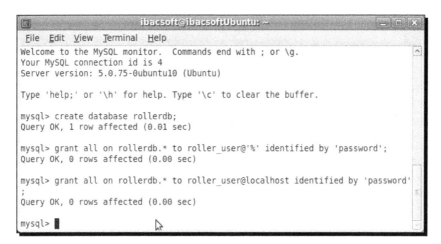

5. Notice the **Query OK, 0 rows affected (X.XX sec)** line after each line you typed. It means there were no errors with the commands you entered. Now type `exit` and press *Enter* to exit the MySQL monitor, then type `exit` to close the Terminal window.

What just happened?

In this last exercise, you used the MySQL monitor to create the `rollerdb` database, and then created a database user named `roller_user`. You then assigned permissions to `roller_user`, so that it can create, modify, and delete tables inside the `rollerdb` database. Note that the password you used for the `rollerdb` database isn't the same as your MySQL root user's password. Remember that the "root" user has access to all the MySQL server configuration, and the user named `roller_user` only has access to your `rollerdb` database.

Roller properties and context files

OK, you downloaded and copied the Apache Roller files to Tomcat, and then you created the `rollerdb` MySQL database. Now it's time to create the `roller-custom.properties` file. Inside this file are all the parameters you can use to fine-tune Apache Roller's behavior during the installation process. After that you'll need to create a file named `Context.xml` for Roller. This file is called a **Context configuration file**, and it's used to describe all the resources (in this case, the JDBC database driver, the JavaMail API, and the JavaBeans Framework API) used inside a context (the Apache Roller blog server).

But that's enough smart-talk for now; let's see how to create the `roller-custom.properties` file first.

The roller-custom.properties file

In the next exercise, you'll create the `roller-custom.properties` file and save it in Roller's `WEB-INF/classes` folder, where Roller can read it.

Time for action – creating roller-custom.properties

In this exercise, you'll create a `roller-custom.properties` file with the basic parameters and I'll show you where it has to be saved.

1. Open a Terminal window (**Applications | Accessories | Terminal**) and type the following lines after the `~$` prompt, pressing *Enter* after each line:

```
cd /usr/local/tomcat/webapps/roller/WEB-INF/classes
sudo gedit roller-custom.properties
```

2. If needed, type the `sudo` password and press *Enter*. The text editor will appear next. Type the following lines inside the blank area, pressing *Enter* after each line:

```
installation.type=auto
database.configurationType=jndi
database.jndi.name=jdbc/rollerdb
mail.configurationType=jndi
mail.jndi.name=mail/Session
```

3. Select **File | Save** from the text editor menu bar to save the `roller-custom.properties` file inside Apache Roller's `WEB-INF/classes` folder:

4. Close the text editor and also type `exit` on the Terminal window to close it.

What just happened?

Roller uses the `roller-custom.properties` file that you've just created to look for the database and mail configuration, in this case, the name of the resources it has to look for in the `Context.xml` file that you'll create in the next exercise.

A word about the `sudo` command in Linux

The `sudo` command in Linux is used to do tasks related to the "root" user, or administrator. As a regular user, you can't save files on certain system folders such as `/usr/share/tomcat6/webapps/roller/WEB-INF/classes`; you need "root" access for writing the `roller-custom.properties` file in there. That's why you need to open a Terminal window and type `sudo` before the `gedit roller-custom-properties` command. If you don't use `sudo`, you won't be able to save that file inside Apache Roller's `WEB-INF/classes` folder.

The Context.xml file

The Context configuration file (`Context.xml`) is used by Roller to read the configuration parameters for the JDBC driver and the mail properties, so that it can communicate with the `rollerdb` database to perform all the required chores for running the blog server, and with the JavaMail API to send e-mail notifications. Now let's see how to create that file.

Time for action – creating Context.xml

In this exercise, you'll learn how to create a `Context.xml` file with all the parameters required for the MySQL `Connector/J` driver and the `activation.jar` and the `mail.jar` files you downloaded before.

You're going to need a valid e-mail address for Roller's e-mail notification features. I chose to use a Gmail account for this exercise, because it lets you send e-mail from your Roller blog server without any problems. So, I recommend you create a Gmail account for your Roller blog server, if you haven't got one already. That way, you'll just need to change the e-mail address and password used in the next exercise, and leave all the other parameters intact.

1. Open a Terminal window (**Applications | Accessories | Terminal**) and type the following lines after the ~$ prompt, pressing *Enter* after each line:

```
cd /usr/local/tomcat/webapps/roller/META-INF
sudo gedit context.xml
```

2. If necessary, type the `sudo` password and press *Enter*. The text editor will appear next. Type the following lines inside the blank area, pressing *Enter* after each line:

```
<Context path="/roller"
    docBase="/usr/local/tomcat/webapps/roller" debug="0">

  <Resource name="jdbc/rollerdb" auth="Container"
    type="javax.sql.DataSource"
    driverClassName="com.mysql.jdbc.Driver"
    url="jdbc:mysql://localhost:3306/rollerdb?
    autoReconnect=true&amp;
    useUnicode=true&amp;characterEncoding=utf-&amp;
    mysqlEncoding=utf8"
    username="roller_user"
    password="password"
    maxActive="20" maxIdle="3"
    removeAbandoned="true" maxWait="3000" />

  <Resource name="mail/Session" auth="Container"
     type="javax.mail.Session"
     username="alromeromx@gmail.com"
     password="password"
     mail.debug="false"
     mail.user="alromeromx@gmail.com"
     mail.password="password"
     mail.smtp.from="alromeromx@gmail.com"
     mail.transport.protocol="smtp"
     mail.smtp.port="465"
     mail.smtp.host="smtp.gmail.com"
     mail.smtp.auth="true"
     mail.smtp.starttls.enable="true"
     mail.smtp.socketFactory.port="465"
     mail.smtp.socketFactory.class=
       "javax.net.ssl.SSLSocketFactory"
     mail.smtp.socketFactory.fallback="false" />
</Context>
```

3. Change the parameters in bold to reflect your own values for the database user password, the e-mail username, password, and SMTP server you're going to use for e-mail notifications (if you're going to use a Gmail account, use the same server).

4. Select **File | Save** from the text editor menu bar to save the `Context.xml` file inside Apache Roller's `META-INF` folder:

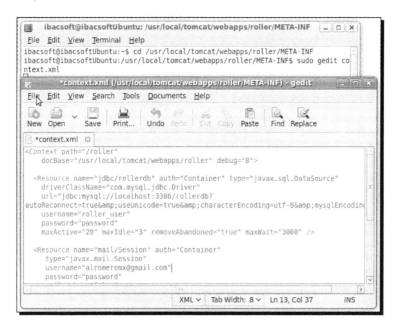

5. Close the text editor and also type `exit` on the Terminal window to close it.

What just happened?

The `Context.xml` file has all the parameters Roller needs to communicate with the `rollerdb` database, and to send e-mail notifications when visitors to your blog leave comments. Now you just need to modify some security settings, and then you can start testing your Roller installation.

Changing keys in security.xml

The `security.xml` file contains some security keys you need to change due to the fact that anyone can get access to Roller's documentation and, if you leave the default values, hackers could infiltrate your blog server.

Time for action – changing key values in security.xml

This is a simple process, you just need to change four key values in the `security.xml` file, inside Roller's `WEB-INF` folder.

1. Open a Terminal window and type `sudo gedit /usr/local/tomcat/webapps/ roller/WEB-INF/security.xml` to open the `security.xml` file with the text editor:

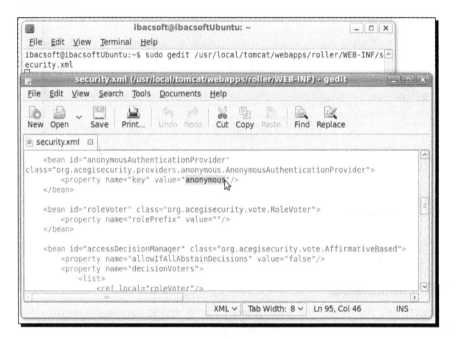

2. Scroll down through the file until you locate the following lines:

```
<bean id="anonymousAuthenticationProvider"
    class="org.acegisecurity.providers.anonymous.
    AnonymousAuthenticationProvider">
        <property name="key" value="anonymous"/>
</bean>
```

Replace the value in bold text (**anonymous**) with any other value of your choice. Use only letters and numbers.

3. Now locate the following lines:

```
<bean id="anonymousProcessingFilter"
    class="org.acegisecurity.providers.anonymous.
    AnonymousProcessingFilter">
        <property name="key" value="anonymous"/>
</bean>
```

Replace the value in bold text (**anonymous**) with the same exact value you used in step 3. These two values must be identical.

4. Now keep scrolling down through the file until you locate the following lines:

```
<bean id="rememberMeServices"
    class="org.acegisecurity.ui.rememberme.
    TokenBasedRememberMeServices">
        <property name="userDetailsService"
                ref="jdbcAuthenticationDao"/>
        <property name="key" value="rollerlovesacegi"/>
        <property name="parameter" value="rememberMe"/>
</bean>

    <bean id="rememberMeAuthenticationProvider"
    class="org.acegisecurity.providers.rememberme.
    RememberMeAuthenticationProvider">
        <property name="key" value="rollerlovesacegi"/>
</bean>
```

Replace the values in bold text (**rollerlovesacegi**) with another value of your liking, but don't use the same one as in steps 3 and 4. Again, use letters and numbers only. You have to use the same value in the two "**rollerlovesacegi**" entries.

5. Save the file, close the text editor, and type `exit` on the Terminal window to close it.

What just happened?

The key values you modified in the previous exercise will prevent hackers from breaking Roller's security and tampering with your site. As anyone can have access to Roller's installation files and documentation, you need to change these key values so that no one besides you has the chance of reading them from your installation files. And, as the `security.xml` file can't be accessed from outside your server, no one will know what values you're using, unless you tell them.

Testing your Roller installation

At last, you made it through the whole installation process. I hope it was as entertaining and valuable an experience for you as it was for me, the first time I installed Roller. Now let's test all the work you've done in the previous sections of this chapter.

Time for action – testing Roller

Now that you have everything installed and waiting for your commands, let's start the testing process.

1. First, open a Terminal window and type

`sudo chown -R tomcat:tomcat /usr/local/tomcat/webapps/roller` to make the `tomcat` user and group owners of that folder:

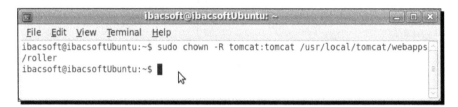

2. Restart your Ubuntu machine and wait for it to boot up. Then open Mozilla Firefox and go to `http://localhost:8080/roller`. You should see the following screenshot:

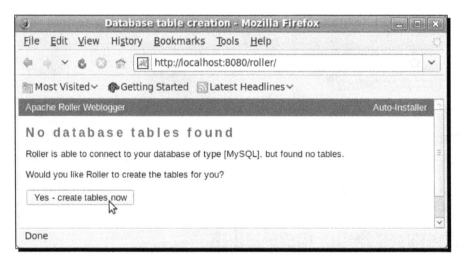

3. This screen indicates that Roller can connect to the JDBC driver you configured before, and so the installation can proceed. Click on the **Yes - create tables now** button to continue.

4. Wait until the **Tables created successfully** page appears, as shown in the next screenshot:

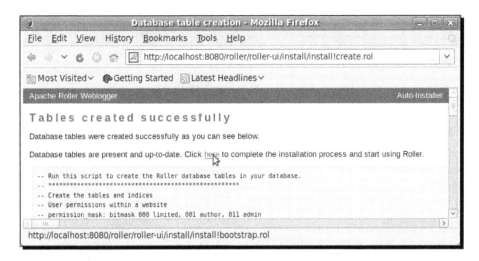

5. Click on the **here** link to complete the installation process. When Roller finishes installing all the required data, the following screen shall appear:

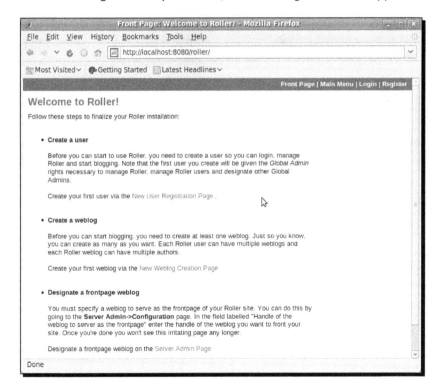

If you get an error page instead of the Welcome to Roller! screen, try refreshing your browser or restart your Ubuntu machine. If the problem persists, send me an e-mail at alromeromx@gmail.com, and I'll be glad to help you out.

6. Now you can be sure that Roller is properly installed on your Linux PC.

What just happened?

You've just tested your Roller installation. Now you're ready for the really fun part, starting to use your Roller blog server. However, before starting with the fun stuff, we need to do a little modification so that Tomcat and the Apache web server can work together with a connector named mod_jk. That way visitors won't have to use the :8080 special notation in the URL address of your blog.

The mod_jk connector for Apache and Tomcat

This little tiny piece of code is the bridge that helps Apache and Tomcat collaborate together to help you host the most powerful web applications from your own PC. Maybe you're wondering, "But why do I need that module?" Well, if you have noticed on the screenshot of step 5 from the previous exercise, to access your Roller homepage you need to type http://localhost:8080/roller. The :8080 part is necessary to access Tomcat, because the Apache web server uses http://localhost to serve web pages. With the mod_jk connector, Apache and Tomcat will share the http://localhost address without conflicts, and you will access your Roller homepage with http://localhost/roller.

Time for action – installing the mod_jk connector

This is the last piece of open source software you'll need to run Apache Roller on your Linux PC. Using the mod_jk connector is considered an advanced topic, but don't worry; I'll guide you through all the steps involved.

1. Open Mozilla Firefox and go to http://tomcat.apache.org/ download-connectors.cgi. Scroll down through the page until you locate the **Tomcat Connectors JK 1.2** section:

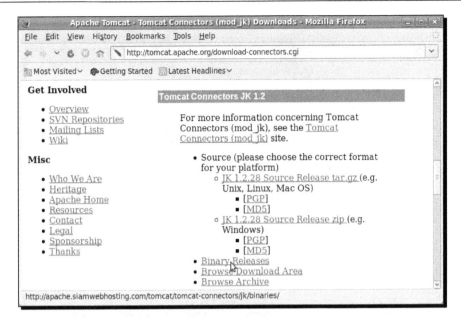

2. Click on the **Binary Releases** link. On the mirror web page, locate the `linux/` folder and click on it:

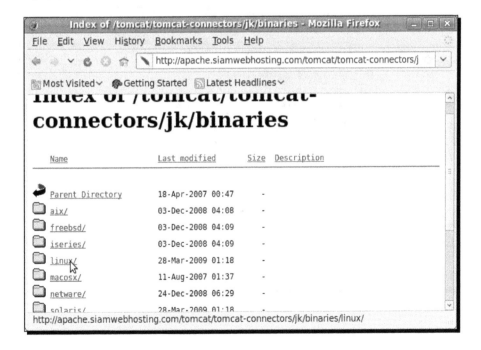

3. Now locate the **jk-1.2.28/** folder and click on its link:

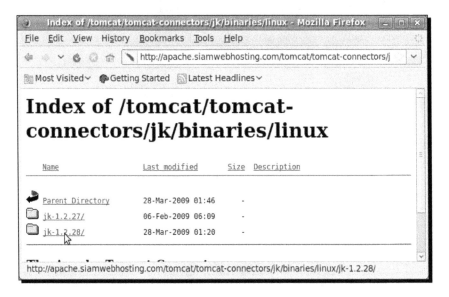

4. On the next web page, locate the **i586/** link and click on it:

5. Now look for the **mod_jk-1.2.28-httpd-2.2.X.so** link and click on it to start downloading the connector:

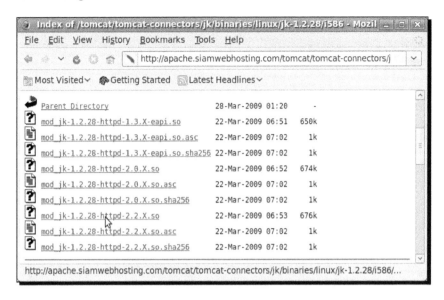

6. The **Opening mod_jk** dialog box will appear next. Click on the **Save File** button to save the mod_jk-1.2.28-httpd-2.2.X.so file on disk.

7. Close Mozilla Firefox, and then open a Terminal window. Type the following lines of code:

```
sudo cp Desktop/mod_jk-1.2.28-httpd-2.2.X.so /usr/lib/apache2/
modules/mod_jk.so
```

This code copies the mod_jk module to the Apache modules folder and renames it to mod_jk.so:

8. Next, type `sudo gedit /etc/apache2/workers.properties` on a Terminal window, and press *Enter*. Then, type the following lines into the text editor's blank area:

```
# Define 1 real worker using ajp13
worker.list=worker1
# Set properties for worker1 (ajp13)
worker.worker1.type=ajp13
worker.worker1.host=localhost
worker.worker1.port=8009
```

9. Select **File | Save** from the menu bar and exit the text editor:

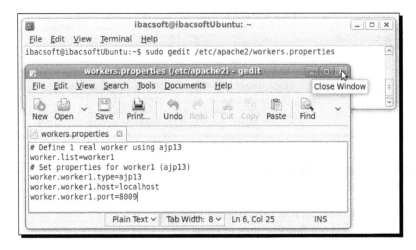

10. The next step is to open the Apache configuration file, `httpd.conf`, with the text editor and add some lines to it. Type `sudo gedit /etc/apache2/httpd.conf` on a Terminal Window.

11. Put the following lines at the end of the file (if it's empty, just put them on the blank area of the editor):

```
# Load mod_jk module
LoadModule jk_module /usr/lib/apache2/modules/mod_jk.so
# Where to find workers.properties
JkWorkersFile /etc/apache2/workers.properties
# Where to put jk shared memory
JkShmFile /var/log/apache2/mod_jk.shm
# Where to put jk logs
JkLogFile /var/log/apache2/mod_jk.log
# Set the jk log level [debug/error/info]
JkLogLevel info
# Select the timestamp log format
JkLogStampFormat "[%a %b %d %H:%M:%S %Y] "
```

12. Select **File | Save** to apply the changes you made to the Apache configuration file:

13. Now type sudo gedit /etc/apache2/sites-available/default to edit the default site configuration file for Apache. Type the following lines on the text editor, below the DocumentRoot /var/www line:

```
# Send everything for context /roller to worker named worker1
JkMount /roller worker1
JkMount /roller/* worker1
```

14. Select **File | Save** on the text editor's menu bar to save the modifications, and close the text editor:

15. The last step is to restart Tomcat and Apache, in that order. Type the following lines in a Terminal window, pressing *Enter* after each line:

```
sudo /etc/init.d/tomcat stop
sudo /etc/init.d/apache2 stop
sudo /etc/init.d/tomcat start
sudo /etc/init.d/apache2 start
```

You should get the following output:

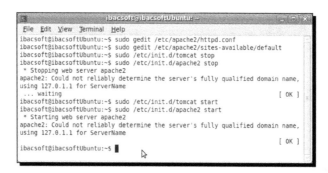

16. Type exit to close the Terminal window, open Mozilla Firefox and go to `http://localhost/roller`. The following screenshot shall appear:

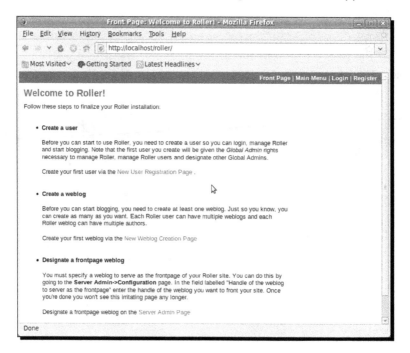

17. You can close Mozilla Firefox now.

What just happened?

This was the last step needed to complete Apache Roller's installation process on your Linux PC. The mod_jk connector helps you to operate Apache Roller seamlessly with your website, without having to type the annoying :8080 port number.

If you're using a different Linux distro, such as Slackware, Fedora, or any other, you can use almost all the steps from the previous exercise. Just be careful because not every Linux system uses different configuration files for Apache. Slackware, for example, uses the httpd.conf file, and that's the only file you need to modify for mod_jk to work. But don't worry, if you have any questions related to any of these exercises and how to adapt them to other Linux flavors, feel free to send me an e-mail. Now you can go to Chapter 4, *How to start working with Roller*, and start with the really fun part of this book.

Pop quiz – installing Roller on Linux

1. The Apache web server lets you:
    a. Create and manage your rollerdb database.
    b. Show your Apache Roller blog to the Internet world.
    c. Change the security parameters of your Roller installation.

2. How can you create a database in MySQL?
    a. Using the mod_jk module to integrate Tomcat and Apache.
    b. Installing the Java SDK and Tomcat.
    c. Opening a Command Prompt window and using the MySQL monitor.

3. Apache Tomcat is:
    a. A web server.
    b. A Java Application server.
    c. A database manager.

4. Deploying Roller means:
    a. Modifying its source code to add bells and whistles.
    b. Integrating Apache with Tomcat through the jk_mod connector.
    c. To download Roller files from the official website, unzip them, and copy the roller folder including all files in it to Tomcat's webapps folder, so that you can access your Roller blog from a web browser.

Have a go hero – doing more with the thing

Well, you have succeeded at installing Roller on your Linux PC. Congratulations! Now, what if you want to use another name for your blog, instead of *roller*? With the examples in this chapter, you can access your blog with the `http://localhost/roller` URL, right? Well, what if you wanted to use `http://localhost/blogging`, `http://localhost/sports`, or just `http://localhost`?

And what about having two different Apache Roller instances? Let's say your name is Rick and you want to create a blog for you, for example, `http://localhost/rick`. You already have `http://localhost/roller` installed. Just follow the same instructions to create an extra installation using *rick* (or your real name, if you're not Rick!).

You can go back to the *Downloading and Installing Roller* section if you need help. Just remember some important points:

- Don't copy the `roller` folder directly on Tomcat's `webapps` folder, because you've already got one in there. You need to rename it first to `rick` and then copy it to `webapps`.

- You also need to create a different database, so use `rickdb` for `rollerdb` and `rick_user` for `roller_user` anywhere they appear in the `roller-custom.properties` and `Context.xml` files, and when creating the database with the MySQL monitor.

- In the `Context.xml`, you'll need to change the `Context path` from `/roller` to `/rick`.

- Also remember to change the `docBase` line in `Context.xml`, from `\roller` to `\rick`.

- You can use the same Gmail account you used for your first Roller installation, unless you really want to use two blogs. In that case, you'll need to create another Gmail account, and change the user and password.

- After that, you need to add some properties to the `roller-custom.properties` file:

  ```
  uploads.dir=${user.home}/rick_data/uploads
  search.index.dir=${user.home}/rick_data/search-index
  log4j.appender.roller.File=${catalina.base}/logs/rick.log
  ```

  The first line defines the folder where Roller stores the files you upload, such as images and other media you plan to use in your blog postings. We didn't use that property before because the default folder is `roller_data`. But now, as you are going to have another Roller installation under the `rick` name, it's necessary to define a separate upload directory named `rick_data`. Be sure to always use a different upload directory for each installation of Roller in your server.

The second line is necessary because you're using the `rick_data` folder as the upload directory, and the third line defines a separate log file for the `rick` blog, so you can track errors and other information about visits, and so on. I recommend you always use the same name as your blog; in this case, `rick.log`.

◆ Oh, and I almost forgot! You need to add the following lines to the `/etc/apache2/sites-available/default` file, below the ones you added in step 12 from the `mod_jk` *Connector for Apache and Tomcat* section:

```
JKMount /rick worker1
JKMount /rick/* worker1
```

◆ This is so that you can use the URL without the annoying `:8080` port number.

Well, that's all you need to know to install another instance of Roller, besides what you've read in this chapter, so if you're up to the challenge, go for it. You'll not regret it. And, if you get stuck somewhere along the process, I'm always an e-mail away.

Summary

In this chapter, you learned how to install Apache Roller on a Linux Ubuntu environment, along with all the supporting software required—Apache web server, JDK SE 6, Tomcat servlet engine, and MySQL database server.

Specifically, we covered:

◆ How to download, install, and test the Apache web server via the Synaptic Package Manager in Ubuntu Linux.

◆ How to download, install, and test the Java SE Development Kit via the Synaptic Package Manager in Ubuntu Linux.

◆ How to download, install, and test the Tomcat servlet engine (also known as Java Application server) in Ubuntu Linux.

◆ How to download, install, and test the MySQL server, Community Edition, via the Synaptic Package Manager in Ubuntu Linux.

◆ How to download, install, and test Apache Roller to make sure it's correctly installed on your Linux PC.

We also discussed the basic Apache Roller properties you need to include in the `roller-custom.properties` file, along with the resources in the `Context.xml` file, so that Roller can communicate with the MySQL database and send e-mail notifications when visitors to your blog leave comments.

Now that you have a functional Roller installation in your PC, you can go to Chapter 4, and start working with your Apache Roller blog. If you read Chapter 2, *Installing Roller on Windows*, you'll notice that installing the supporting open source components for Roller (Apache, Tomcat, MySQL, JDK) is easier in Windows. That's because when you work in Linux, as a regular user you can't just go and install anything your little heart desires. No! You need administrator rights to do that kind of stuff. The Administrator user in Linux is called the "root" user. In Linux Ubuntu, for example, you work as a regular user and you can't modify anything inside the system folders. That's why you need to use the `sudo` command. Think of it as a super power invested in you by a high cyber authority.

Anyways, I think that's enough smart-talk for now. It's time to read Chapter 4, and start building your blog.

4

How to Start Working with Roller

In this chapter, you'll learn to create users and weblogs, along with all the adjustments and modifications needed to start blogging like a pro! In Chapters 2 and 3, you learned how to install Roller and all the required software. Now you'll finally start to add content to your weblog, create categories for your posts, and adjust some of the basic settings of the entire site or your weblog.

In short, you will:

- ◆ Create your first user, your first weblog, and designate it as the front page
- ◆ Adjust your server's basic settings
- ◆ Create/edit your first blog entry
- ◆ Define categories for your weblog
- ◆ Adjust your weblog's basic settings
- ◆ Create and edit bookmarks (blogroll)
- ◆ Use a rich-text editor to write your weblog posts

And now, let's begin our enlightening journey!

Your first steps with Roller

The very first thing you need to do after successfully installing Apache Roller is to create your first user and weblog. And why is that? Well, the first user created in Roller after the installation process becomes the Administrator—the one and only supreme ruler of your little virtual world. Imagine what would happen if someone else entered into your blog and created the first user! That's why you need to do these chores immediately after the Roller installation.

Creating your first user and weblog

Once the first user is created, you may take a break and leave the rest for later. But I know you're pretty anxious to start writing in your brand new weblog, so keep on reading with me. I guarantee you won't regret it!

Time for action – creating your first user and weblog

OK, you finished installing Roller. The next step is to create your first user and weblog. As I said before, the first user is going to be the blog server administrator, and the first weblog will be the front page of your whole website, so I hope you've already decided about your blog name (don't worry if you haven't decided yet; use the example data provided in the meantime, and later we'll see how to modify that information, or start a new Roller installation from scratch):

1. Open Mozilla Firefox or your favorite web browser, and go to your website's address (`http://localhost/roller`, for example). The **Welcome to Roller!** screen will appear:

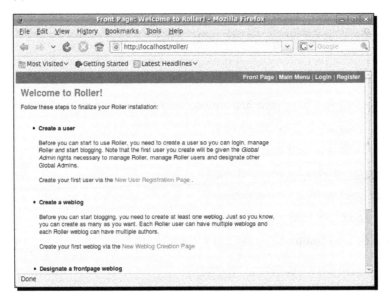

2. Select the **New User Registration Page** link. The **New User Registration** screen will appear. Fill in the **Username**, **Password**, and **Password (Confirm)** fields with the username and password you want to use as the blog administrator. In the **Screen Name** field, type the username you chose. Then fill the **Full Name** and **Email** fields with your full name and e-mail address, respectively. *The e-mail address must be the same one that you used in the installation process.* You can leave the default values for **Locale** and **Timezone**:

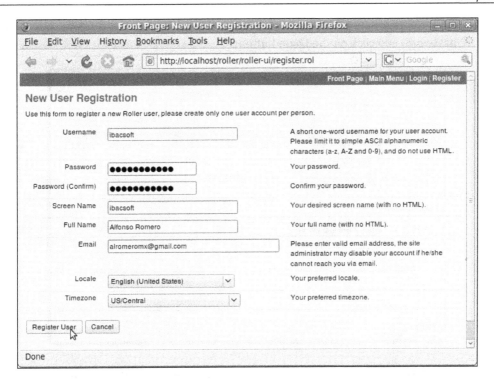

3. Now, click on **Register User**. The message **Your new user account has been created** will appear. Select the **Click here** link to log in with your newly created username and password:

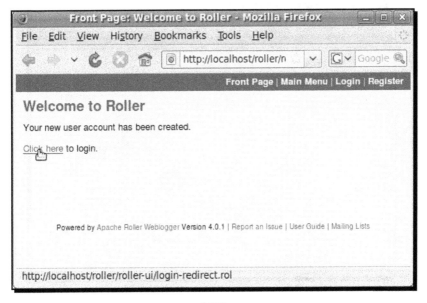

4. Fill in the **Username** and **Password** fields with your respective username and password, and click on the **Login** button:

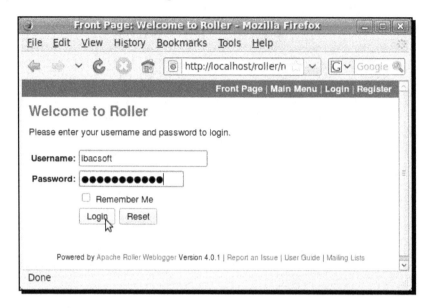

5. The **Main Menu** screen will appear next. Click on the link in the **You've got a user account, but no weblog. Would you like to create one?** message to create your first weblog:

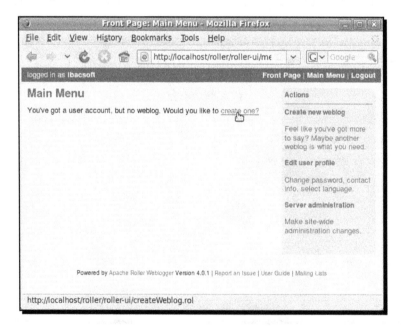

6. In the **Create Weblog** screen, you need to fill in the **Name** field with a good title for your weblog, and the **Description** field with a brief description to give your visitors a concise idea of what you intend to write. Be careful with the **Handle** field; you must use a short alphanumeric name because it will be used in your weblog's URL. The **Email Address** field is already filled in with the e-mail you used in the installation process. Leave the default values for **Locale** and **Timezone**, as Roller adjusts them automatically based on your location. For now, use the **Basic** theme. Later we'll see how to change themes and customize them. The following screenshot shows an example with all the information I used for my weblog:

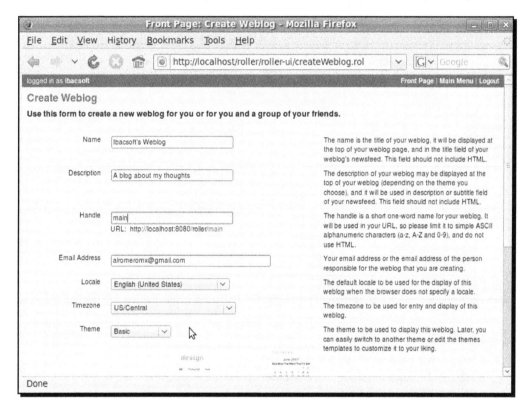

7. When you're ready to continue, scroll down to the bottom of the web page and click on the **Create Weblog** button. Roller will create your first weblog and take you back to the **Main Menu** screen, where you will see some details about your newly created weblog:

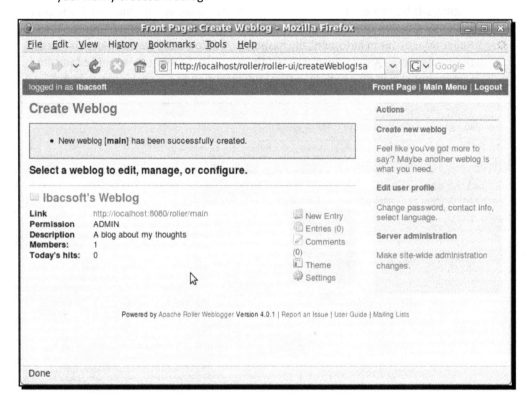

What just happened?

Well, it wasn't that hard, don't you agree? As you can see, the user interface in Roller is very friendly and gives you enough information on-screen about the tasks you can do. The process for creating more users and weblogs is the same; later we'll see how to manage several weblogs and one or more users.

The weblog **handle** is a unique identifier for your weblog; once you create it, you won't be able to change its handle, so choose well. Visitors will use that handle to access your weblog posts, along with the URL of your site. We'll talk more about this in later chapters.

Now that you have your first user (the blog admin) and your first weblog (the front page of your blog), let's explore the other basic tasks you need to do as the blog administrator.

Adjusting basic server settings

Roller has a lot of settings that you, as the blog admin, can manipulate to change the appearance of a single weblog, or the whole blog server. In the previous exercise, you created the admin user and the weblog that we're going to use as the front page of the whole website. In this next exercise, you'll learn to adjust Roller's basic global settings.

Time for action – basic server settings

Before you can start populating your blog with all the things you want to write, it's necessary to adjust some basic settings for your entire blog site and for your front page weblog:

1. If you've just finished the last exercise and Roller's **Main Menu** is still open, select the **Server administration** link on the right-hand side of the screen (underneath the **Actions** section). Otherwise, open a web browser, type your blog's URL (`http://localhost/roller`), and then fill in your **Username** and **Password**. In the **Welcome to Roller!** page, select the **Server Admin Page** link at the bottom of the screen (under **Designate a frontpage weblog**):

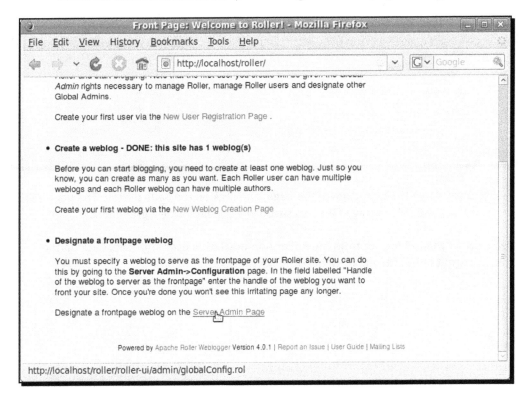

2. The **Roller Configuration** screen will appear next. At this moment, you only need to fill in several fields in the **Site Settings** section. Use the example data shown in the following screenshot; just remember to use your own e-mail address, instead of mine!

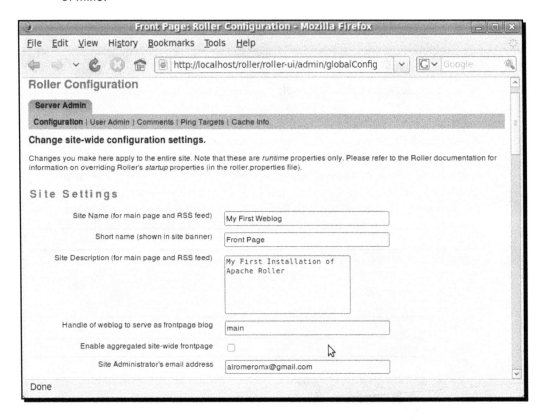

Scroll down to the bottom of the page, and click on the **Save** button. The page will reload and the message **Changes saved** will appear inside a green box.

3. Now you can log out from the Roller Administration user interface. Click on the **Logout** link at the upper-right corner of the screen.

What just happened?

In this last exercise, you adjusted the following server settings:

Server setting	Definition	Tip
Site Name (for main page and RSS feed)	The name that shows in the front page when someone visits your blog.	Try to use an attractive name that best describes the topics you're going to write about in your blog. We'll talk about RSS feeds later.
Short name (shown in site banner)	The front page link that shows up at the upper-right corner on every page of the Roller user interface.	You can leave the default value (**Front Page**) or use the name of your blog. For the exercises in this book, you can leave the default value.
Site Description (for main page and RSS feed)	This description shows up on the front page of your blog, and on site-wide RSS feeds.	Use a short but concise description, to give your readers a good idea about your blog's content.
Handle of weblog to serve as frontpage blog	Specifies what weblog is going to show up to your visitors when they visit your website.	This is the most important setting you need to define from the beginning, and it can't be changed. Later, we'll see how you can create or delete more weblogs, and choose which one to use as the front page blog.
Site Administrator's email address	The e-mail address used by the blog administrator to send/receive e-mails. It also shows up on site-wide newsfeeds.	Make sure you use the same e-mail address as in the `roller-custom.properties` file to avoid problems when connecting to your SMTP provider.

Up until now, we've only covered five of the nine settings in the **Site Settings** section of the **Server Admin Configuration** page. These are the most basic settings every Roller admin needs to adjust, so that regular users can start working on their blogs. In this case, you're going to be the user and the admin, but in Chapter 9, I'll show you how to manage group blogs, so you can invite a couple of friends or colleagues—or maybe a thousand—to blog with you; Roller is very powerful, as we'll see in later chapters. Later on, we'll talk about the other settings in this section, and the rest of the settings in the other sections as well (**User Settings**, **Weblog Rendering Settings**, **Comment and Trackback Settings**, **File Upload Settings**, **Theme Settings**, and **Spam Prevention**). Remember I'm using a "learn by doing" approach in this book, so you'll get to use each one of these settings when you need them.

Sometimes, if you leave the Roller admin interface open without doing anything for a while, and then you try to make some action (for example, clicking on the **Save** button in the **Roller Configuration** screen), Roller will ask for your username and password again. This security measure is used in a lot of web applications nowadays, in case you forget to close your web browser and someone tries to tamper with your account. Don't worry; you will not lose information or configuration settings, because once you type in your username and password, Roller will log you in again and the action you made will take effect.

Creating/editing your first entry

Now it's time to begin the writing process on your blog. I hope you have a lot of material ready! First I'll show you how to write a sample post, and then we'll see how to create and edit categories for all of your posts.

Time for action – creating/editing entries

Have you decided yet what you are going to write? In the meantime, let's do an exercise with a sample post, so you can get the feeling:

1. In the previous exercise, you logged out of Roller's Administration user interface. If you closed your web browser, open it and go to your blog's URL (`http://localhost/roller`). Your weblog's front page will appear next:

2. Scroll down the page until you find the **Login** link, at the bottom-right corner of the screen, under the **NAVIGATION** section of your weblog's front page, and click on it:

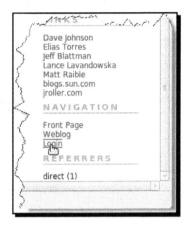

3. In the **Welcome to Roller** screen, enter your username and password. As you only have one weblog, Roller will take you directly to the **New Entry** page, where you can start writing a new post:

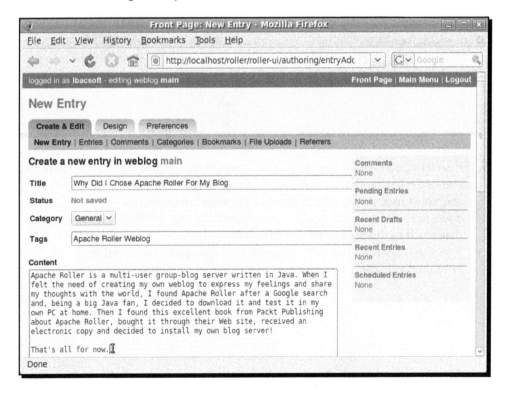

4. Use the sample data in the previous screenshot to write your first post. Fill in the **Title**, **Tags**, and **Content** fields only. Then scroll down to the end of the page and click on the **Save as Draft** button. Roller will save your draft, adding information to the **Status** and **Permalink** fields, as shown in the following screenshot:

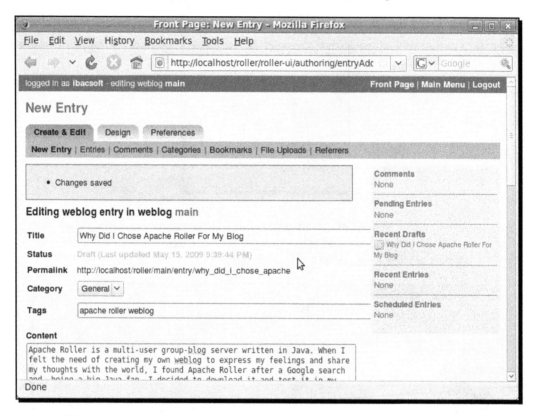

5. Now let's publish your first post. In the **Content** field, move the text cursor to the end of the last sentence (**That's all for now.**), press *Enter* twice, type the text **Stay tuned on my blog, because I'll update it frequently!**, scroll down to the bottom of the page, and click on the **Post to Weblog** button that's next to the **Save Draft** button you used previously. In the following screenshot, you can see that the **Status** field changed from **Saved** to **Published** indicating that your post was successfully published:

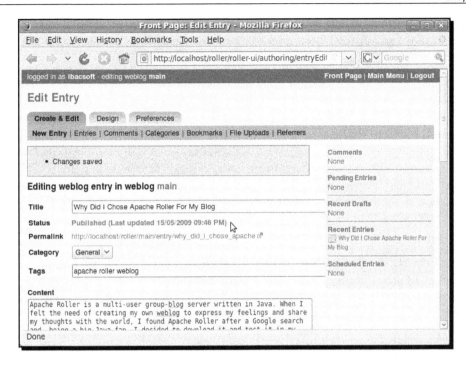

6. To see how your published entry is going to look in your weblog, click on the **Front Page** link at the upper right corner of the screen to go to your blog's front page:

7. You can close your web browser now.

What just happened?

At last, you wrote your first post! As you can see from the previous exercise, Roller's user interface for adding content to your weblog is very friendly. In the last screenshot, we can see that the title of your post is used as the **Permalink**—a permanent link to your weblog entry. Roller sets the permalink of an entry once it is saved for the first time, and it can't be changed after that. Although, you can change the post's title after you publish it, I don't recommend doing so. You have to be *very careful* when choosing a title for a post, because it's going to be there forever! But this does make sense, as you want people to read your posts, don't you? The permalink shows up in Google, Digg, Technorati, and the rest of the search engines and blog aggregators when you publish a new post in your blog (later on, we'll see how to do that). If you could change the permalink for a post, the same post would show up twice with different titles on search engines and aggregators, and that would be a huge mess!

If you look closely, you'll notice two important differences between the permalink and the title: the use of underscores (_) instead of spaces, and the use of lowercase. This is the format used by Roller. WordPress, b2evolution, and other popular blogging applications use similar formats for their permalinks.

Notice that in step 4 you only saved a **draft** of your post; this means it wasn't published yet. You can tell that from the **Status** field. In the screenshot from step 3, it was **Not Saved**. Then, in the screenshot from step 4 it was something like **Draft (Last updated date & time)** and finally, when you clicked the **Post to Weblog** button in step 5, the **Status** field was **Published (Last updated date & time)**.

Save drafts of your posts periodically

Better to be safe than sorry. And this is more important when dealing with long posts. That way, you can write several ideas in your blog and save drafts of your posts before publishing them, so you can make modifications (or add more information) at a later time.

Defining weblog categories

With the previous exercise you learned how to create/edit and publish posts on your blog. Now you can start writing about anything you want! However, before you start cluttering up your newly created blog, I'm going to show you how to define categories for your posts, so visitors to your blog can wander throughout your writings.

Time for action – define a category for your blog

In Roller, it's very easy to organize your blog's content. You can create new categories, choose from the ones already created or edit them to your liking, and delete categories you don't need:

1. Open your web browser and go to your blog's URL (`http://localhost/roller`). Your weblog's front page should appear, showing the post you published in the previous exercise. Scroll down the web page until you locate the **Login** link under the **NAVIGATION** section, and click on it. If the login page shows up, type your password and hit *Enter*. You'll be taken to the **New Entry** web page.

2. Click on the **Categories** link from the **Create & Edit** tab. The **Categories** web page will show up with a table of categories for your weblog:

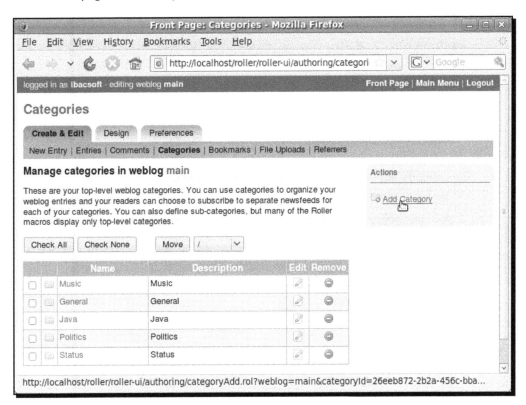

3. Click on the **Add Category** link in the **Actions** section at the right-hand side of the screen. On the **Add Category** web page, fill in the **Name** and **Description** fields with **Roller** and **Weblog entries related to Apache Roller**, respectively, and then click on the **Save** button, as shown in the following screenshot:

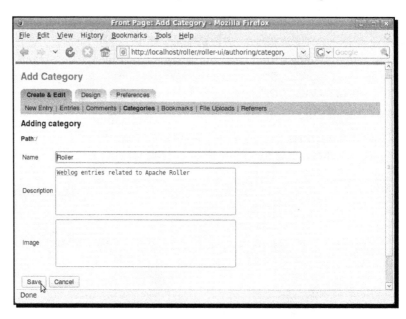

4. The **category added** message will appear on the **Add Category** web page, and the category you've just created will be added to the categories list for your weblog:

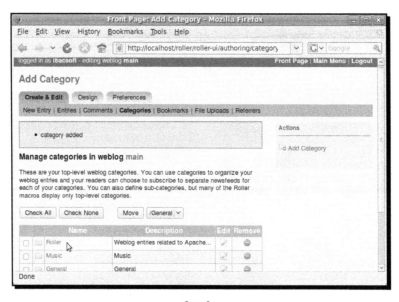

5. Now scroll down the page until you locate the **Politics** category, and click on the **Remove** button (the red circle with the white "-" sign):

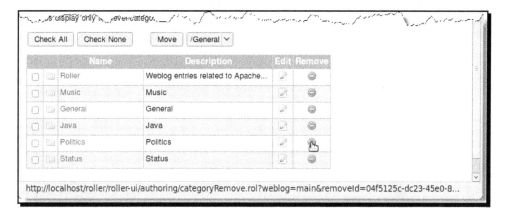

6. Roller will ask if you want to delete the **Politics** category. Click on the **Yes** button. When the categories list shows up, you'll see that the **Politics** category isn't included anymore. Now click on the **Edit** button (the little blank page with a pencil) for the **Status** category, to change its name and description:

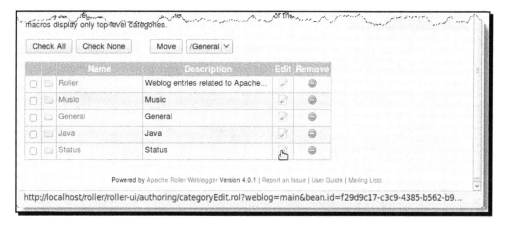

7. Double-click inside the **Name** field and replace its contents (**Status**) with **Open Source**. Do the same with the **Description** field, and type **All things related to Open Source software** to replace its contents, as shown in the following screenshot:

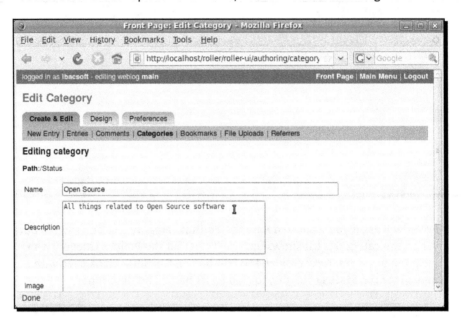

8. Click on the **Save** button to save the modifications you've just made to that category. Roller will show the **category updated** message inside a green box in response:

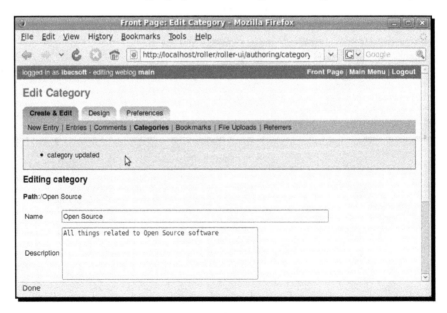

9. You can logout from Roller now, clicking on the **Logout** link in the upper-right corner of the screen.

What just happened?

In this last exercise, you saw how to manage categories for your blog, so that you can classify your posts and readers can concentrate on their areas of interest. You can add new categories, and modify or delete the existing ones. Up to this point, your blog only has one post and, in case you didn't notice, it's under the *General* category. That's the default category Roller selects for you when you add a new entry in your blog. Later on, we'll see how to change that post's category, to include it in the Roller-related posts.

Deleting non-empty categories

If you want to delete a category containing one or more posts, you have to move those posts to another category first. Fortunately, Roller does this for you automatically. You just have to select the category where you want to move those posts to, and Roller takes care of the rest!

Categories have a field called **Image**, where you can write a URL pointing to an image and Roller can show it along with the category's title, but at the present time there aren't any Roller templates that make use of this field. However, you could make your own template and add this feature—that's an advanced subject that we'll cover in Chapter 6, *Roller Themes*.

Enhancing your weblog

Now that you've learned how to create and publish entries on your blog, and how to define categories for them, it's time to start customizing the look and feel of your front page, along with the way you're going to write your thoughts for the world. Let's begin with some basic settings you can twist on your blog to enhance its appearance.

Server settings versus weblog settings

In the *Adjusting basic server settings* section, we saw how to manage Roller's global settings. In this section, we'll see how to manage settings for each one of your weblogs. Just remember that the server settings affect some of the weblog settings, as we'll see in a moment.

Adjusting basic weblog settings

In Roller, a regular user can have one or more weblogs, and each one of them has several settings you can adjust to fulfill your needs. In the next exercise, you'll learn about the basic weblog settings you can tweak to customize your blog's title, the e-mail address where you'll receive comment notifications, and some other basic elements.

Time for action –basic weblog settings

Each weblog has separate configuration settings that you, the owner, can adjust to your liking. Now let's see how to do that:

1. Open your web browser and go to your blog's URL (`http://localhost/roller`). Scroll down the home page until you locate the **Login** link under the **NAVIGATION** section, and click on it. As this is the only weblog you have at the moment, Roller will take you to the **New Entry** page, as shown in the following screenshot:

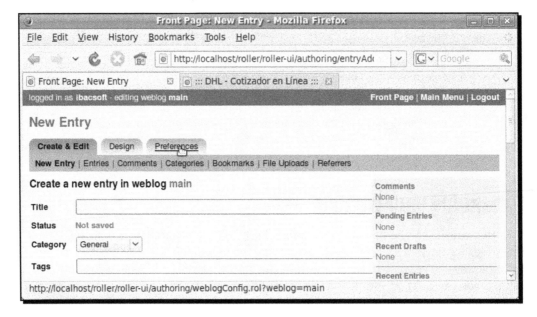

2. In this web page, there are three tabs: **Create & Edit**, **Design**, and **Preferences**. Click on the **Preferences** tab, and Roller will show you all the configuration settings available for your weblog:

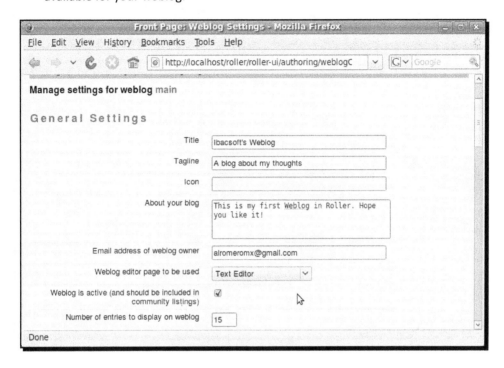

3. The **Title**, **Tagline**, and **Email address of weblog owner** fields should already contain the values you typed when creating the weblog. You can change them at this time, in case you want to use another e-mail or another title for your blog. In the **About your blog** field, type a short description of your blog contents. You can use the example text from the previous screenshot. Also check that the **Weblog is active** option is enabled; otherwise, it means you're not going to post new entries, and aggregators such as Technorati won't update their listings to show your new posts.

4. Now, scroll down to the **Internationalization Settings** section. The **Locale** and **Timezone** fields must contain the values you chose when creating your weblog:

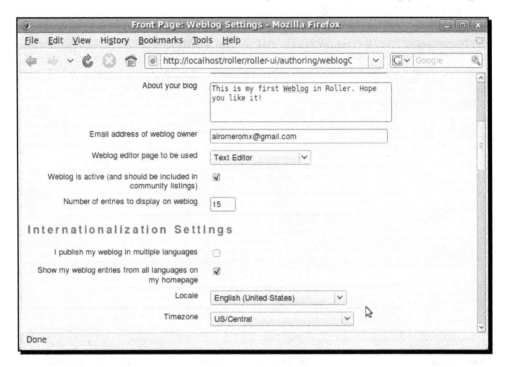

5. Now suppose you want to write posts in two or more languages; you can use the **I publish my weblog in multiple languages** option to select a different locale for each entry in your post. To see it in action, click on this option to enable it and make sure the **Show my weblog entries from all languages on my homepage** is enabled, so that all your posts in different languages show up in your blog's home page. Then scroll down the page until you find the **Update Weblog Settings** button, and click on it.

6. Roller will show you the **Saved changes to weblog settings** message inside a green box, to confirm that the changes are made.

7. Click on the **Create & Edit** tab to go to the **New Entry** page. There should now be a **Language** field under the **Tags** field, as shown in the following screenshot:

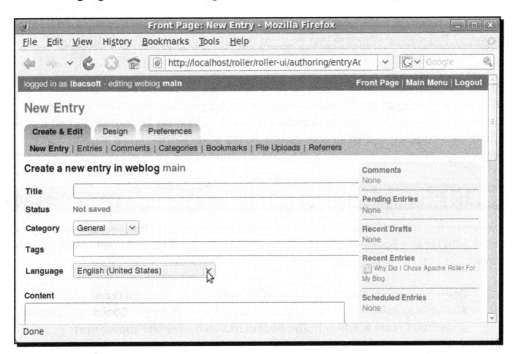

8. You can select another language from this drop-down list, and write a post in Spanish, French, German, or any other language of your choice. Now click on the **Preferences** tab again, go to the **Internationalization Settings** section and deselect the **I publish my weblog in multiple languages** checkbox to continue with the exercises in this book. You can logout from Roller and close your web browser, if you don't want to continue with the rest of the chapter for now.

What just happened?

There are several configuration settings for each weblog in Roller. In this last exercise, we saw the *General Settings* and *Internationalization Settings* sections. As you can adjust each weblog's settings, you can assign blogs to different users; for example, if you work in a company with 10 or more people, you could install Roller and create a main weblog for the company, and then assign to each employee a blog of his/her own. That's what a lot of companies such as Microsoft and Sun are doing nowadays, because a blog can bring a lot of benefits to their businesses: a team of developers can use blogs to share information between each other or with other teams, managers can see their employee's progress on some project or duty, and the company can open its doors to prospective clients by means of promoting new products on the blogosphere. And this is only the tip of the iceberg!

Roller can also be very helpful if you intend to write posts in different languages. Imagine you work in a company that has several offices around the world, and needs to communicate with its customers in different languages. What could be better than using Roller to create multi-language blogs, where employees from different countries could publish posts in different languages? This is a real situation that happens to many enterprises around the world!

Creating/editing bookmarks (blogroll)

In blog jargon, a **blogroll** is a list of your favorite weblogs and websites. Each website included in a blogroll is called a **bookmark**. You can show that list on your blog's home page, to share your bookmarks with all your visitors. In the next exercise, you'll learn to manage your weblog's blogroll by means of Roller's Bookmarks section.

Time for action – managing bookmarks in Roller

As we've seen in previous exercises, Roller's user interface is very friendly. Now you're going to work with Roller's Bookmarks section, where you can add, edit, and delete bookmarks to maintain your very own blogroll!

1. Open your web browser, go to your blog's URL (`http://localhost/roller`) and log into Roller. Or, if you're already logged in, click on the **Bookmarks** section, under the **Create & Edit** tab. The **Bookmarks** web page will appear next:

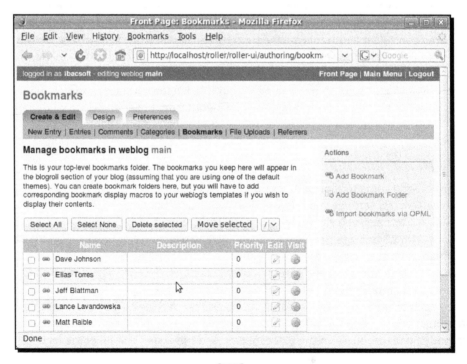

2. When you install Roller for the first time, the installation routine adds several predefined bookmarks for you. You can add, edit, delete, or visit any bookmark from the list. Click on the **Visit** link of the first bookmark (**Dave Johnson**) to go to that bookmark's web page:

3. The bookmark's web page will show up in the same window:

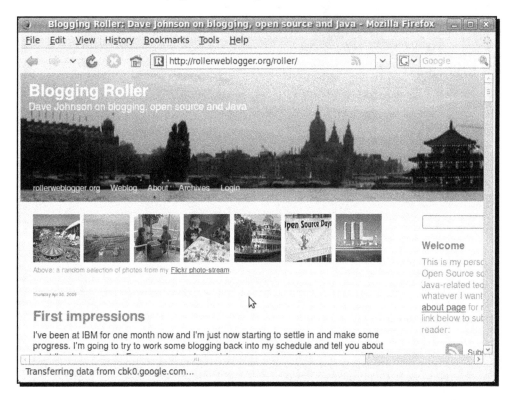

4. Click on your web browser's **Back** button ( ) to return to the **Bookmarks** page on your weblog, and then click on the **Edit** link of the second bookmark:

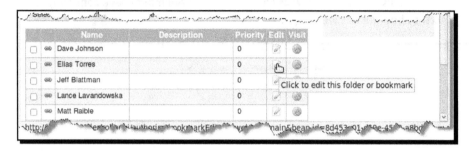

5. Roller will take you to the **Edit Bookmark** page, where you can modify the **Name**, **Description**, **Bookmark URL**, and **Newsfeed URL** fields. Use the following screenshot to edit this bookmark, and click on the **Save** button when finished:

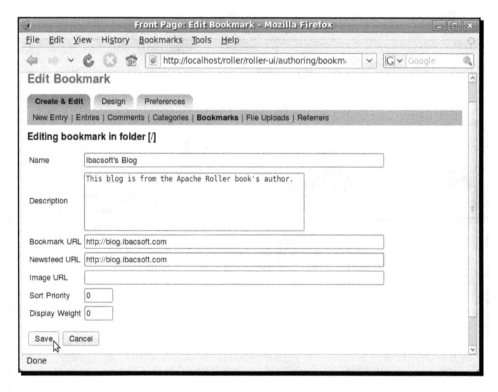

6. Roller will show the same **Edit Bookmark** page with the **bookmark updated message** inside a green box, indicating that your changes were saved.

7. Click on the **Bookmarks** section again, to return to the **Bookmarks** page. Now click on the checkboxes to the left of the last five bookmarks, and then click on the **Delete selected** button above the bookmarks to delete them:

8. The **Delete selected bookmarks** dialog will appear. Click on the **OK** button to delete the bookmarks you selected. Roller will show the **Bookmarks** page again, with the list updated to reflect the deletions you've just made:

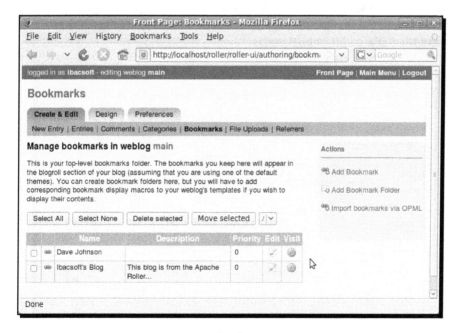

9. Click on the **Add Bookmark** link, under the **Actions** section in the right part of the **Bookmarks** page. Roller will take you to the **Add New Bookmark** page. Use the example data from the following screenshot to fill in the **Name**, **Description**, **Bookmark URL**, **Newsfeed URL**, and **Image URL** fields:

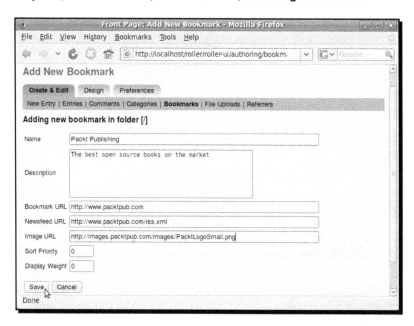

10. Click on the **Save** button to add the new bookmark to your blogroll. Roller will take you to the bookmarks page, showing **bookmark added** inside a green box and the updated list of bookmarks:

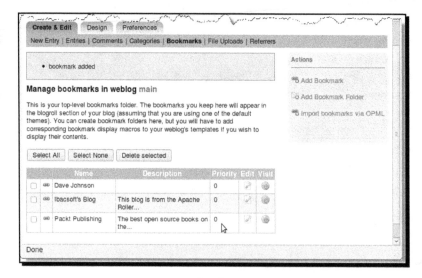

11. Now click on the **Front Page** link at the upper-right corner of the page to see your bookmarks in action.

12. Your weblog's front page will show up in the web browser's window. Scroll down until you locate the **LINKS** section, at the right part of the screen, between the **SEARCH** and **NAVIGATION** sections:

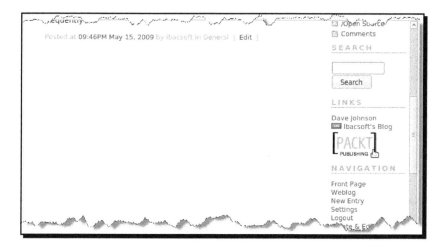

13. There should be three bookmarks. The first two show their names, and the last one shows the image from the **Image URL** field you used in step 9 of this exercise. Now scroll down the page until you locate the **Create & Edit Bookmarks** link under the **NAVIGATION** section, to return to Roller's weblog administration interface:

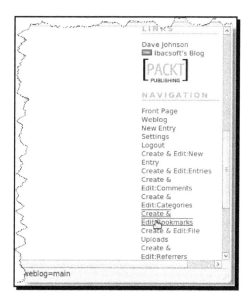

14. In the **Bookmarks** page, click on the **Edit** link from the **Packt Publishing** bookmark, delete the URL address in the **Image URL** field, and click on the **Save** button to apply the changes:

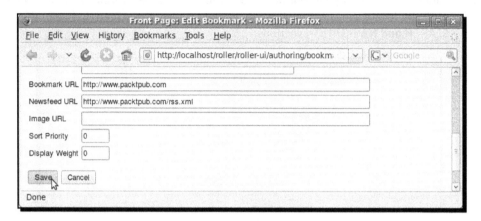

15. Roller will show the **bookmark updated** message in a green box. Click on the **Front Page** link again (at the upper-right corner of the screen), and when your weblog's front page appears, scroll down to the **LINKS** section to see how this modification you've made affects the way Roller shows a bookmark:

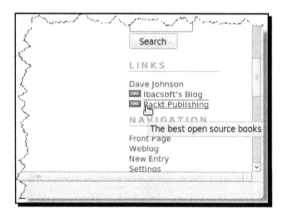

16. As you can see from the previous screenshot, the **Packt Publishing** bookmark shows up just like the other two bookmarks: when you include an image URL for a bookmark, the image from this URL shows up in the blogroll, and if you leave the **Image URL** field blank, the **Name** field contents show up instead. Now click on the **Create & Edit** link from the **NAVIGATION** section again, to return to the **Bookmarks** page.

17. Click on the **Edit** link from the first bookmark (**Dave Johnson**), type **The creator of Roller** in the **Description** field, and replace the **0** in the **Sort Priority** field with a **1**, as shown in the following screenshot:

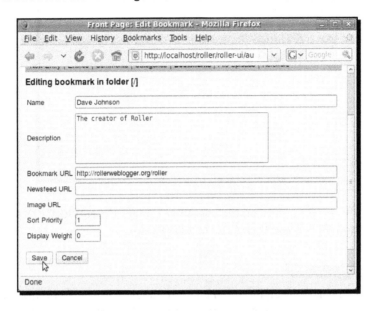

18. Click on the **Save** button to apply the changes, and then click on the **Bookmarks** link from the **Create & Edit** tab, to return to the **Bookmarks** page. Then, click on the **Edit** link from the second bookmark (**Packt Publishing**), replace the **0** in the **Sort Priority** field with a **2**, and click on **Save** to apply the changes you made:

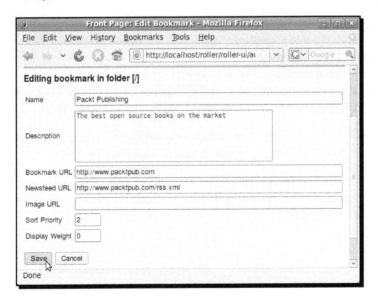

19. Click on the **Front Page** link again, to see how the changes you made affect the way Roller shows bookmarks:

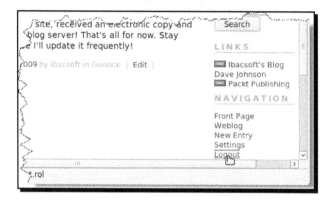

20. To end this exercise, click on the **Logout** link under the **NAVIGATION** section to logout from Roller, and then close Mozilla Firefox.

What just happened?

Wow! It sure was a lengthy exercise, wasn't it? But I bet you learned a lot from it! Now you know how to create, edit, or delete bookmarks for your blogroll. You also learned that, if you type the URL of an image in the **Image URL** field of a bookmark, Roller shows that image instead of the bookmark's name under the front page's **LINKS** section (the name of this section may vary, depending on the template you're using; it can be *Links*, *Blogrolls*, or anything related). The URL you used in step 9 of the previous exercise belongs to the Packt Publishing website. You can use any URL of your choice, as long as it points to a valid image URL.

If you take a look at the screenshot in step 9, the first and last bookmarks have a little XML icon to the left, and the second bookmark doesn't. This icon shows up on a bookmark when you fill in the **Newsfeed URL** field, and if you click on it you can see the RSS feed and subscribe to it, if you wish. We'll talk about RSS feeds in Chapter 9.

Also, if you look at the screenshot in step 15, you'll notice that when you move your mouse over a bookmark, a tool tip box shows that bookmark's description.

In Chapter 5, we'll see how to upload images to your Roller weblog, so you can use them in bookmarks and posts to spice up your weblog. As people like to say, sometimes an image is better than a thousand words!

You also learned how to change the order in which the bookmarks show up in your front page, thanks to the **Sort Priority** field. The number you type into this field determines the order the bookmark is going to have on the blogroll. "0" is the highest priority, and the bigger the number, the lower the priority.

I also showed you how to use the **Front Page** link at the menu bar located in the upper-right corner of Roller's user interface, to see how changes in your bookmarks' fields reflect in your weblog's front page.

And last, but not least, we saw how to use the **NAVIGATION** section to go directly to the **Bookmarks** page from your weblog's front page. If you haven't noticed yet, this section expands its content when you're logged into Roller. For example, the following screenshot shows the **NAVIGATION** section of your weblog's front page when you're not logged into Roller:

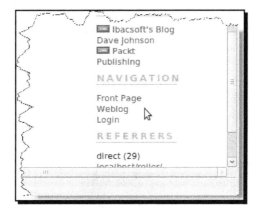

And the following screenshot shows the **NAVIGATION** section—well, in this case just part of it—when you're logged into Roller:

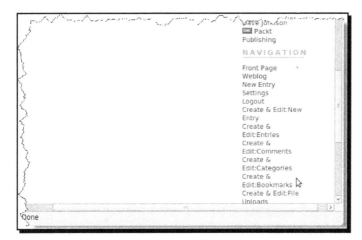

From this section, you can go back to any configuration page inside your weblog's administration interface. We'll keep using this section on further examples throughout the book, because it's one of the most useful features Roller has to offer when alternating between making changes to your blog's settings, and returning to the front page to see the effects of those changes.

> Bookmarks have another field, **Display Weight**, that we didn't cover in the previous exercise. The purpose of this field is to differentiate one bookmark over the other ones with a bolder font, for example. But to see the effects of this setting, you have to manipulate it programmatically; at this time the Roller default templates for your weblog don't include this functionality by default, so we're not going to cover it.

Using a Rich Text Editor

In this chapter, you learned how to create and edit entries in your weblog. As you may have noticed, the only entry we've made so far is made up of plain text. That's because we used the default plain Text Editor. Roller also includes a Rich Text Editor, so we can use different fonts, sizes, and colors in our posts, along with links, images, tables, and a lot of other stuff you usually find in word processors like Microsoft Word or OpenOffice Writer. Think of a post as a web page—you can include HTML tags and even use the HTML mode to manipulate HTML tags directly.

Time for action – using Roller's Rich Text Editor

In the following exercise, you'll select the Rich Text Editor through Roller's administrator user interface, and then you'll create a post using the tools included in this editor:

1. Open your web browser and log into your Roller blog. The **New Entry** page will appear next. Click on the **Preferences** tab to go to the **Weblog Settings** page, and scroll down until you locate the **Weblog editor page to be used** setting, as shown in the following screenshot:

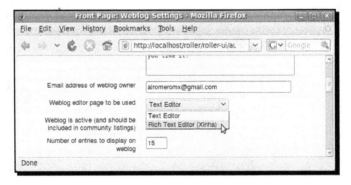

2. Click on the drop-down list and select the **Rich Text Editor (Xinha)** option, then scroll down to the end of the web page and click on the **Update Weblog Settings** button to apply the changes you made. Roller will respond with the following success message:

> - Accepted 0 string and 0 regex blacklist rules
> - Saved changes to weblog settings

3. Now click on the **Create & Edit** tab to add a new entry to your weblog. Type **Testing the Rich Text Editor** in the **Title** field, click on the **Category** field's drop-down list and select the **Roller** category, and type **Apache Roller Rich Text Editor** in the **Tags** field. Use the following screenshot as a guide to fill the **Content** field for your new entry:

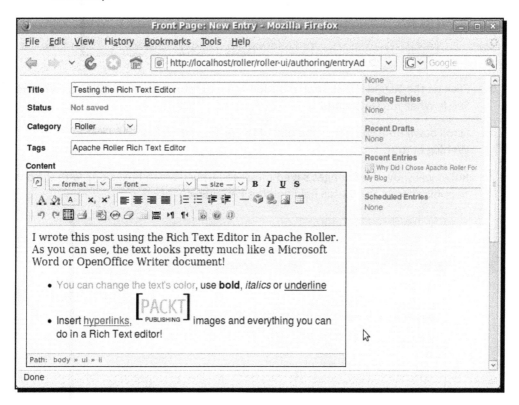

4. Click on the **Toggle HTML Source** button on the Rich Text Editor's control interface to enter **TEXT MODE** and see the HTML code behind the **Content** field of your post:

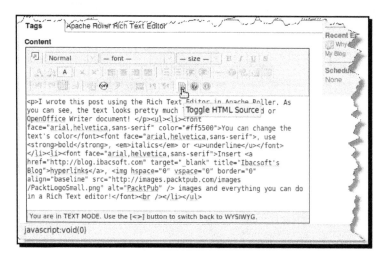

5. Click on the **Toggle HTML Source** button again to return to the **WYSIWYG** (What You See Is What You Get) mode.

6. Scroll down until you get to the end of the page, and click on the **Post to Weblog** button.

7. Roller will show the **Changes saved** message inside a green box, along with the date of publication in the **Status** field and the **Permalink** field:

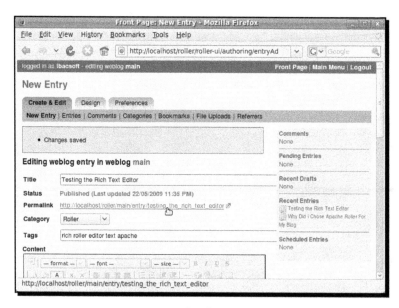

8. Click on the permalink to see how your post shows up in your weblog's front page:

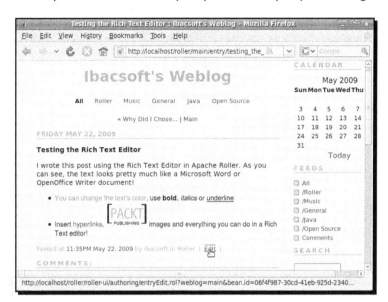

9. You can logout from Roller and close your web browser now.

What just happened?

Isn't the Rich Text Editor great? With this powerful tool, you can create very complex web pages and publish them in your blog, as if they were simple posts! The Rich Text Editor interface is just like the MS Word or OpenOffice Writer, so if you have any experience working with these two word processors, you won't have any problems with the editor.

If you're into HTML programming, you can enter the HTML mode and create complex scenarios inside your posts—the possibilities are endless!

The Summary field

When you create or edit an entry in Roller's administration interface, you need to fill several fields: *Title*, *Category*, *Tags*, and *Content*, as we saw in the previous exercise. There is another optional field called *Summary*, and if you type text in it, Roller will show its contents instead of the complete post on your weblog's front page. This field is used when you have a very long post and don't want it to occupy a lot of space on your weblog's front page, so users can see your other posts as well, without having to scroll down the page. To avoid this, you type a summary of that post and, if visitors to your site want to read its full contents, they click on its permalink and Roller shows them only that post.

Time for action – using the Summary field

In this exercise, you'll see the differences between using the **Summary** field and leaving it blank:

1. Open your web browser and go to your weblog (`http://localhost/roller`). The front page will show the last post you published:

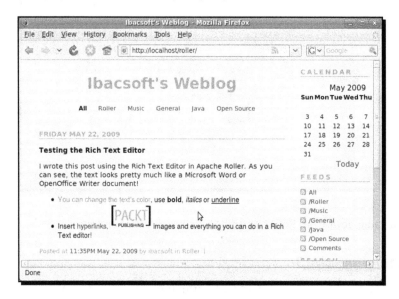

2. If you scroll down the page, you'll notice that the first post you created also shows up in Roller's front page:

3. Click on the **Login** link under the **NAVIGATION** section of your weblog's front page. The **New Entry** page should appear. Click on the **Entries** link that's next to the **New Entry** link, under the **Create & Edit** tab:

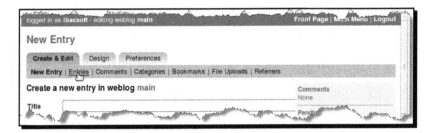

4. The **Edit Entries** page should appear. Click on the **Edit** link from the first entry that shows up in the list (**Testing the Rich Text Editor**):

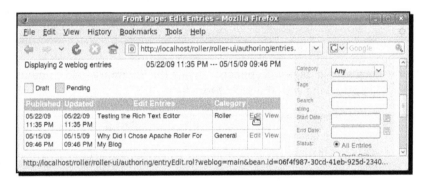

5. Scroll down the **Edit Entry** page until you locate the **Summary** field. Use the following screenshot as an example to fill in your post's **Summary** field:

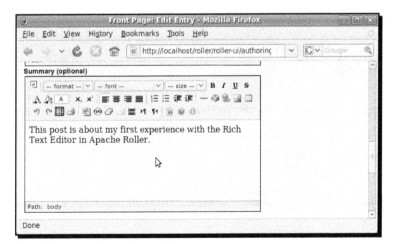

6. Scroll down the page and click on the **Post to Weblog** button to apply the changes to your post.

7. Roller will show the **Edit Entry** page again, with the **Changes saved** message inside a green box. Now, click on the **Front Page** link at the upper-right corner of the screen:

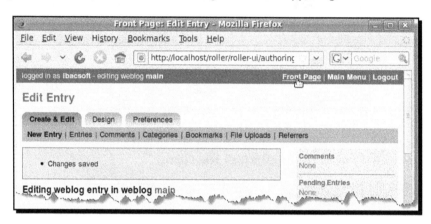

8. Your weblog's main page will appear, showing the **Summary** field contents instead of the full post, along with the **Read More** link:

9. To see the full post, click on the **Read More** link:

10. You can logout from Roller and close your web browser now.

What just happened?

As you saw in the previous exercise, the *Summary* field is useful when you have a lot of posts in your blog, and don't want them to show up in full, occupying your precious front page space. Imagine what would the length of your front page be if you had 100 posts, and each one of them was two or three paragraphs long? That's what the *Summary* field is for: you can have a lot of posts, and by showing only their summary, visitors to your site will have the chance to see more of them without having to scroll down through a lengthy front page.

Pop quiz – working with Roller

1. The weblog handle is:

    a. The link to a post.

    b. A unique identifier for your weblog.

    c. The description of a weblog, that you can change later.

2. In Roller, the first weblog you create becomes:

    a. The front page of your weblog.

    b. A summary of all your weblogs.

    c. Your worst nightmare!

3. The Summary field in an entry is for:

    a. Writing short posts.

    b. Showing a brief description of your weblog.

    c. Showing only a summary of that entry in the front page.

4. How would you change the order of your bookmarks?

    a. Deleting them and re-creating them in the order you want.

    b. Changing your server's settings.

    c. Through the Sort Priority field of each bookmark.

5. What would be the best way to manage a blog with posts in English and Spanish?

    a. Creating two Roller installations, one for the Spanish blog and the other for the English blog.

    b. Using Roller's Internationalization Settings to add a Language field on each post.

    c. Changing the Time Zone on each post.

Have a go hero – doing more with the thing

Now that you've got some knowledge about publishing posts, categorizing them, and managing your blogroll, it would be a great idea to start writing your own content and experiment with all the tools that Roller has to offer. For example, if you're planning to write about a hobby, you can start building a good blogroll of other sites related to this subject.

If you start building your weblog's skeleton now, when you finish reading Chapter 5, you will have the opportunity to edit your posts and add images, maybe even videos of you showing your skills to the world!

So don't be afraid, get your hands dirty and have a lot of fun with your Roller weblog! And if you need some assistance, remember I'm always an e-mail away!

Summary

In this chapter, you learned the basics about blogging with Apache Roller, and how to manage the blogroll, an important element of every blog that shows up in the front page. You also saw how to maximize your front page's space, by means of the Summary field.

Specifically, we covered:

- How to create your first user and weblog
- How to adjust basic settings for your server and weblog
- How to create and edit weblog entries (posts)
- How to manage categories for your weblog
- How to manage your weblog's blogroll (creating, editing, and deleting bookmarks)
- How to use the Rich Text Editor included in Roller in order to enhance the appearance of your posts
- How to use the Summary field when creating a post in order to show only a summary of that post in the front page, instead of showing the full post

These are the basic operations you can do in a weblog.

In Chapter 5, you'll learn to add multimedia content to your weblog (images, sounds, video) and about some interesting tools from Google, YouTube, and SlideShare. So what are you waiting for? Go on and start reading Chapter 5, you won't regret it!

5
Spicing Up Your Blog

*In this chapter, you're going to see some ways to spice up your posts
with images, sounds, videos, and maps. There is a special section about
using Google Maps, inserting YouTube videos, and embedding SlideShare
presentations in your weblog's posts. In Chapter 4, How to Start Working with
Roller, you learned how to adjust several basic settings for your blog server and
your main weblog. You also learned how to create, edit, and publish posts, and
how to manage your blogroll as well. Now it's time for you to learn how to add
multimedia capabilities to your blog.*

Basically, in this chapter we shall:

◆ Upload files (images, sounds, and videos) to your weblog, so that you can use them
in your posts

◆ Change the file upload size limit for your weblog server

◆ Include content from Google Maps, YouTube, and SlideShare in your weblog to give
your visitors a more pleasant experience

◆ Manage Roller's weblog entry plugins and editor add-ins

Before the action begins

Before starting with this chapter's exercises, you need to download the support files
(screenshots, videos, sounds, and so on) from the book's web page, and then unzip them
into a folder—`C:\ApacheRollerBook`, for example—on your hard drive. All these files
are zipped in a file named `chapter05.zip`. Inside this file, there's an image file
(`chapter05_01.jpg`), a sound file (`seaontherocks.mp3`), and several files for the
video example (`showvbox.mp4`, `showvbox_controller.swf`, and `FirstFrame.png`).

Uploading files to your weblog

Now that you have the basic knowledge about how to manage your weblog, it's time to make things more interesting for you and your future visitors. So, how can we do that? Well, multimedia files (audio or video) are always a good addition to a web page, because they can express much more than using text-only posts. Imagine what you could offer to your clients, if you had an online specialty store. You could show your new items in your Roller weblog with full color photos, and you could also embed videos of your items in your posts, to give visitors a complete virtual tour of your store! To top that, you could show them a custom Google Map, where they could get directions from their location to your store! What else could you ask for?

Using images on your posts

An image can say a thousand words and if you include some of them in your posts, imagine the space you can save. Roller has a very friendly interface to help you upload and include images in your posts, and now you're about to learn how to do it!

Time for action – uploading images into Roller

In this exercise, I'll show you how to use Roller's file upload interface, so that you can add an image to an entry (post) in your blog:

1. Open your web browser and log into Roller. The **New Entry** page will appear. Then click on the **File Uploads** link, under the **Create & Edit** tab:

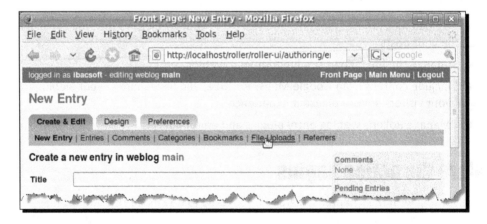

2. The **File Uploads** page will appear next, as shown in the following screenshot:

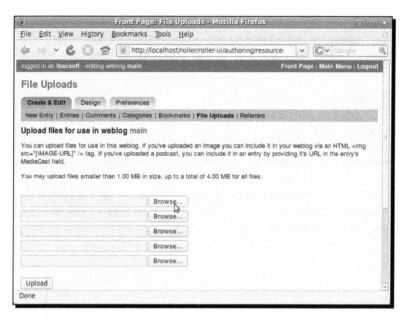

3. Click on the **Browse...** button of the first text field, and the **File Upload** dialog will appear. Go to the folder where you downloaded this chapter's support files, and double-click on the chapter5_01.png image to select it. The name of the file you selected will show up in the first textbox of the **File Uploads** page:

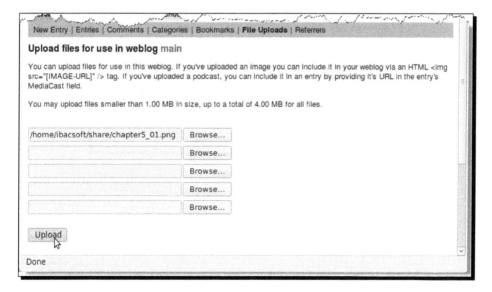

4. Click on the **Upload** button to upload the image to your blog. Roller will respond with a success message as shown in the next screenshot:

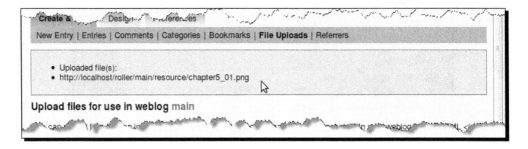

5. Take note of the URL shown in the previous message, because you'll use it when inserting the image inside a post in your blog. Now click on the **New Entry** link from the **Create & Edit** tab, and use the following screenshot as an example for your new post:

6. Press *Enter* after the last line of text (**Here's a screenshot of the official Web site:**) and click on the text editor's **Insert/Modify Image** button:

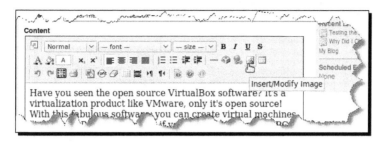

7. The **Insert Image** dialog will show up. Type the URL of the image you uploaded to Roller (`http://localhost/roller/main/resource/chapter5_01.png`) inside the **Image URL** field, and click on the **Preview** button to see a small preview of the image. Then, type **VirtualBox Web site** in the **Alternate text** field and click on the **OK** button to insert the image in your post:

8. You'll be taken back to the **New Entry** page again. To see the image, click on the **Maximize/Minimize Editor** button:

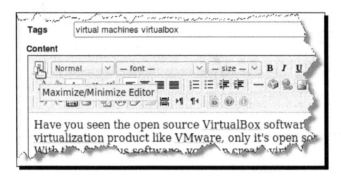

9. The editor will fill up your web browser's entire workspace area and you will be able to see the image, as shown in the following screenshot:

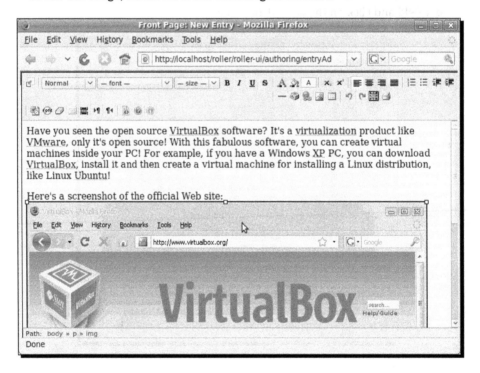

10. Click on the image to select it and change its size by dragging the little white square at the upper-right corner:

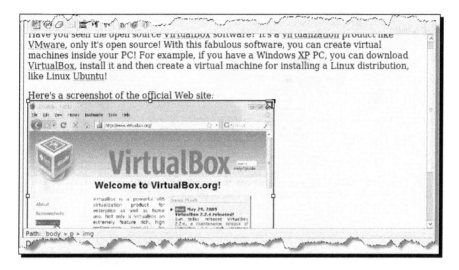

11. Click on the **Maximize/Minimize Editor** button again to change the text editor to its original size. The image will now fit inside the text editor, as shown in the following screenshot:

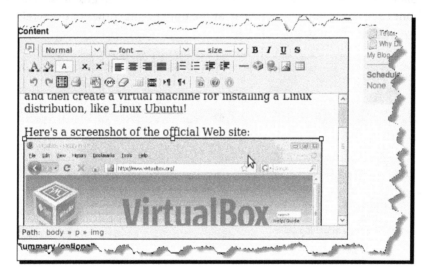

12. Use the down and right arrow keys to position the text cursor at the end of the post, press *Enter* and type the text shown in the following screenshot:

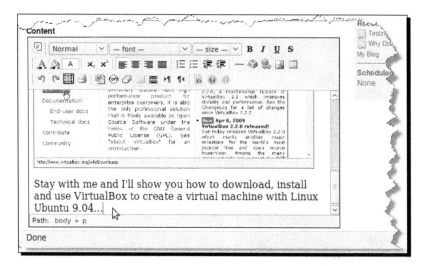

13. Exit the text editor and scroll down the **New Entry** page until you locate the **Post to Weblog** button, and click on it to publish the post to the blog.

14. Roller will show the **Changes saved** message inside a green box. Now click on the **Front Page** link in Roller's menu bar, at the upper-right corner of the screen, to go to your blog's front page:

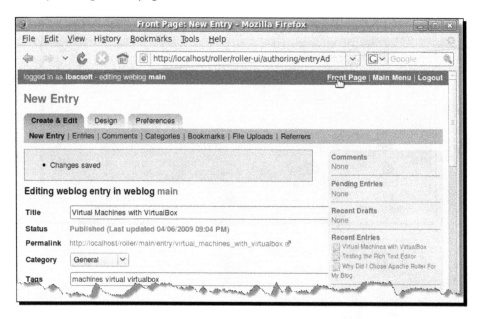

15. Your new post will appear on your weblog's front page, as shown in the following screenshot:

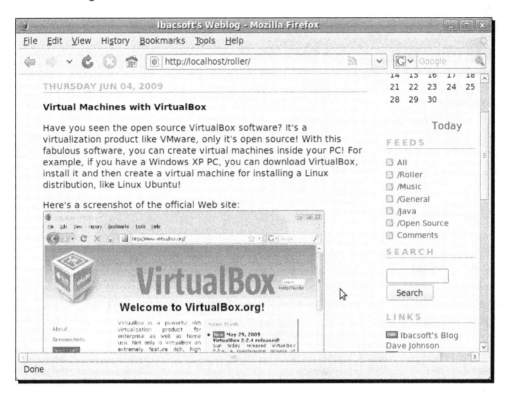

16. You can logout from Roller and close your web browser now.

What just happened?

Now you know how to upload images to your Roller weblog and guess what? You can use the same **File Upload** page to upload videos and sound files, too! You can also upload Word, Excel, PowerPoint, and almost every other file type you can imagine. The only restriction is file size—1 MB or less for each file you want to upload. However, what if you want to increase the size limit for uploading files? Well, we'll see how to deal with that problem in the following subsection.

You also learned how to use the **Insert/Modify Image** and **Maximize/Minimize Editor** buttons from the Rich Text editor. With these two buttons you can insert images and, if they are too big to see in the editor, you can maximize the editor to cover all your workspace area, so that you can manipulate images more easily.

The **Insert/Modify Image** button lets you insert an image on an entry. In the **Image URL** field, you can type the URL of an uploaded image, or you can type the URL of an image located anywhere on the Internet.

Changing file upload size limit

Previously, you learned how to upload an image to Roller and include it in a post. The **File Upload** page lets you upload up to four files, and each one of them must be smaller than 1 MB. What happens if you want to insert a video in one of your posts, and its size is greater than 1 MB? Well, there are two things you need to modify—Roller's **File Upload Settings** and a property called `struts.multipart.maxSize` in the `struts.properties` file of your Roller installation.

File upload settings

The first thing you need to do is change the size limit for file uploads in the **File Upload Settings** section from Roller's Global Server settings. The default size limit is 1 MB, to protect your weblog server in case an intruder tried to upload a very big file that could make the server crash or run out of storage space. If you plan to have other users in your weblog server, be careful with this setting because maybe someone could upload too many videos for your weblog server to handle!

Time for action – changing Roller's file upload settings

In the following exercise, I'll show you how to change the size limit for file uploads.

1. Open your web browser and log into Roller. The **New Entry** page will appear. Click on the **Main Menu** link from Roller's menu bar:

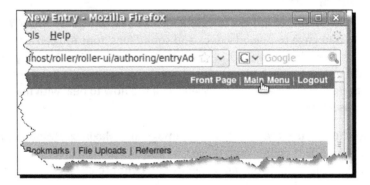

2. The **Main Menu** page will appear next, showing you a list of all your blogs:

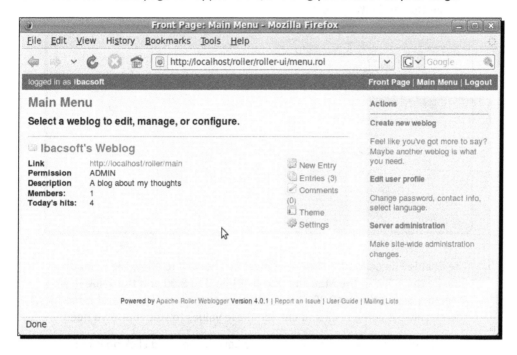

3. Now click on the **Server Administration** link under the **Actions** panel to go to your blog server's settings:

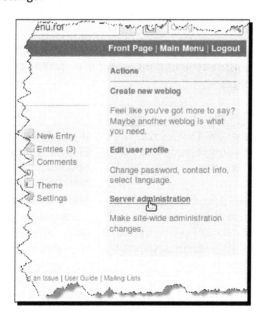

4. The **Roller Configuration** page will show up. Scroll down this page until you locate the **File Upload Settings** section:

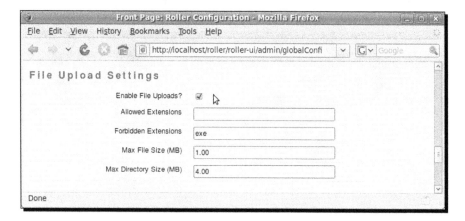

5. The **Enable File Uploads?** checkbox must be checked to allow file uploading. Change the value in the **Max File Size (MB)** field to **8.00** and the value in **Max Directory Size (MB)** to **40.00**, just to allow enough space for several video files. You can always come back and change these values to suit your own needs.

6. Scroll down the page until you locate the **Save** button and click on it to save your new settings. Roller will respond with the **Changes saved** message inside a green box. You can logout from Roller and close your web browser.

What just happened?

The previous exercise taught you how to change the size limit for file uploads, among other things. The following table lists all the options available in the **File Upload Settings** section of the **Roller Configuration** page:

Option	Definition	Tip
Enable File Uploads?	Enables or disables file uploading in your blog server.	If you don't want users to upload files for security reasons, disable this option and upload the files you need manually, with an FTP client.
Allowed Extensions	In this field, you can type all the extensions you want to allow for uploading files to your blog server, separated by spaces.	If you want to allow jpeg or png file uploading only, type **jpeg** in this field, followed by a space, and then type **png**.

Option	Definition	Tip
Forbidden Extensions	In this field, type the file extensions that you don't want being uploaded to your blog server.	The default value for this field is **exe**, because all files with .exe extensions are potentially dangerous in a Windows environment. If you want to forbid **.mov** and **.wmv** files, you need to include the mov and wmv extensions in this field (without the dot), separated by a space.
Max File Size (MB)	The maximum size for files that are being uploaded to the blog server.	The default value for this field is 1 MB, as most of the image files can be compressed to occupy less than 1 MB. You can change this field to a bigger number, so that you can upload images, videos, and sound files greater than 1 MB.
Max Directory Size (MB)	The maximum size for each individual subdirectory inside the main upload directory.	You can create directories that have several categories for all your uploaded files. For example, videos, audio, and images.

You can change the file and directory size limits to suit your own needs. Just be sure to allow enough space for all the files you want to upload.

The struts.properties file

As Roller is based on the Struts Web Framework (http://struts.apache.org/), there's a property named struts.multipart.maxSize that controls the size limit for uploading files. By default, the value of this property is 2,097,152 bytes. So, for example, if you try to upload a video file of 3,725,268 bytes, Roller will show the following error message:

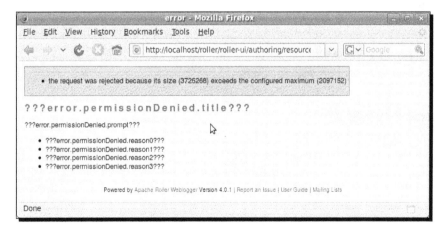

In the following exercise, I'll show you how to modify the property's value, so that you can upload videos and files of any size.

Time for action – modifying the struts.multipart.maxSize property

The `struts.properties` file is inside Roller's `WEB-INF/classes` folder. If you are using Windows, you can just open and edit the file; but if you're using Linux, remember you need to have "root" privileges to modify this file.

1. Go to Roller's `WEB-INF/classes` folder and open the `struts.properties` file. Add the following line at the end of this file: `struts.multipart.maxSize=104857600`.

2. The following screenshot shows the `struts.properties` file with the `struts.multipart.maxSize` property, in a Linux Ubuntu environment:

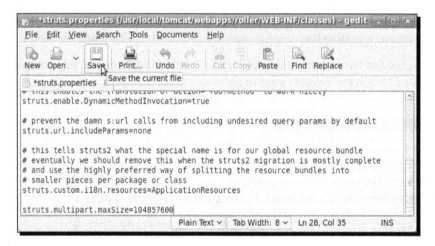

3. Save your changes and close the file. You'll need to logout from Roller and restart Tomcat to apply the new size limit.

What just happened?

Now you can upload videos or files up to 100 MB in size. However, don't forget the **Max File Size** limit in the **File Upload Settings** section. This setting only allows a maximum size of 8 MB for each uploaded file. Just remember that the setting with the smallest value will determine the maximum size of each file to be uploaded. In this case, the **Max File Size (MB)** setting is just 8 MB, it doesn't matter if the `struts.multipart.maxSize` is 10 MB or 100 MB, the maximum file size you can upload is 8 MB.

If you look at the screenshot in step 2 of the previous section, the `struts.multipart.maxSize` is `104857600` bytes, or 100 MB (100 x 1024 x 1024). You could also use `100000000` as an approximate value for 100 MB, but if you want to use exact values, apply the following formula:

Total bytes = Value in Megabytes * 1024 * 1024

Be careful when changing the size limit for uploading files
As I said earlier, you need to be very careful with this setting, because your weblog server could be seriously affected if one or several users start to upload big files. It's better to leave the default size limit and create accounts on YouTube, SlideShare, and other services available on the Internet to upload videos and presentations, and then embed them in your weblog. We'll talk about this in the *Google Maps, YouTube, and SlideShare* section.

Using videos in your posts

OK, you changed the space limit for uploading files to your blog server. Now it's time to learn how to insert video files in your posts. You can just insert one as an HTML link, but who does that anymore? It's a good way to drive your prospective readers away! In today's world, you need to offer your spectators the easiest, quickest, and most attractive way to see what you have to offer. My job is to show you how to do that with your Roller weblog, so let's get to it!

Time for action – uploading and inserting videos on your posts

In this exercise, I'll show you how to upload a video file to your blog server and then insert it into a post using Apache Roller:

1. Open your web browser and log into Roller. The **New Entry** page will appear. Click on the **File Uploads** link from the **Create & Edit** tab. Scroll down the **File Uploads** page until you locate the **Manage Uploaded Files** section. Type **video** in the **New Directory** field and click on the **Create** button, as shown in the following screenshot:

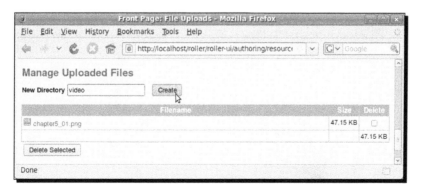

2. Roller will show the following success message:

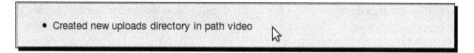

3. Scroll down the page again until you locate the `video` folder in the **Manage Uploaded Files** section, and click on it:

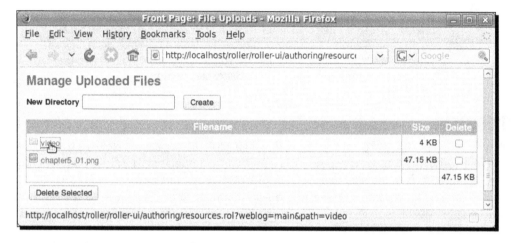

4. Roller will take you to the same **File Uploads** page, but this time you'll be inside the `video` directory. Now click on the first **Browse...** button of the **Upload files for use in weblog main** section. On the **File Upload** dialog, go to the folder where you downloaded the support files for this chapter, and double-click on the `FirstFrame.png` image to select it. The name of this file will show up on the first textbox of the **File Uploads** page.

5. Now click on the second **Browse...** button and double-click on the `showvbox.mp4` file, so that its name appears in the second textbox of the **File Uploads** page.

6. Repeat the process with the third **Browse...** button and the `showvbox_controller.swf` file. Your **File Uploads** page must look like the following screenshot:

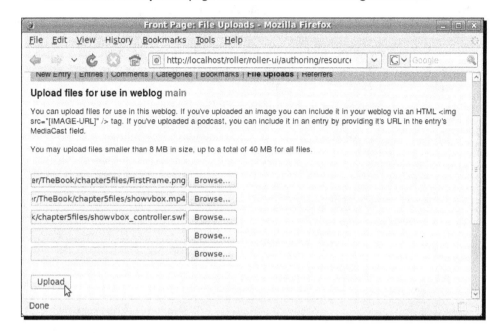

7. Click on the **Upload** button to upload the three files to the `video` directory in your blog server. Roller will return the following success page:

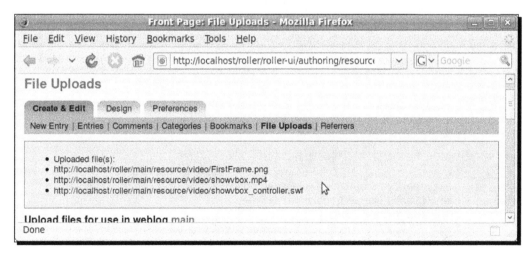

Don't forget to write down the three URLs from the previous Roller message; you'll need them when inserting the video into an entry (post).

8. Click on the **New Entry** link from the **Create & Edit** tab to go to the **New Entry** page and create a new post for your blog. Type **Ubuntu Linux Virtual Machine Inside a Windows XP PC** in the **Title** field, select **Open Source** in the **Category** field, type **virtualbox windows xp linux ubuntu** in the **Tags** field. In the **Content** field, and type **Here's a sample video of my Ubuntu Linux Virtual Machine, running inside a Windows XP PC with VirtualBox:** as shown in the following screenshot:

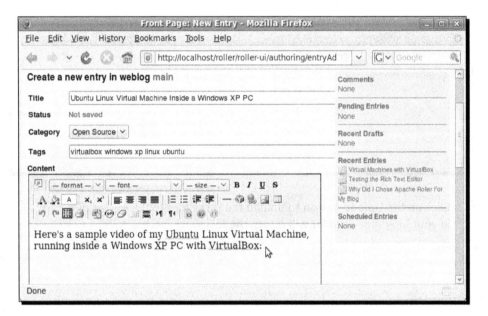

9. Click on the **Toggle HTML Source** button from the HTML editor (⬚) and write the following code below the text you typed in step 8 (the text in bold must correspond to the URLs from step 7's screenshot):

```
<object height="498" width="640" id="csSWF"
  classid="clsid:d27cdb6e-ae6d-11cf-96b8-444553540000"
  codebase="http://download.macromedia.com/pub/shockwave/
  cabs/flash/swflash.cab#version=9,0,115,0">
    <param name="src"
           value="http://localhost/roller/main/
                     resource/video/showvbox_controller.swf" />
    <param name="bgcolor" value="#1a1a1a" />
    <param name="quality" value="best" />
    <param name="allowScriptAccess" value="always" />
    <param name="allowFullScreen" value="true" />
```

```
<param name="scale" value="showall" />
<param name="flashVars" value="autostart=false" />
<embed height="498" width="640" name="csSWF"
        src="http://localhost/roller/main/resource/
            video/showvbox_controller.swf"
        bgcolor="#1a1a1a" quality="best"
        allowscriptaccess="always"
        allowfullscreen="true" scale="showall"
        flashvars="autostart=false&amp;
        thumb=http://localhost/roller/main/resource/
            video/FirstFrame.png&amp;
        thumbscale=45&amp;color=0x000000,0x000000"
        pluginspage="http://www.macromedia.com/
                shockwave/download/
                index.cgi?P1_Prod_Version=ShockwaveFlash"
    />
</object>
```

10. Click on the **Save as Draft** button, to save a draft of your post. Then scroll down the page and click on the **Full Preview** button, to see how your post will look in your blog before publishing it. The preview will open in a new tab in your web browser:

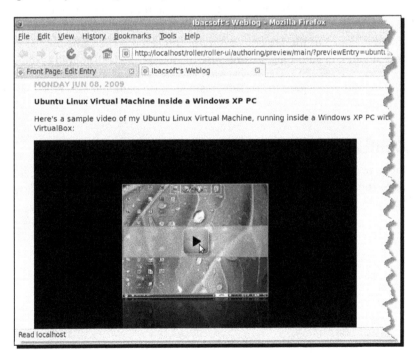

11. Click on the play button and the video will begin to playback. When finished, close the preview tab and click on the **Post to Weblog** button to publish your new post. You can logout from Roller now.

What just happened?

The previous exercise showed you how to upload a video to your blog server and insert it in a post. As you can see, videos are a little more complicated than plain images. In this case, we used the following files:

- `FirstFrame.png`: This is the thumbnail image that shows up before the video begins to playback

- `showvbox.mp4`: The video file

- `showvbox_controller.swf`: The controller that plays back the `showvbox.mp4` file

The video was produced with Camtasia Studio, an excellent screen recording software application from TechSmith (`http://www.techsmith.com`). If you want to practice with your own videos, you can download a 30-day free trial version of Camtasia Studio from the following URL: `http://www.techsmith.com/download/camtasiatrial.asp`.

What would happen if you wanted to embed a video from your camera or cell phone? Well, you can embed it directly in your blog, but the best thing to do is use a software application such as Camtasia Studio to create the `.swf` controller and the HTML code to embed into your post automatically. Then you just need to change the `.swf` controller and thumbnail URLs, as you did in step 9 of the previous exercise. You can use the same embed code to insert a different video in your blog; just be sure to change the URL in bold text.

You could also upload your video to YouTube instead of uploading it into Roller, as we'll see later in this chapter.

Using sound files in your posts

There are times when you need to express something with audio. For example, if you've ever wanted to run your own radio show, Roller can help you with that! Just follow the next exercise and you'll be ready for action!

Time for action – uploading and inserting sound files in your posts

In the following exercise, I'll show you how to insert a sound file in one of your posts, and how to use **Play Tagger** from Delicious, so that your visitors don't need to download your sound files to hear them:

1. Open your web browser and log into Roller. The **New Entry** page will appear. Click on the **File Uploads** link from the **Create & Edit** tab to go to the **File Uploads** page. Click on the **Browse...** button of the first text field, and the **File Upload** dialog will appear. Go to the folder where you downloaded this chapter's support files, and double-click on the seaontherocks.mp3 file to select it. The name of the file you selected will show up in the first textbox of the **File Uploads** page. Click on the **Upload** button to upload the sound file to your weblog server. Remember to write down the URL of the file you've just uploaded, for future reference.

2. Use the following screenshot as an example to create a new post:

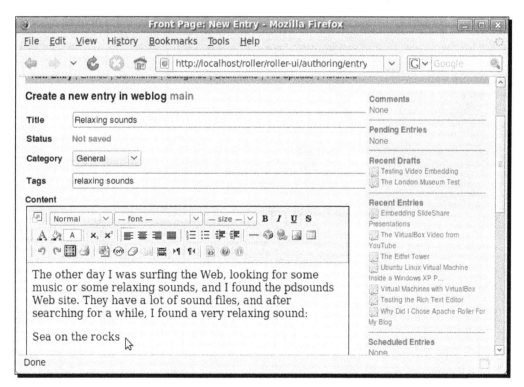

3. Drag your mouse over the **Sea on the rocks** text to select it, and then click on the **Insert Web Link** button from the text editor's toolbar:

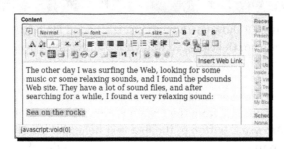

4. In the **URL** field of the **Insert/Modify Link** dialog, paste the URL of the sound file that you uploaded in step 1, type **Sea on the rocks** in the **Title (tooltip)** field, and click on the **OK** button:

5. Now scroll down the **New Entry** page and click on the **Post to Weblog** button, to publish your new post. Roller will show you the **Changes saved** message in a green box. Click on the **Permalink** field to see the new post on your weblog's front page:

6. If you click on the **Sea on the rocks** link, your web browser will try to use a media player installed on your PC to play the sound file. Now click on the **Edit** link, near the bottom-right area of the screen:

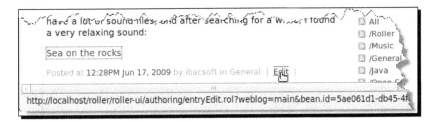

7. In the **Edit Entry** page, scroll to the **Content** field and click on the **Toggle HTML Source** button of the Rich Text editor's toolbar to see the following HTML source code:

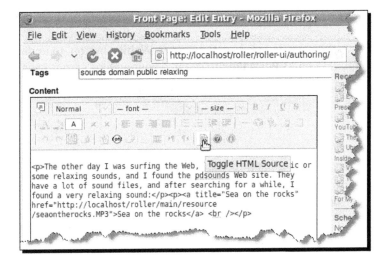

8. Type `<script type="text/javascript" src="http://static.delicious.com/js/playtagger.js"></script>` before all the text in the **Content** field, as shown in the following screenshot:

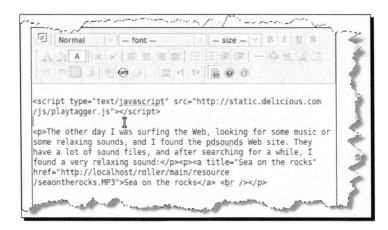

9. Scroll down the page and click on the **Post to Weblog** button, to update your post. Then, click on its **Permalink** to see it in your weblog's front page:

10. There will be a **listen** icon at the left of the **Sea on the rocks** link. If you click on this icon, you'll start hearing the sound file directly from your blog post, and the "link" icon will change, as shown in the following screenshot:

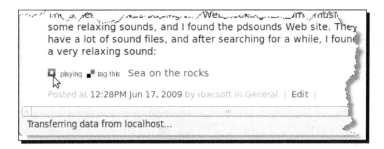

11. You can click on the **stop** button or wait until the sound finishes playing. Log out of Roller and close your web browser, if you wish.

What just happened?

In this exercise, you learned how to insert a sound file in one of your weblog's posts. In this case, there are two ways in which your visitors can hear your sound files—via an external media player installed on their PC, or using the Play Tagger tool from Delicious (http://delicious.com/help/playtagger). By using the latter one, your visitors will be capable of hearing your sound files without the need for an external media player.

As you can see, everything you upload into Roller can be pasted in a post via the URL assigned to it. In this example, we used a .mp3 file, but you can upload any other audio file type, and insert it in a similar way. If you use the Play Tagger tool, your visitors won't have to download and use an external media player to play your files. Now you can write and speak to your weblog visitors. They can see you as well, if you embed a video. This is why blogs are becoming so popular and powerful as a communication tool nowadays. Now let's get on to the next section, where you'll see how to take advantage of web services such as Google Maps, YouTube, and SlideShare.

Google Maps, YouTube, and SlideShare

There are a lot of Internet and web services which you can use along with your blog to make your content more interesting for your viewers. With a good digital camera and video production software, you can make your own videos and presentations quickly and easily, and embed them in your posts with just a few clicks! For example, with Google Maps, you can add photos of your business to a custom map, and post it in your blog to attract customers. There are a lot of possibilities, and it all depends on your creativity!

Including Google Maps in your posts

Using **Google Maps** in your blog is a good way of promoting your business because you can show your visitors your exact location. Or you can blog about your favorite places and show them as if you were there, using your own photos.

Time for action – using Google Maps

There are a lot of things you can do with Google Maps, one of them is including maps of your favorite places in your blog, as we'll see in a moment:

1. Open your web browser and go to Google Maps (`http://maps.google.com`). Type **Eiffel Tower** in the search textbox, and click on the **Search Maps** button or press *Enter*. Your web browser window will split in two areas, as shown in the following screenshot:

2. Click on the **Eiffel Tower** link at the bottom-left part of the screen to see the Eiffel Tower's exact position in the map at the right panel:

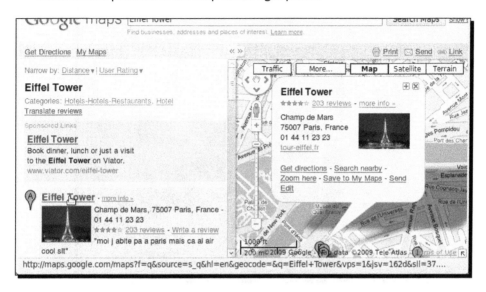

3. Now click on the **Satellite** button to see a satellite image of the Eiffel Tower:

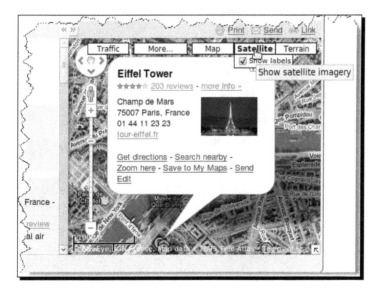

4. Drag the Eiffel Tower upwards using your mouse, to center it on the map area:

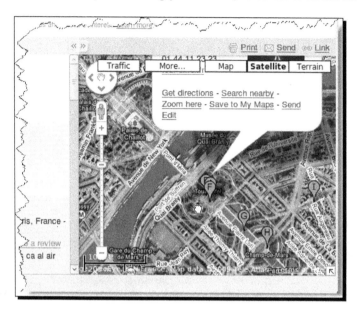

5. Click on the **Zoom here** link inside the Eiffel Tower caption to see a closer image:

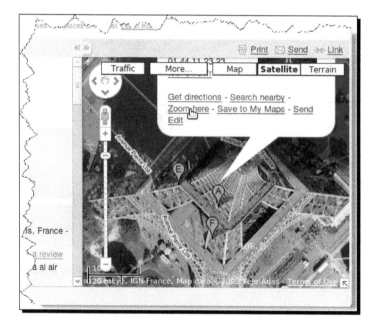

6. If you look closely at the previous screenshot, you'll notice three links above the map: **Print**, **Send**, and **Link**. Click on **Link** to open a small window:

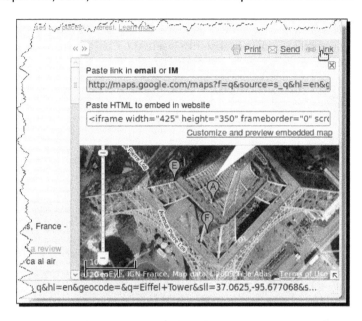

7. Right-click on the **Paste HTML to embed in website** field to select the HTML code, and then click on the **Copy** option from the pop-up menu:

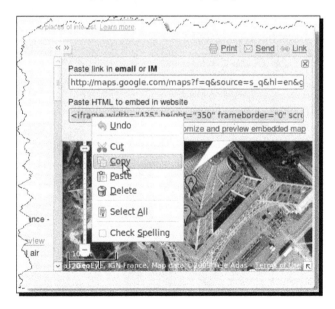

8. Open a new web browser window and log into your Roller weblog. In the **New Entry** page, type **The Eiffel Tower** inside the **Title** field, and **Eiffel Tower Google Maps** inside the **Tags** field. Then click on the **Toggle HTML Source** button in the Tich Text editor toolbar, type **This is an Eiffel Tower satellite image, courtesy of Google Maps:
** inside the **Content** Field, press *Enter*, and paste the code you copied from the Google Maps web page:

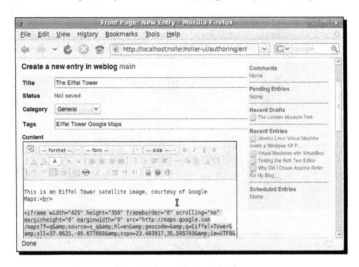

9. Scroll down the **New Entry** page and click on the **Post to Weblog** button. Then click on the **Permalink** field's URL, to see your Google Maps image posted in your blog.

10. Click on the **Zoom here** link once to see a close-up of the Eiffel Tower, as shown in the following screenshot:

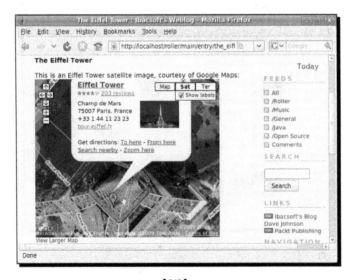

What just happened?

Now you can add Google Maps functionality inside your blog! Isn't that great? You just need to copy and paste the HTML code that the Google Maps produce automatically for you. If you want a bigger or smaller map, you can click on the **Customize and preview embedded map** link to customize the HTML code that you're going to paste into your blog:

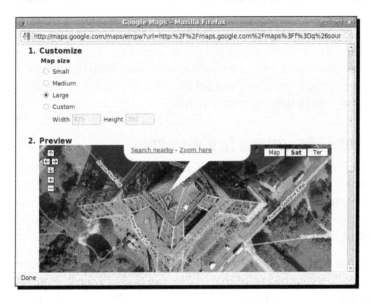

Then you just copy the HTML code produced by Google Maps and paste it into your blog post:

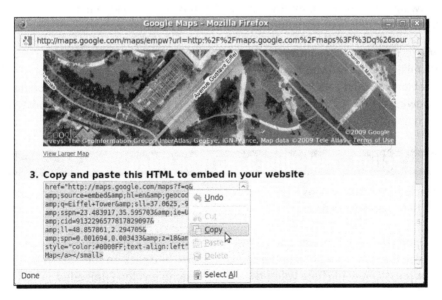

If you have a Google Maps account, you can create customized maps and show them to your visitors, add photos and videos of places you've visited, and even write reviews about your favorite restaurants and hotels.

Have a go hero – explore Google Maps

Now that you've seen how to embed Google Maps in your weblog, it would be a great idea to create your own Google Maps account, and start exploring all the things that you can do—inserting photos and videos about places you've visited in your own custom maps, adding reviews of restaurants and other businesses in your locality, and so on. You can explore other users' maps, too. Once you get the hang of it, you'll be traveling around the world and meeting new people from your own PC.

Including YouTube videos in your posts

YouTube is one of the most popular video sharing websites in the world. You can include your favorite videos in your blog, or make your own videos and show them to your visitors. However, before you start complaining that we have already seen how to insert videos on your weblog, let me tell you that the big difference between uploading a video to your own blog server and uploading a video to a YouTube server is **bandwidth**.

When someone plays back a video from your weblog, the blog server transfers the video data to your visitor's web browser, so that he/she can begin to see it, even before the video downloads completely. This is known as **video streaming**. Now, imagine you have 1,000 visitors, and each one of them is viewing the same video from your weblog! There would be a big amount of data flowing from your weblog to each visitor's web browser! That amount of data flowing from one PC to another is called **bandwidth**. You would need a very broad connection to be capable of transmitting your video to all those visitors.

That's where YouTube comes into play. They have lots of bandwidth available for you and the other millions of users who share videos daily! So, if you plan to include a lot of videos in your weblog, it would be a great idea to get a YouTube account and start uploading them. In the following exercise, I'll show you how to include a YouTube video in your post, without having to upload it to your weblog.

Time for action – including a YouTube video

You can include YouTube videos from your account or from other YouTube users; just be sure to ask for their permission first!

1. Open your web browser and go to YouTube (http://www.youtube.com). Type **ibacsoft virtualbox** in the search textbox, and click on the **Search** button or press *Enter*. YouTube will show you the example video I uploaded:

2. Click on the **Using Linux Ubuntu with Sun VirtualBox** link and you'll be taken to a web page where you can see the video, and also copy some HTML code to insert into your blog:

3. Select the HTML code in the **Embed** field from the gray information box, right-click on it and select **Copy** from the pop-up menu.

4. Open another web browser window and log into your Roller weblog. Use the following screenshot to create an example post and paste the code you copied from the video inside the **Content** field:

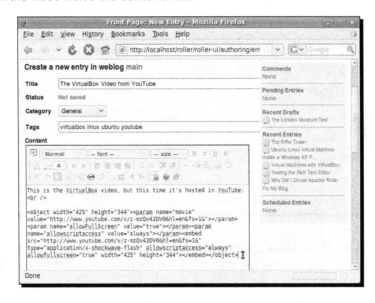

5. Scroll down the page and click on the **Post to Weblog** button. Then, click on the **Permalink** URL to see your post in your weblog's front page:

6. Click on the play button to confirm that it's the same video you posted before on your weblog.

What just happened?

Although you get the same result as uploading a video to your own weblog server, using YouTube is better because you won't be limited by your Internet connection speed. It's better to open a YouTube account and start uploading your own videos, and then copy the HTML code that YouTube generates automatically to embed them to your weblog posts. You'll even get more publicity for your videos, as YouTube will include them in their listings!

Like Google Maps, YouTube also has a **Customize** option, next to the **Embed** field:

With this option, you can change the color, size, and appearance of the YouTube container for your video. You can also uncheck the **Include related videos** option, to avoid showing related videos after your visitors have seen your video.

If you're serious about broadcasting a lot of videos in your weblog to visitors from the Internet, you can pay for a premium account on Screencast (`http://www.screencast.com`) or any other dedicated content sharing web page. However, if you're planning to post videos on a blog server inside your company, without broadcasting them to the Internet, it's better to upload them to your blog server and take advantage of your high-speed LAN.

Have a go hero – explore YouTube

If you haven't created a YouTube account yet, what are you waiting for? Go on and start uploading videos, it's as easy as embedding them in your blog! YouTube takes care of all the conversion and rendering processes, so you only need to copy the HTML code and paste it in your post in order to embed your YouTube videos.

Now that you also have a Google Maps account, why don't you start embedding YouTube videos in your custom Google Maps? I'm pretty sure you'll find out how to do it! If you have any doubts or questions, remember I'm just an e-mail away!

Including SlideShare presentations in your posts

PowerPoint, OpenOffice, and PDF presentations are a very popular communication media nowadays. People use them to transmit their thoughts, ideas, and experiences to other people. For example, software developers use presentations to introduce their software products in conferences. Business managers use them to show new business objectives and marketing plans to their subordinates in meetings. You can use presentations with pictures and diagrams in your blog as well. Your visitors will be more attracted to your blog and what you have to say, trust me on that one.

Time for action – including a SlideShare presentation

You can make your own SlideShare presentations and include them in your weblog, or you can include presentations from other SlideShare users. Just be sure to ask them for permission first.

1. Open your web browser and go to SlideShare (`http://www.slideshare.net`). The SlideShare front page will show up:

2. Click on the **Take a tour** link to see the **Why you should use SlideShare?** presentation:

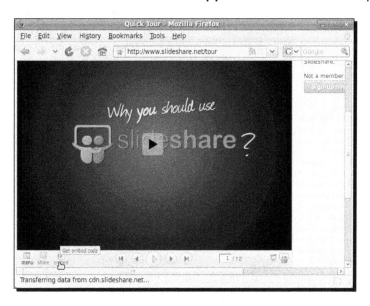

3. Click on the **embed** button in the SlideShare control bar. The **Embed** tab will show up in the SlideShare presentation area, along with the HTML code needed to embed the presentation in your weblog. Click on the **Copy** button to copy the HTML code into the clipboard:

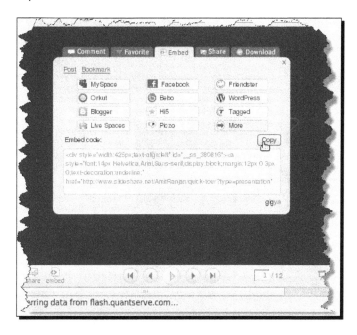

4. Open a new web browser window and log into Roller. The **New Entry** page will show up. Type **Embedding SlideShare Presentations** in the **Title** field, **embedding slideshare presentations apache roller** in the **Tags** field, and **This post shows how to embed a SlideShare presentation into an Apache Roller weblog post:</br>** into the **Content** field. Then press *Enter* and paste the code you copied in the previous step of this exercise. Your screen should look like the following screenshot:

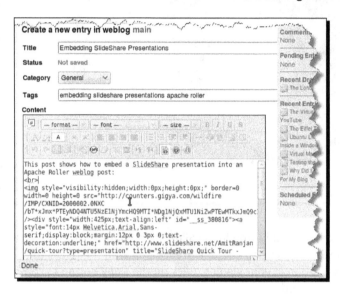

5. Scroll down the page and click on the **Post to Weblog** button. Then click on the **Permalink** field URL to see the new post in your weblog's front page, with the SlideShare presentation embedded:

6. Click on the SlideShare presentation's **Play** button, to verify that it works as expected. If you wish, you can log out from Roller and close your web browser.

What just happened?

In the last exercise, I showed you how to embed a SlideShare presentation in your post. You can use PowerPoint presentations, MS Word or OpenOffice documents, and PDF files. So, if you need to share a presentation or document with other people, you can use your Roller blog and SlideShare to get the job done.

Have a go hero – explore SlideShare

As with Google Maps and YouTube, it would be great if you create a SlideShare account and start adding your own content, to embed it in your blog and share it with all your visitors. If you are planning to use Roller to promote your business or to write about your activities at work, start planning on several presentations to begin with. Oh, and let me know if you have any questions or doubts about using SlideShare, okay?

Pop quiz – images, sounds, and videos

1. You've just captured your first video on your digital camera! What would be the best way to show it in your blog?

    a. Insert it as an HTML link.

    b. Upload it to YouTube and then copy the HTML embed code in your post.

    c. Call 911 for help!

2. If you wanted to post a ten-minute talk about self-improvement daily, what would you need to do in order to broadcast that talk to all your friends and colleagues through the Internet?

    a. Get the software to record your voice in your PC, upload that audio file to your Roller blog, create a new entry, insert the audio file as an HTML link, and use the Play Tagger tool from Delicious, so that visitors can play that audio file directly from your blog.

    b. Hire some web programmer to do it for you.

    c. Send an e-mail to each one of your listeners, with the audio file attached.

3. Your boss wants you to use the PowerPoint presentation for the new product that the Graphic Design Department finished just yesterday. However, there's just a little problem, you need to show that presentation to 20 or 30 people from 10 different companies, at the same time tomorrow! How could you use your Roller blog to solve this problem?

    a. Rent a conference room in the nearest hotel and send an e-mail to everyone, telling them to be on time for tomorrow's presentation!

    b. Upload the presentation to your SlideShare account, use the embed code produced by SlideShare to embed the presentation inside a post in your weblog, and send the Permalink URL to everyone who must see that presentation, so that they can visit your blog and see it from their own PCs!

    c. Capture a screenshot of every slide in the presentation, upload all the images, and create a new post in your weblog to insert them.

Summary

In this chapter, you learned about all the different tools available on the Internet, which can help you build a very attractive weblog for your visitors.

Specifically, we covered:

- How to upload files to your blog, and use the rich text editor to insert images, sound files, and videos
- How to change the file uploading size limit for your blog server in order to upload bigger files
- How to use Google Maps, YouTube, and SlideShare to embed maps, videos, and document presentations in your blog

Now you have lot of tools at your service to make your blog stand out in the crowd. All that stands between you and the sweet smell of success is the time you'll need to turn your ideas and imagination into impressive posts that will knock the socks off your visitors.

In Chapter 6, *Roller Themes and Blog Promotion*, you'll learn about Roller themes, and how you can use them to change your weblog's appearance, to complement what you learned in this chapter and Chapter 4. I hope you've liked it so far, because there are a lot of interesting things you still have to learn about Roller, to explore it to its fullest potential.

6
Roller Themes and Blog Promotion

Wow, we're finally over the hill! I hope you've enjoyed the chapters we've seen in this book so far. In this chapter, we're going to talk about Roller Themes and how to promote your weblog on all the popular social bookmarking websites such as Technorati, Digg, Delicious, and StumbleUpon.

A theme is a small set of templates, and a template is just a web page with HTML and Velocity code embedded inside it. In Chapter 7, Working with Templates, we'll see some basics about Velocity. For now, let's just concentrate on these basic definitions and start working with all the cool examples I've designed for you!

Basically, in this chapter you will:

♦ Learn how to choose a weblog theme

♦ Download and install new weblog themes

♦ Learn about port forwarding in order to open the web port (80) on your PC and show your Roller weblog to the Internet world

♦ Learn how to promote your weblog on some popular social bookmarking websites

I guarantee that you'll learn a lot of useful stuff to enhance your weblog and attract a lot of visitors!

Before the action begins

Before starting with this chapter's exercises, you need to download the `chapter06.zip` support file from the book's website and then unzip its contents into a folder—`C:\ApacheRollerBook`, for example—on your hard drive. There's only one image file inside this ZIP file: `image01.jpg`.

Choosing a weblog theme

Up until now, we've been working with the same Roller theme: *Basic*. When you install Roller for the first time, there are several themes already installed for you to choose from: *Basic*, *Brushed Metal*, *Frontpage*, and *Sotto*. In this section, you'll see how to choose any of these weblog themes from Roller's admin interface.

Time for action – choosing a Roller theme

OK, it's time to give your weblog a total makeover with just a few clicks:

1. Open your web browser and log into Roller. The **New Entry** page will appear. Click on the **Design** tab to go to the **Weblog Theme** page:

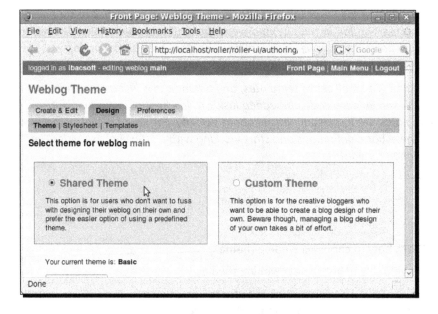

2. The **Shared Theme** option will be selected. Scroll down the page until you see the theme selector drop-down listbox and a thumbnail of your current theme:

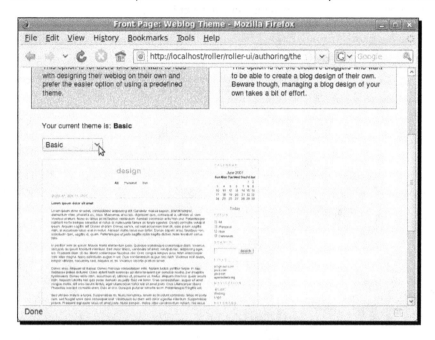

3. Click on the drop-down list to see all the available Roller themes, and select the **Brushed Metal** theme. The thumbnail will change to reflect the new theme you selected:

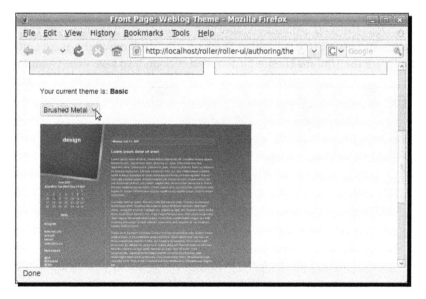

4. Scroll down the page until you locate the **See how your blog will look with this theme** link, and click on it. Roller will open a new web browser window to show you how the new theme will look in your weblog:

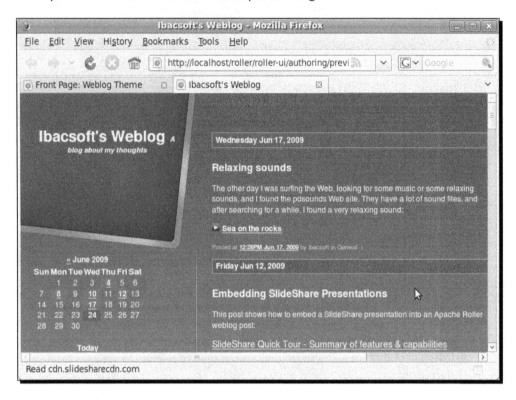

5. Now, close the web browser window that Roller opened to show you the new theme, and return to the **Weblog Theme** page. Scroll down this page until you locate the **Update Theme** button, and click on it to save your changes:

6. Roller will show the **Successfully set theme to - Brushed Metal** message inside a green box. You can logout from your weblog now and close your web browser.

What just happened?

As you saw in the previous exercise, it's pretty easy to change themes in Roller. All you need to do is log in, go to the **Weblog Theme** page, and select one theme from the list. And the minute you click on the **Update Theme** button, the whole appearance of your blog will change, without you having to do anything complicated, such as HTML programming! That's the beauty of using Roller themes!

Exploring the differences between themes

All these theme-changing features sound great, but as you may have noticed, there are several differences between one theme and the other. So let's do a little exercise to show you how choosing a different theme may affect the way your weblog displays information.

Time for action – differences between the Brushed Metal and Basic themes

Now that you've changed your first theme, let's see how some differences between the *Brushed Metal* and *Basic* themes may affect the way you and your visitors see your weblog:

1. Open your web browser and go to your weblog's front page (http://localhost/roller). Scroll down until you locate the **Controls** section at the left-hand side of the screen:

2. Click on the **Login** link to log into Roller. The **New Entry** page will show up. Now click on the **Front Page** link in Roller's menu bar:

3. Roller will take you again to your weblog's front page. Scroll down and take a look at the **Controls** section again:

4. As you can see, there are more links in this section when you're logged in: **Front Page**, **Weblog**, **New Entry**, **Settings**, and **Logout**.

5. Click on the **Settings** link to return to the administrator interface. Roller will take you to the **Weblog Settings** page (**Preferences** tab). Now click on the **Design** tab to see the **Weblog Theme** page, select the **Basic** theme, and click on the **Update Theme** button. Then click on the **Front Page** link in Roller's menu bar to see your weblog with the Basic theme, and scroll down the page until you locate the **NAVIGATION** section, at the right-hand side of the screen:

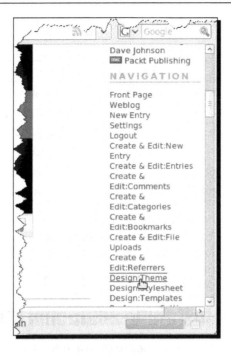

6. As you can see, this theme shows a lot more options in the **NAVIGATION** section than the **Control** section in the *Brushed Metal* theme. Now click on the **Design:Theme** link to return to the **Weblog Theme** page, select the **Brushed Metal** theme from the drop-down listbox, and click on the **Update Theme** button to change your weblog theme back to Brushed Metal.

What just happened?

The first thing you must have noticed in the previous exercise is that the *Basic* and the *Brushed* **Metal** themes show different names for the same sections, such as the **NAVIGATION** section in the *Basic* theme and the **Control** section in the *Brushed Metal* theme. If you take a closer look at both themes, you'll notice that all sections have different names. And if you try out the other two default themes, there will be noticeable differences in the way they show your weblog's data.

Don't use the *Frontpage* theme for your personal weblog; this is a special theme to be used when you run a community of several users and weblogs on your blog server, and you want to show all their newest and more popular posts combined in your front page.

The next table sums up the three default themes you can use for personal weblogs, and their corresponding sections:

Basic	Brushed Metal	Sotto
Calendar	No name	No name
Feeds	Newsfeeds	No name
Search	Not included	No name
Links	Blogroll	No name
Navigation	Controls	Editor Menu
Referrers	Not included	Not included

In short, you can use Roller themes to change your weblog's visual appearance, but you have to be careful when choosing the best one for your needs because each theme shows your weblog's information in a different way. If you keep on reading, I'll show you how to get a lot more themes in the next section.

Downloading and installing additional themes

After installing Roller, you have four themes to choose from: *Basic*, *Brushed Metal*, *Frontpage*, and *Sotto*. I know it's a pretty darn small set of choices, but that's why I'm going to show you how to get more themes for your weblog in the next exercise.

Time for action – getting additional themes for your weblog

The `https://roller.dev.java.net/` website has a lot of additional themes you can download for your weblog. Let's find out how to do that:

1. Open your web browser and type `https://roller.dev.java.net/files/ documents/190/73198/opt-themes-roller-4.0.tar.gz` in the **Address** bar to download the optional themes file. Your web browser will ask if you want to open or save this file. If you're using Windows, click on the **Save** button; if you're using Linux, select the **Save File** option, and click on the **OK** button to start downloading the file.

2. Once the file has downloaded, extract it to see all the additional Roller themes, each one inside its own subdirectory:

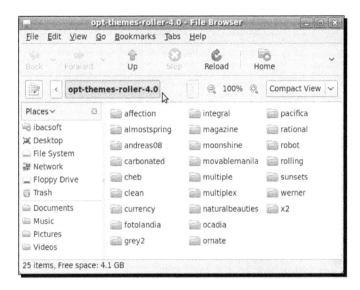

3. Now, select all these directories and copy them to the `themes` directory, inside Roller's main directory. In Ubuntu Linux, open a terminal window, go to the `opt-themes-roller-4.0` directory you've just extracted, and type `sudo cp -R * /usr/local/tomcat/webapps/roller/themes` to copy all the themes' directories into the Roller `themes` directory:

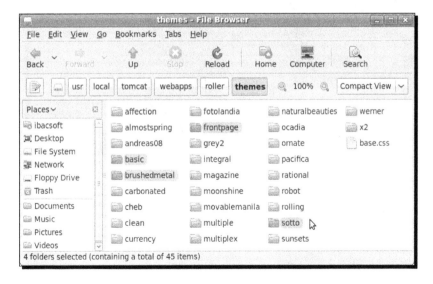

4. Now open your web browser and log into Roller. Click on the **Design** tab to go to the **Web Themes** page, and click on the theme selector drop-down listbox to see all of the available themes:

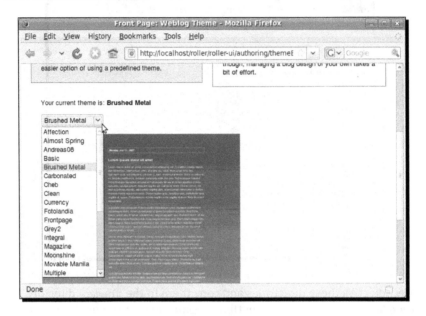

5. Select the **Carbonated** theme, click on the **See how your blog will look with this theme** link to open a new web browser tab, and take a look at your new weblog theme:

6. Close the preview tab and click on the **Update Theme** button to apply the changes to your weblog:

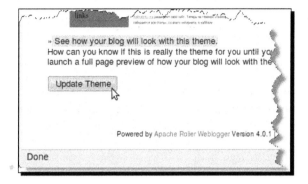

7. Roller will show you the **Successfully set theme to – Carbonated** message to confirm that your theme was successfully changed.

What just happened?

Now you have a good set of themes to choose from! All you need to do in order to add a new theme to your Roller weblog is copy its directory to the `themes` directory inside Roller's main directory. In the screenshot from step 3 of the previous exercise, you can see that there's a directory for each theme; for example, inside the `carbonated` directory, there are several files and subdirectories that make up that theme, as shown in the following screenshot:

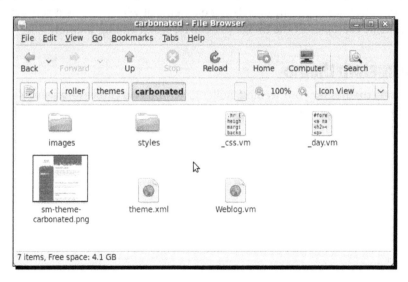

A theme can have additional files and directories besides the ones shown in the previous screenshot, but in general these are the most common files you'll see inside a theme's directory. In the next section, I'll show you how to edit the *Carbonated* theme, to adjust it to your own needs.

Editing themes

OK. You've learned how to change your Roller theme, and how to download additional themes. You've chosen the Carbonated theme for now, but if you look at the front page closely, you'll notice that the weblog categories don't fit in the header:

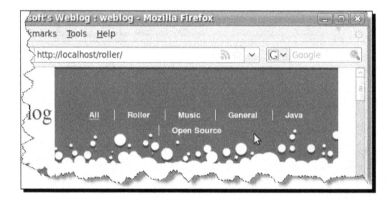

And, what if you want to use some feature that you saw in the *Basic* theme in your *Carbonated* theme, or in any other theme whatsoever? Well, that's why Roller lets us edit any theme to customize it, adding or deleting elements at will. In the next subsections, we'll see some specific examples of the things you can do when editing themes.

Using a custom theme

When choosing themes for your weblog, Roller gives you two choices—a *shared* theme or a *custom* theme. Until now, we've been using **Shared Themes** only. In the next exercise, you'll learn how to use **Custom Themes**.

 You'll need to use image01.jpg in this next exercise. It's the support file included inside chapter06.zip.

Time for action – editing a custom theme

In this exercise, you'll learn how to edit the *Carbonated* theme, although you can use the same process for any other theme:

1. Open your web browser and log into Roller. Click on the **Design** tab to go to the **Weblog Theme** page, and select the **Custom Theme** option:

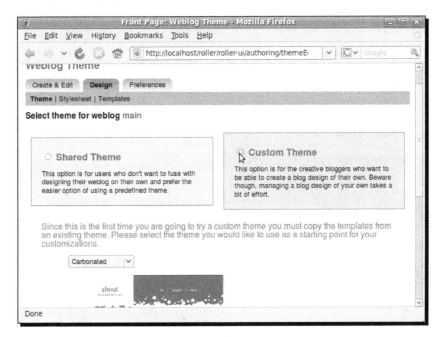

2. Select the **Carbonated** theme, scroll down until you locate the **Update Theme** button, and click on it to copy the *Carbonated* theme templates to your custom space. Roller will respond with the following success message:

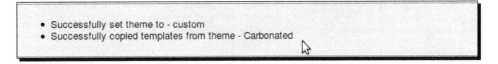

3. Now click on the **Start editing your blog templates** link to start editing your new theme:

4. Roller will take you to the **Templates** page. Here you can see a list of all the templates used in the *Carbonated* theme:

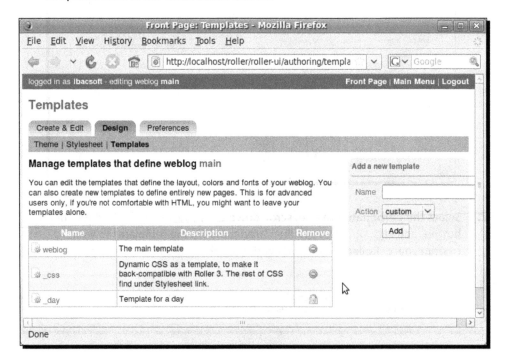

5. Select **File | New Tab** on your web browser to open a new tab, and type your weblog's URL to see the front page (http://localhost/roller):

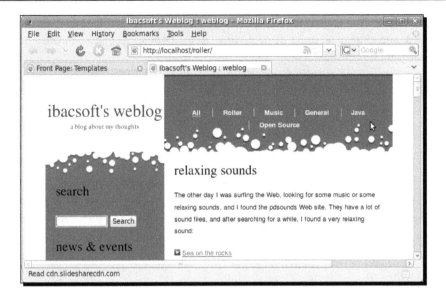

6. In the previous screenshot, we can see that there are two tabs: **Front Page:
   Templates** (Roller's admin interface) and **Ibacsoft's Weblog : weblog** (the front
   page of your weblog). In your case, the second tab will show the name you
   selected for your weblog. In the blue area of the front page's header, we can
   see all the categories for the weblog, but they can't fit into a single line.

7. Now return to the **Front Page: Templates** tab and click on the second template (**_css**)
   to edit the width of the blue area. Roller will show you the **_css** template contents:

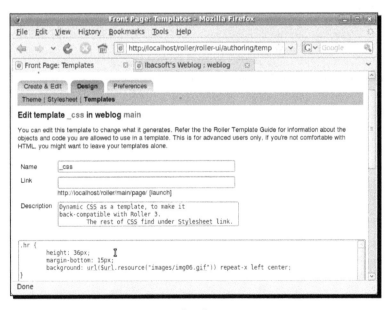

8. Scroll down the page until you locate the #menu { line. Scroll down two more lines, and change `width: 460px;` to `width: 560px;` as shown in the following screenshot:

```
                                        e., ;cytesne. / Tink.

        margin bottom  rspx;
        background: url($url.resource("images/img06.gif")) repeat-x left center;
}

#menu {
        float: right;
        width: 560px; I
        height: 147px;
        background: #0065CC url($url.resource("images/img01.gif")) no-repeat left bottom;
        border-top: 3px solid #000099;
}

/* Page */

#page {
        width: 700px;
        margin: 0 auto;
        background: url($url.resource("images/img03.gif")) repeat-y;
}

#sidebar {
Done
```

9. Now locate the #page{ line, scroll down two more lines and change `width: 700px;` to `width: 800px;` as shown in the following screenshot:

```
/* Page */

#page {
        width: 800px; I
        margin: 0 auto;
        background: url($url.resource("images/img03.gif")) repeat-y;
}

#sidebar {
Done
```

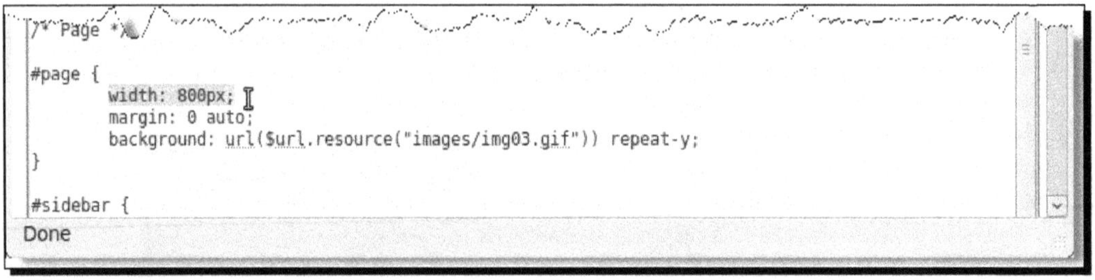

10. Keep scrolling down the page until you locate the **Save** button, and click on it to save your modifications:

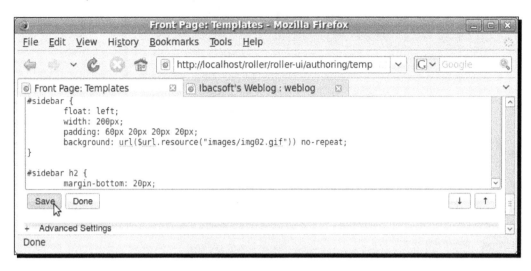

11. Roller will show you a success message inside the classic green box, indicating that your modifications were saved:

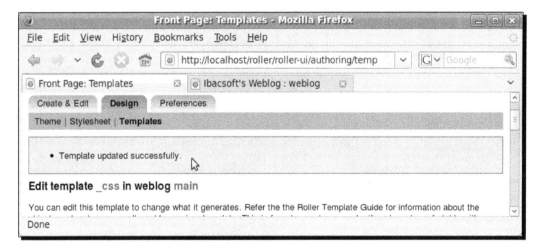

12. Now click on the **Stylesheet** link, between the **Theme** and **Templates** links:

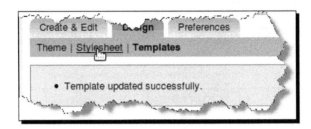

13. Roller will take you to the **Stylesheet** page. Scroll down until you locate the /* Header */ section, and change the width: 700px; line to width: 800px; as shown in the following screenshot:

```
/* Header */

#header {
        width: 800px;
        height: 150px;
        margin: 0 auto;
}
Done
```

14. Scroll down again until you locate the /* Content */ section, and change the width: 420px; line to width: 520px; as shown in the following screenshot:

```
/* Content */

#content {
        float: right;
        width: 520px;
        padding: 20px;
}
Done
```

15. Keep scrolling down until you locate the **Save** button, and click on it to save your modifications. Roller will show you the following success message:

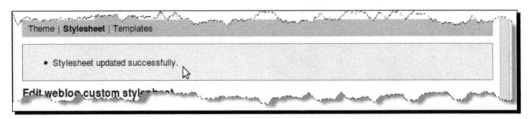

16. To see the changes in your theme, select the second tab of your web browser window (in my case, **Ibacsoft's Weblog : weblog**) and hit the **Reload** button:

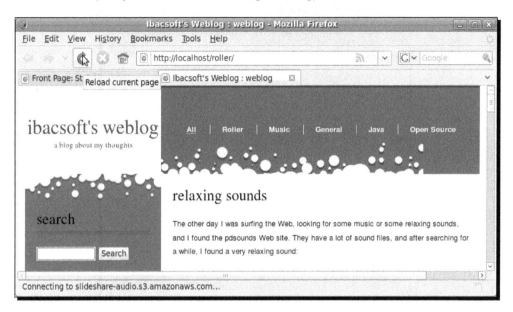

17. As you can see from the previous picture, all your weblog's categories now fit in one line (**All**, **Roller**, **Music**, **General**, **Java**, and **Open Source**), but the bubbles image below them doesn't fit the whole blue area. To solve this problem, select the first tab (**Front Page: Stylesheet**) on your web browser window to go to your weblog's admin interface, click on the **Create & Edit** tab, and select the **File Uploads** link. Roller will take you to the **File Uploads** page. Scroll down to the **Manage Uploaded Files** section and click on the **images** folder:

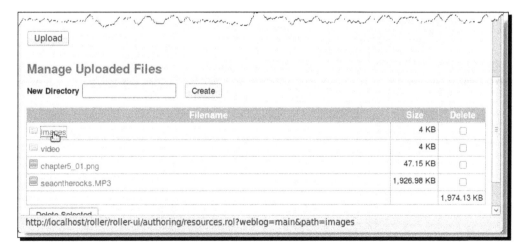

18. Click on the first **Browse...** button, go to the folder where you extracted the image01.jpg file, and select it. Now click on the **Upload** button to upload the file to your images directory, and replace the old image01.jpg file:

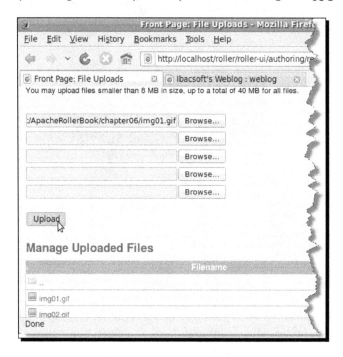

19. Roller will show a success message indicating that your file was uploaded successfully:

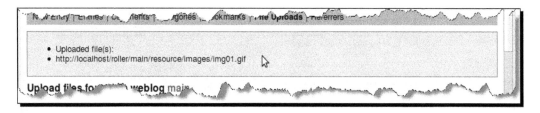

20. To see the change you made to the *Carbonated* theme, select the second tab of your web browser window (in my case, **Ibacsoft's Weblog : weblog**) and hit the **Reload** button:

21. The bubbles image must fit in the whole blue area now, as you can see in the previous screenshot. Leave your web browser open for the next exercise.

What just happened?

Congratulations! You've just edited your first Roller theme! In this case, we focused on changing the width of the area where your weblog categories show up, but you can tweak any other value thanks to CSS, or Cascading Style Sheets. The Carbonated theme has a template called _css that you edited in steps 7-10 of the previous exercise, and a default.css file that you can edit thanks to the **Stylesheet** link that we learnt how to use in step 12 of the previous exercise.

These two files contain the *stylesheet language* code that describes the visual appearance of the HTML documents used in the *Carbonated* theme. All of the other Roller themes contain similar CSS files to describe the colors, fonts, images, and every other visual element that's going to appear in your weblog. If you plan to carry on some intensive editing on your weblog theme to suit your needs, you need to learn more about CSS and HTML. I recommend that you search for tutorials or information on Google, or you could go to http://www.packtpub.com and buy a good book about CSS and HTML!

The themes you've been using up until now are *shared*. What does that mean? In your case, you've been using only one weblog as of this moment, but with Roller you can have more than one weblog, or you can invite some friends to make a community of weblogs in your Roller blog server. When Roller has several weblogs or users, if two or more weblogs use the same theme, they share the same files that make up that theme. For example, if you use the *Carbonated* theme on two weblogs, each one of them shares a copy of the theme's files that are located inside the `themes/carbonated` directory of your Roller installation.

And if you want to edit the *Carbonated* theme on one of your weblogs, you need to copy its files to your custom space, using the **Custom Theme** option as in step 1 of the previous exercise. In Chapter 7, we'll see much more about template editing and custom themes. In the next section, we'll see how to add some interesting stuff to your weblog, using the theme-editing features built inside Roller.

Adding a Twitter widget to your custom theme

In the next exercise, you'll learn to add a twitter box to your Roller theme. If you don't have a twitter account, go on and create one at `http://www.twitter.com`! You won't regret it!

Time for action – adding a Twitter box

With a twitter box, your visitors will see your latest tweets on your weblog side panel.

1. Open your web browser and go to the **Twitter Widgets** page at `http://www.twitter.com/widgets`. You'll need to log into your Twitter account, and then Twitter will take you to a web page where you can choose the type of website you plan to put the widget in. Select the **Other** option and click on the **Continue** button:

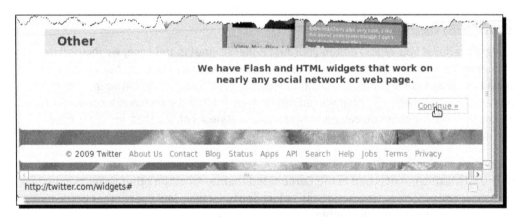

2. Now you have to choose the type of widget you want for your weblog. Select the **Flash Widget** option and click on **Continue**:

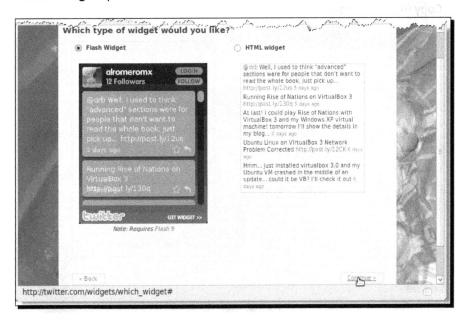

3. The next page will ask what type of Flash widget you want for your weblog. Select the **Interactive widget** option and click on **Continue**:

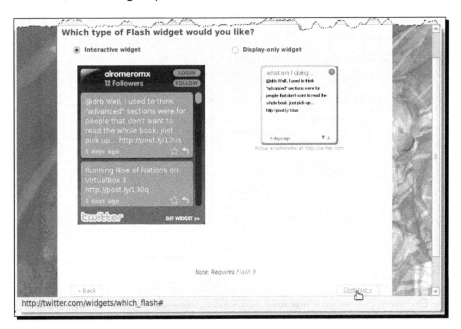

4. On the next page, Twitter will show you the HTML code for the widget you selected. Drag your mouse over all the HTML code to highlight it, right-click over it, and select **Copy** from the pop-up menu:

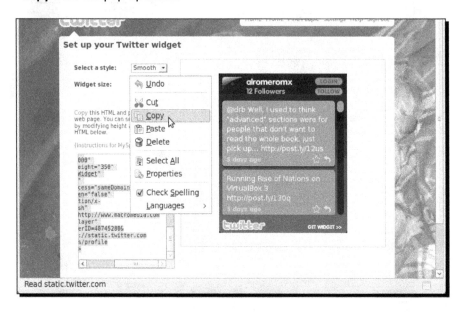

5. Open a new web browser window and log into Roller. Click on the **Design** tab and select the **Templates** link to see the template list for your custom theme. This time, click on the **weblog** template to open it:

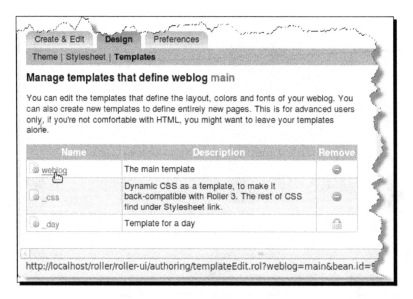

6. Scroll down the weblog template until you locate the `<ul>` line right after
`<div id="sidebar">`. Add the following two lines after the `<ul>` line,
as shown in the following screenshot:

```
<li>
</li>
```

7. Now paste the HTML code for your widget between the `<li>` and `</li>` lines
you've just added, and click on the **Save** button to save your changes:

8. Go to your weblog's front page, to see your Twitter widget in action:

9. Oops! The Twitter widget is too wide to fit in your weblog's sidebar! Click on your web browser's **Back** button to return to the weblog template, scroll down until you locate the Twitter widget HTML code you pasted before, change the two occurrences of width="290" height="350" to width="200" height="300", and click on the **Save** button, as shown in the following screenshot:

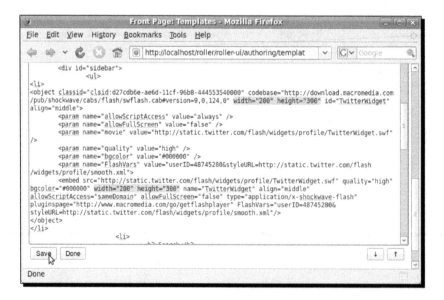

10. Go to your weblog's front page again, and this time the Twitter widget will have the appropriate width for your Roller theme:

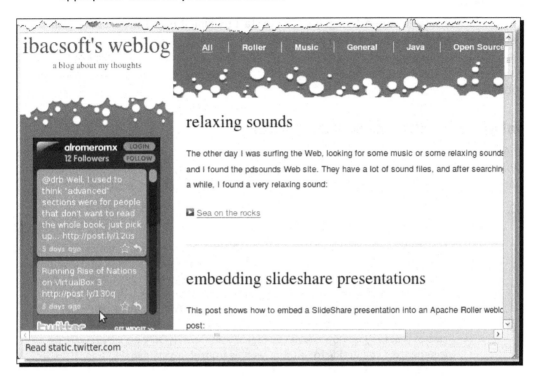

11. You can log out from Roller and close your web browser now.

What just happened?

See how easy it is to add new functionality to your weblog, thanks to the theme-editing features included in Roller? Now you can show your tweets on your very own weblog! With Roller, it's very easy to customize your own themes, adding your personal touch to your weblog. There are a lot of things you can tweak on your custom theme besides adding Twitter widgets, so keep on reading this chapter!

Have a go hero – explore Twitter widgets and custom themes

Now that you've inserted your first Twitter widget in your custom theme, it would be a great idea to experiment with the different options available; just go to the Twitter widgets web page and play with all the available options, paste the HTML code in your weblog template, and see the results! Or you could try using the Twitter Widget on another custom theme.

Promoting your blog on Technorati, Digg, StumbleUpon, and Delicious

OK, you have a state-of-the-art blog. It's time to start making it popular! And what could be better than adding a few buttons so your visitors can promote your weblog on Technorati, Digg, StumbleUpon, and Delicious? Well, in the next few exercises, you'll learn how to let visitors from the Internet see your weblog, and how to get it promoted on the most popular social bookmarking websites!

Get a free dynamic DNS service account

The first thing you need to do to make your weblog reachable to Internet surfers is get a free dynamic **DNS (Domain Name System)** service account. In short, this type of service lets you run a web server—in this case, your Roller weblog—from your own PC at home!

Dynamic versus static DNS service

In today's world, almost all home and small office PCs use a DSL broadband connection to the Internet. That means you get a dynamic IP address, and if you want to host a Roller weblog from your own PC, you'll need to get a free dynamic DNS service and open the port 80 in your firewall. If, on the other hand, you have the resources to get a hosting provider for your Roller weblog, you won't need to follow the next two exercises, because your hosting provider will take care of that for you. However, if you feel adventurous, it will be a very rewarding experience if you decide to run your weblog from your very own PC! And I'll always be an e-mail away for any help that you may need along the way!

Time for action – open a No-IP.com account

There are several Dynamic DNS providers available, and you can get a free account from almost any of them. In this exercise, I'll use the No-IP.com Dynamic DNS provider to show you how to run your Roller weblog from a PC connected to the Internet through a firewall:

1. Open your web browser and go to the No-IP.com free service web page at `http://www.no-ip.com/services/managed_dns/free_dynamic_dns.html`. Type your e-mail address (the same one that you're using for your Roller weblog) and click on the **Sign Up Now!** button:

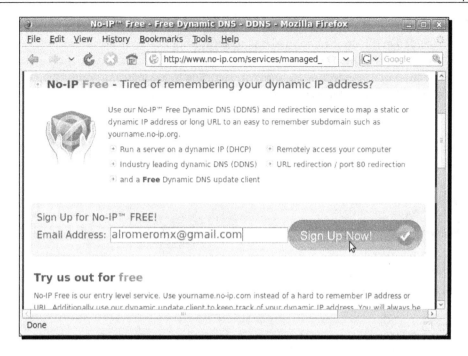

2. The **Create Your No-IP Account** page will show up next. Fill in all the required fields (password, first and last name, security question, and so on), read the **Terms of Service**, and click on the **I Accept, Create my Account** button to create your No-IP account:

3. No-IP will send you a confirmation e-mail. You need to click on the link included in this confirmation e-mail to verify your e-mail address and login to your NO-IP account. Once you've verified your account, go to the `http://www.no-ip.com/login/` link to log in, using your e-mail address and password. Once you log in, the **Your No-IP** page will show up. Click on the **Add a Host** button to add your Roller weblog:

4. In the **Add a host** page, fill in the **Hostname** field with the name you want to use for your weblog. Leave the default **DNS Host (A)** value in the **Host Type** field. The **IP Address** field will be filled in automatically with your IP address, as shown in the following screenshot:

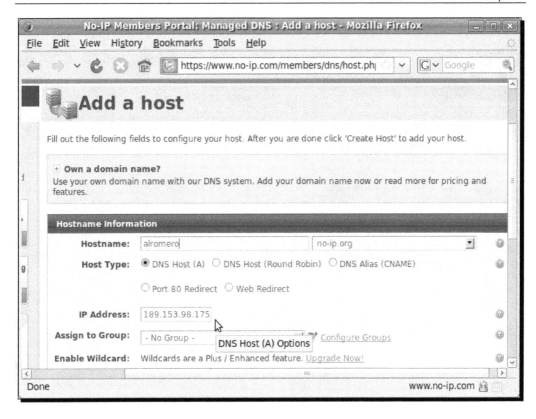

5. Scroll down the page until you locate the **Create Host** button, and click on it to create your Roller weblog host:

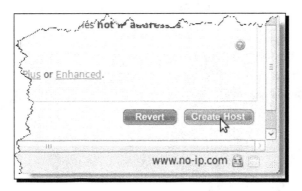

6. Once your host is successfully created, the following page will appear:

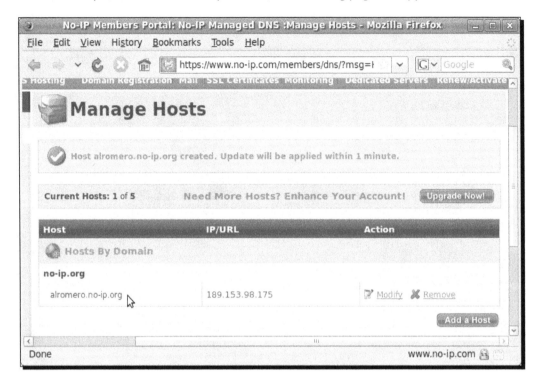

7. To test your new dynamic hostname, open a **Terminal** window in Linux or a **Command Prompt** window in Windows and type `ping hostname`, using the hostname you've just created, as in the following example:

```
Microsoft Windows XP [Version 5.1.2600]
(C) Copyright 1985-2001 Microsoft Corp.

C:\Documents and Settings\ibacsoft>ping alromero.no-ip.org

Pinging alromero.no-ip.org [189.153.98.175] with 32 bytes of data:

Reply from 189.153.98.175: bytes=32 time=5ms TTL=254
Reply from 189.153.98.175: bytes=32 time=2ms TTL=254
Reply from 189.153.98.175: bytes=32 time=3ms TTL=254
Reply from 189.153.98.175: bytes=32 time=4ms TTL=254

Ping statistics for 189.153.98.175:
    Packets: Sent = 4, Received = 4, Lost = 0 (0% loss),
Approximate round trip times in milli-seconds:
    Minimum = 2ms, Maximum = 5ms, Average = 3ms

C:\Documents and Settings\ibacsoft>_
```

8. The IP address you'll get in the previous window will be the dynamic IP address your ISP assigned to your PC. Now you can log out from your No-IP account.

What just happened?

In the previous exercise, you created a No-IP account, so that you can show your weblog to all the Internet audience out there! Now you can call your friends and brag about your Roller weblog! Well, you'll need to write a few more posts to make it really interesting, don't you think so?

The Dynamic DNS service lets you run a web server (in this case, your Roller weblog) from your home or any other place with a DSL, Cable, or Dial-up Internet connection where the ISP assigns a dynamic IP address. Instead of having to write an IP address such as 189.153.98.175, visitors to your site use a dynamic hostname such as alromero.no-ip.org, and if for any reason your ISP changes the IP address assigned to your PC, you just need to log into your No-IP account to update the IP address used for your weblog server.

Have a go hero – install the No-IP Dynamic Update Client

No-IP has a *Dynamic Update Client* you can use to update your IP address automatically, in case your ISP assigns you another one. You can download the No-IP Dynamic Update Client from http://www.no-ip.com/downloads.php, and follow the instructions to install it on your machine. Remember, if you have any trouble or doubts, just e-mail me and I'll do my best to help you!

Open up your web port (80) to the world

Now that you have your free dynamic hostname, it's time to open up port 80 (Web) on your Internet inbound connection, so visitors can see your weblog; and how can we do that? Well, it all depends on your Internet connection—if you're using a hardware router, or if your PC is connected directly to the DSL/Cable modem, and so on. In this chapter, I'll show you how to use port forwarding with a 1700HG 2Wire DSL modem/router, but the process is almost the same with any other Cable/DSL modem/router available nowadays.

Time for action – forwarding port 80

There are several ways to run your own web server from a Cable/DSL Internet connection, but the basic process is the same—opening up the web port on your firewall. In the next exercise, I'll show you how to open up the web port on a hardware firewall, used in the vast majority of homes and small offices with a Cable/DSL Internet connection (the most popular connections available at the time of this writing):

1. The first step is finding out your router's IP address. In Windows, open a **Command Prompt** dialog, type `ipconfig`, and look for the **Default Gateway** value:

```
Select Command Prompt                                                    _ □ ×
C:\Documents and Settings\ibacsoft>ipconfig

Windows IP Configuration

Ethernet adapter VMware Network Adapter VMnet8:

        Connection-specific DNS Suffix  . :
        IP Address. . . . . . . . . . . . : 192.168.195.1
        Subnet Mask . . . . . . . . . . . : 255.255.255.0
        Default Gateway . . . . . . . . . :

Ethernet adapter VMware Network Adapter VMnet1:

        Connection-specific DNS Suffix  . :
        IP Address. . . . . . . . . . . . : 192.168.128.1
        Subnet Mask . . . . . . . . . . . : 255.255.255.0
        Default Gateway . . . . . . . . . :

Ethernet adapter Local Area Connection:

        Connection-specific DNS Suffix  . :
        IP Address. . . . . . . . . . . . : 192.168.0.1
        Subnet Mask . . . . . . . . . . . : 255.255.255.0
        Default Gateway . . . . . . . . . :

Ethernet adapter VirtualBox Host-Only Network:

        Connection-specific DNS Suffix  . :
        IP Address. . . . . . . . . . . . : 192.168.56.1
        Subnet Mask . . . . . . . . . . . : 255.255.255.0
        Default Gateway . . . . . . . . . :

Ethernet adapter Wireless Network Connection:

        Connection-specific DNS Suffix  . : gateway.2wire.net
        IP Address. . . . . . . . . . . . : 192.168.1.3
        Subnet Mask . . . . . . . . . . . : 255.255.255.0
        Default Gateway . . . . . . . . . : 192.168.1.254

C:\Documents and Settings\ibacsoft>_
```

2. In this example, the Windows PC is connected to the router via a wireless card, so in the **Ethernet adapter Wireless Network Connection** section, you can find the **Default Gateway** value: `192.168.1.254`. If you're using Linux, remember to open a Terminal window and use the `route -n` command instead of `ipconfig`:

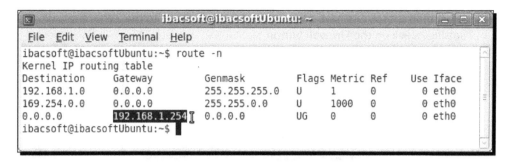

3. Once you've got the router's IP address, you can enter its web admin interface. Open your web browser and type your router's IP address to see its home page:

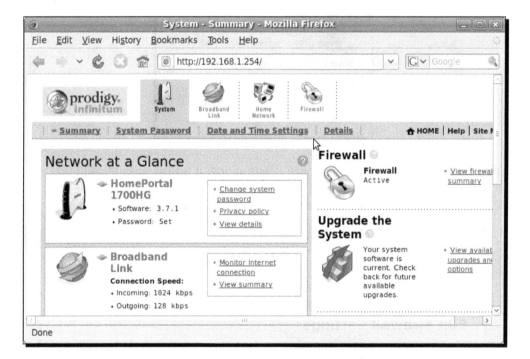

 You should find your router's IP address inside its documentation. Usually you need to type a username/password combination to log in. Check with your ISP or your router's documentation if you need more information.

4. Most modern routers have an integrated firewall. To go to the 2Wire firewall settings, click on the **Firewall** button:

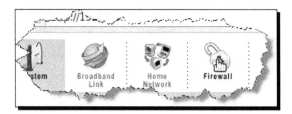

5. The **View Firewall Summary** page will appear. Click on the **Firewall Settings** link to continue:

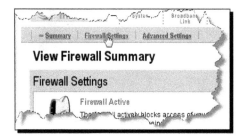

6. On the **Edit Firewall Settings** page, select your PC's hostname or IP address, depending on your router's configuration. In this example, the hostname of the PC that runs the Roller weblog server is **ibacsoftUbuntu**:

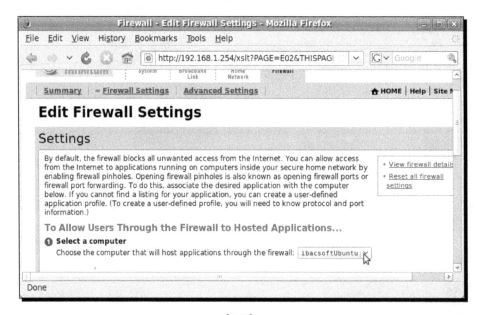

7. Now select the **Allow individual application(s)** option, scroll down the listbox until you find the **Web Server** application, and click on the **ADD** button to add it to the **Hosted Applications** list:

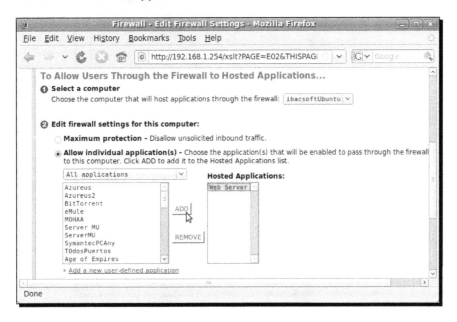

8. Scroll down the page until you locate the **DONE** button and click on it to save your changes:

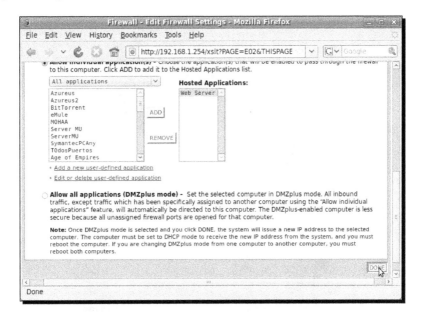

9. The **View Firewall Summary** page will show the **Web Server** application allowed for the **ibacsoftUbuntu** computer:

10. To test your dynamic DNS service, type the dynamic No-IP hostname you configured in the previous exercise (in my case, I used the `alromero.no-ip.org` dynamic hostname):

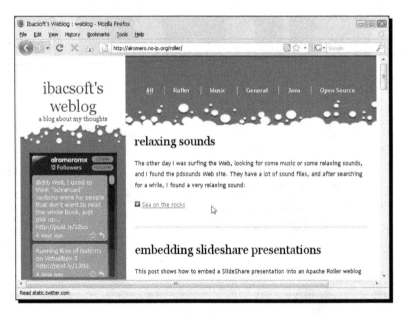

11. Now everybody will be able to access your Roller weblog from your LAN or from anywhere on the Internet!

What just happened?

How about that? Your Roller weblog is just about to enter the cyberspace! It wasn't all that complicated, right? And it doesn't matter if you own a router of another brand because the port forwarding process is basically the same for all routers. Just search on Google for your router's brand and model number, to get information about configuring your firewall to forward port 80 (the web port), and you'll be blogging to the world in no time! Or e-mail me and I'll help you with the port forwarding process!

Adding a Digg It button to your weblog

Now that your weblog can be seen by all the Internet users out there, it would be very convenient to include a *Digg It* button in your weblog posts, so that visitors can click on it. This will make your weblog stand out from the crowd!

Time for action – adding a Digg It button

The Digg It button lets your visitors submit—or "dig"—your blog's posts to `Digg.com`. This is an excellent way to promote your blog!

1. Open your web browser and go to the `http://digg.com/tools/integrate` web page. Scroll down until you locate the **"Digg This" with Submit Capability** section, select the HTML code with your mouse, right-click on it, and select **Copy** from the pop-up menu:

2. Open a new web browser window and log into your Roller weblog. The **New Entry** page will show up. Click on the **Design** tab and select the **Templates** link to see your custom theme's template list. Now click on the **weblog** template link to edit this template's contents and scroll down the page until you locate the `#showWeblogEntryComments($entry)` line:

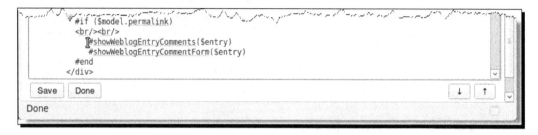

```
    #if ($model.permalink)
    <br/><br/>
      #showWeblogEntryComments($entry)
      #showWeblogEntryCommentForm($entry)
    #end
    </div>
```

Save   Done

Done

3. Position your mouse at the beginning of this line, right-click on it, and select **Paste** on the pop-up menu to paste the HTML code for the Digg It button:

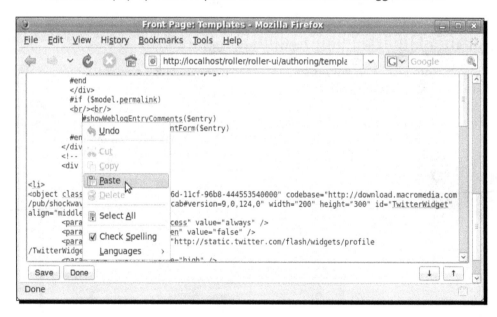

4. The HTML code will appear before the `#showWeblogEntryComments($entry)` line. You can add some indentation to the code to keep it neat, as shown in the following screenshot:

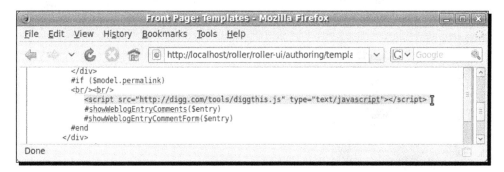

5. Scroll down the page, click on the **Save** button to save your modifications, and go to your weblog's front page (remember to use your new dynamic hostname):

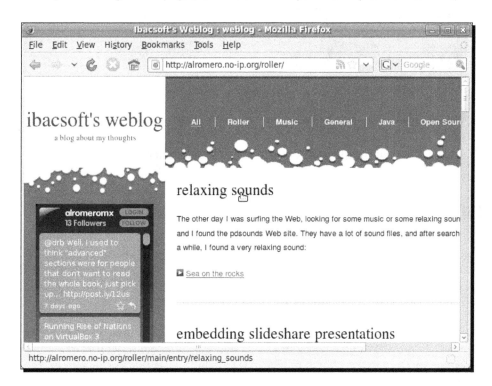

6. The Digg It button will show up when someone clicks on one of your posts. To test it, click on the first link (**relaxing sounds**) to see the individual post:

7. The Digg It button will show up right above the **Comments** section, just as we planned!

What just happened?

Now your visitors will have the opportunity to use the Digg It button and promote your weblog on Digg.com! This is one big step ahead for your weblog's success! With all the excellent tools available to promote your weblog, it's really easy to edit your Roller custom theme to include buttons and widgets from Digg.com and all the other popular social bookmarking sites, such as Technorati, Delicious, and StumbleUpon.

In the last exercise, I showed you how to put a Digg It button just above the **Comments** section, which only shows up when someone is seeing a complete post. That's because every post in your weblog must be able to provide a Digg It button so visitors can vote for their favorite posts individually. In Chapter 7, we'll see more about templates and the Velocity template language, so you can manipulate elements such as `#showWeblogEntryComments` `($entry)` in order to show what you want on your weblog.

Have a go hero – adding Technorati, StumbleUpon, and Delicious buttons

Digg.com is a great social bookmarking website, but if you want to attract all the attention you can for your weblog, you'll need to add Technorati, StumbleUpon, and Delicious buttons to let your visitors promote your weblog among all the popular social bookmarking sites in the world. Follow the same procedure as with the Digg It button: just paste the code from the other buttons below it. For example, I added the Technorati code to the weblog template as shown in the following screenshot:

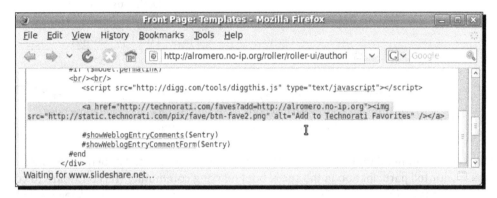

When you click on a link to see a post in my weblog, the **Technorati** button shows up next to the **Digg It** button:

Now it's time for you to add all these cool buttons to your weblog, and start writing good posts to attract visitors! The following table lists the URLs that you need to visit in order to get the code for these buttons:

URL	Description
http://technorati.com/account/favbuttons	"Fave this blog on Technorati" button
http://delicious.com/help/savebuttons	"Bookmark this on Delicious" button
http://www.stumbleupon.com/buttons.php	"Stumble It!" or "Thumb This Up!" button

 At the time of publication, the http://technorati.com/account/ favbuttons link wasn't working as Technorati recently made some huge changes to their site, but it should work again soon.

I definitely recommend that you create an account on all these social bookmarking sites because your full participation in the social bookmarking community will contribute to your weblog success in the long run. Trust me on this one! If you're consitent and keep your blog updated, you'll get good results with these social bookmarking services!

Pop quiz – editing themes and promoting your weblog

1. Your boss just loved your Roller weblog presentation, but wants to use the **Andreas08** theme instead of the **Carbonated** theme for the company blog. He also wants you to add the company's Twitter account to the weblog's front page. What do you need to do?

    a. Tell the boss it's better to use the **Carbonated** theme because you can copy the book's exercises directly to your company weblog!

    b. Select **Andreas08** as your new theme, and click on the **Custom Theme** option to copy the templates to your custom space, so you can edit them.

    c. Get a web designer and pay him/her for the custom modifications to the **Andreas08** theme.

2. Your new client wants to use a weblog to promote his business, but he doesn't want to spend too much at the beginning, because he still doesn't fully understand how a weblog can help him to get more customers. What could you do to help him?

    a. Use a cheaper, slower, and less customizable weblog server, based on the PHP language.

    b. Show him how to get a free dynamic DNS service to use a dynamic hostname for his Apache Roller weblog, and how to open up port 80 to run Apache Roller from a PC inside his own office.

    c. Tell him to go and get the Apache Roller book, so he can learn how to do all the dirty work himself.

3. If you want to change the background color of your weblog theme, you:

    a. Edit the weblog template.

    b. Change the Carbonated theme to the Basic theme.

    c. Use your dynamic DNS service to edit your dynamic host settings.

Summary

In this chapter, you learned how to change your Roller weblog theme, download additional themes, and promote your weblog on all the popular bookmarking services.

Specifically, we covered:

◆ How to choose a weblog theme from Roller's administration interface

◆ How to download additional themes and install them on your Roller weblog server

◆ How to create an account in No-IP.com, which is a dynamic DNS service provider used to run your Roller weblog from your own PC

◆ How to open the web port (80) via port forwarding on your DSL modem/router firewall

◆ How to add a Digg It button to your weblog, so visitors can vote for your posts on the Digg.com social bookmarking website

From now on, everything you do on your weblog can be seen by anyone connected to the Internet, so be careful and write good posts to attract all the visitors you can! Also be sure to check all the popular social bookmarking sites and search engines regularly, to see if your weblog is gaining popularity and to add more buttons for additional social bookmarking services.

In the next chapter, we'll cover some basic stuff about the Velocity template language and the Roller template system, with several exercises on creating themes and templates, so you can learn to create your very own themes from scratch, or use a predefined theme as a starting point to create an enhanced version. Who knows, maybe someday you'll become a Roller theme designer and contribute your themes to the Apache Roller community!

7

Working with Templates

*In the previous chapter, you learned to use Roller themes and made some tiny modifications to the **weblog** template, and added a Digg It button and a Twitter widget to your weblog. In this chapter, you'll see all the basics about the Velocity Template Language, and how you can use it in your Apache Roller templates to enhance your theme, or even build one from scratch!*

Basically, in this chapter you shall:

- Learn how to create and edit your first template
- Learn about the Velocity Template Language and how you can use it in your Roller templates
- Work with Roller's model and data objects to access your weblog's data from custom templates
- Create a Roller theme from scratch!

If you liked the exercises in Chapter 6, this chapter's exercises will take you to the next level regarding Roller themes and templates!

Your first template

We already talked about Roller themes and templates in Chapter 6. In essence, a *theme* is a set of templates, and a *template* is composed of HTML and Velocity code. You can make your own templates to access your weblog's data and show this to your visitors in any way you want.

Creating and editing templates

In Apache Roller, you can create, edit, or delete templates via the **Frontpage: Templates** page. Let's see how to use this wonderful tool to create and edit your own templates!

Time for action – creating your first template

In this exercise, you'll learn to create and edit your first custom template via Roller's admin interface:

1. Open your web browser, log into Roller, and go to the **Templates** page, under the **Design** tab:

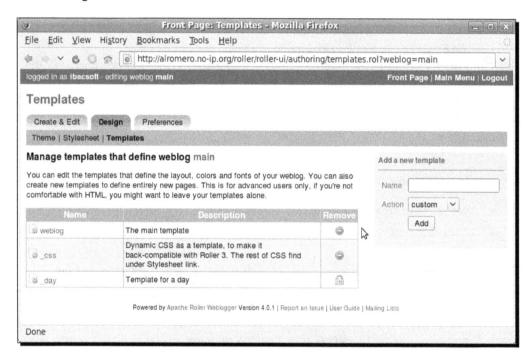

2. On the **Add a new template** panel, type **mytemplate** in the **Name** field, leave the default **custom** value in the **Action** field, and click on the **Add** button:

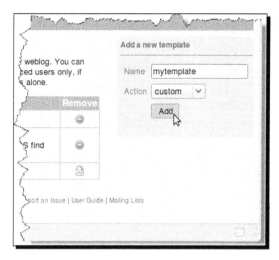

3. The **mytemplate** template you've just created will show up in the templates list:

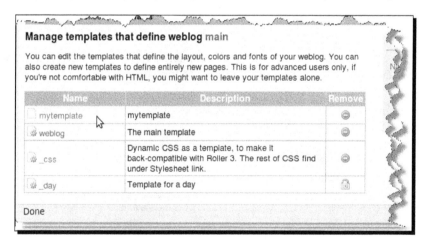

4. Now click on the **mytemplate** link under the **Name** field, to open the **mytemplate** file for editing:

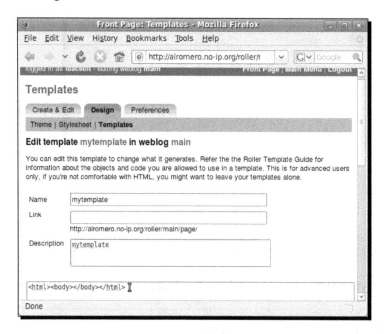

5. Leave the **mytemplate** value for the **Name** field, type **mytemplate** in the **Link** field, and type **My First Template in Apache Roller!** in the **Description** field:

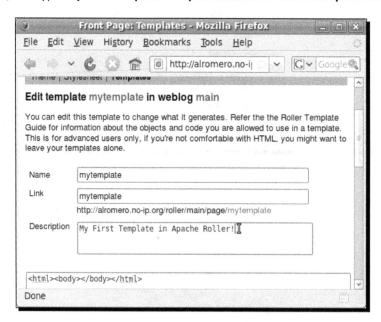

6. Then replace the `<html><body></body></html>` line with the following HTML code:

```html
<html>
  <body>
    Welcome to my blog, <b>$model.weblog.name</b> </br>
    This is my first template </br>
    My weblog's absolute URL is: <b>$url.absoluteSite</b> </br>
  </body>
</html>
```

This is shown in the following screenshot:

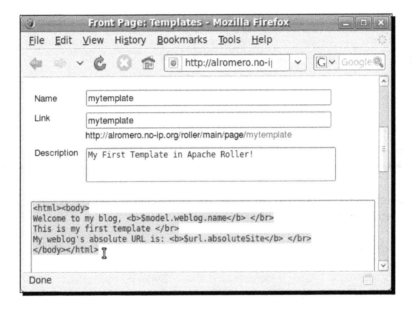

7. Scroll down the page and click on the **Save** button to apply the changes to your new template. Roller will show the **Template updated successfully** message inside a green box to confirm that your changes were saved:

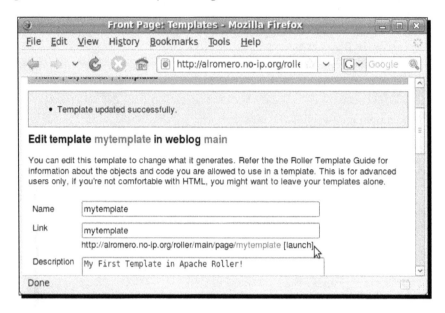

8. Now click on the **[launch]** link under the **Link** field to open a new tab in your web browser and see your template in action:

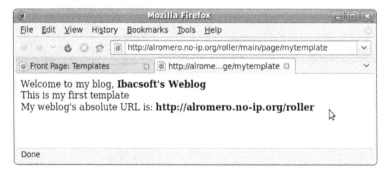

9. You can close this tab now, but leave the **Frontpage: Templates** window open for the next exercise.

What just happened?

Now you know how to create your own templates! Although the previous example is very simple, you can use it as a starting point to create very complex templates, such as the ones inside the *Carbonated* theme that we used in Chapter 6. As I said before, templates are composed of HTML and Velocity code.

The template we wrote in the previous exercise uses a few basic HTML elements, or tags:

HTML tag	Definition	Tip
`<html>`, `</html>`	Defines the start/end of an HTML document.	You must write these tags at the beginning/end of each Roller template.
`<body>`, `</body>`	Defines the start/end of an HTML document's body.	All the code that you write for your templates must go between the `<body>` and `</body>` tags.
`<b>`, `</b>`	Shows text in bold.	Example: `<b>Hello</b>` shows up as **Hello**
`</br>`	Indicates a line break.	Example: `Hello</br>World` shows up as `Hello` `World`

Also, there are some elements from the Velocity Template Language, along with an example from the previous exercise:

Velocity element	Definition	Example
`$model.weblog.name`	Shows the name of your weblog.	`<b>$model.weblog.name</b>` shows up as **Ibacsoft's Weblog**.
`$url.absoluteSite`	Shows the absolute URL of your weblog.	`<b>$url.absoluteSite</b>` shows up as `http://alromero.no-ip.org/roller`.

These are just some of the basic HTML tags and Velocity elements you'll learn to use for your templates. In the following sections, we'll see some more, along with elements from the Velocity Template Language.

The Velocity template language

All templates in Roller use HTML tags, along with Velocity code. In the next subsections, you'll learn about some of the most widely used Velocity elements in your Roller templates.

Using Velocity macros in your Roller weblog

A **macro** in Velocity is a set of instructions that generate HTML code based on data from your weblog. They are very helpful when you need to do the same task more than once. In the following exercise, you'll learn to use some macros included in Roller in order to show your weblog data to your visitors.

Time for action – showing your weblog's blogroll and most recent entries

Now you will use the Velocity Template Language to show your weblog's bookmarks (blogroll) in your custom template, along with the most recent entries:

1. Go to your custom template editing page, and type the following code just above the `</body></html>` line:

```
</br>
These are my favorite Web sites: </br>
#set($rootFolder = $model.weblog.getBookmarkFolder("/"))
#showBookmarkLinksList($rootFolder false false)
```

2. The entire code of your template should look like the following screenshot (the code you have to add is highlighted):

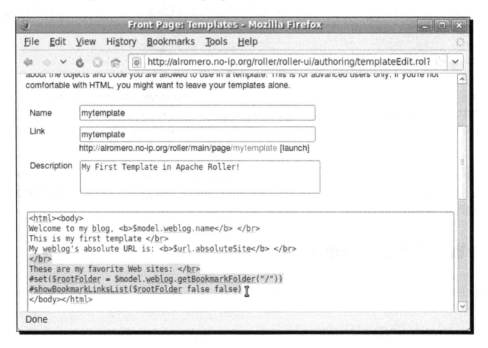

3. Save your changes and click on your template's **[launch]** link to open a new tab in your web browser and see how your template will look like:

4. Now close the results tab to return to the **Front Page: Templates** window, and add the following lines of code right after the code you added in steps 1 and 2 of this exercise:

```
</br>
And these are the most recent entries in my weblog: </br>
#set($entries = $model.weblog.getRecentWeblogEntries("nil", 5))
#showWeblogEntryLinksList($entries)
```

5. Now your template's code should look like the following screenshot:

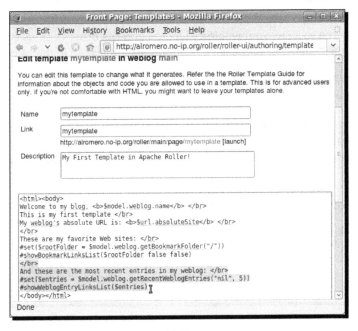

6. Save your changes and click on your template's **[launch]** link to open a new tab in your web browser and see the results:

7. You can close this tab now, but leave the **Frontpage: Templates** window open for the next exercise.

What just happened?

In Velocity, a *macro* starts with the # character. In the previous exercise, you used two Velocity macros: one to show your weblog's blogroll and the other to show your weblog's most recent entries. There are two Velocity statements implicated in the blogroll macro:

```
#set($rootFolder = $model.weblog.getBookmarkFolder("/"))
#showBookmarkLinksList($rootFolder false false)
```

The first line gets the root bookmark folder (represented by "/") and assigns it to the $rootFolder variable. The second line is the showBookmarkLinksList macro, which uses the value in $rootFolder to generate a bookmarks list and show it in your template:

The two false arguments after `$rootFolder` indicate that we are not using subcategories inside the bookmark links list. If you want more information about these arguments, check the Roller template guide included in the Roller installation.

There are two more lines involved in the recent entries macro:

```
#set($entries = $model.weblog.getRecentWeblogEntries("nil", 5)
#showWeblogEntryLinksList($entries)
```

The first line gets the 5 most recent entries from your weblog and assigns the result to `$entries`. The "nil" parameter specifies that Roller must get the five most recent entries from all categories. If you want to get the most recent entries from a specific category, just replace "nil" with the name of that category.

The next line is the `showWeblogEntryLinksList` macro, which uses all the entries included in `$entries` to generate a list with links:

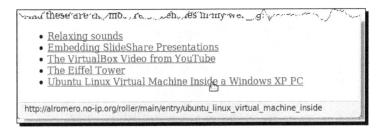

In the next subsection, we'll see some of the Velocity elements used in Roller to display data from your weblog.

Velocity model and data objects in Apache Roller

There are several standard model and data objects you can use in Apache Roller to access your weblog's data. Some of the most widely used are `$config`, `$model`, `$url`, `$utils`, `$weblog`, `$weblogCategory`, and `$weblogPage`. We already saw the `$model` object in action in previous exercises, when we used `$model.weblog.name` to show the name of our weblog. We also used the `$url` object to show our weblog's absolute URL with `$url.absoluteSite`. In the following exercise, you'll get to work with the `$config` object.

The $config object

This model is used to access Roller's site-wide configuration parameters, such as the e-mail address of Roller's administrator, the name of the Roller site, and so on.

Time for action – properties of the $config model object

The following exercise will show you how to use some properties of the $config model object inside your custom template:

1. Go to your custom template editing page, and replace the six lines of code below the `<body><html>` line with the following lines:

```
Welcome to my blog, <b>$model.weblog.name</b> --> <i>$config.
siteDescription</i> </br>
I'm using Apache Roller Version <b>$config.rollerVersion</b> </br>
You can e-mail me at <b>$config.siteEmail</b> if you run into any
problems in this site. </br>
This is my first template </br>
My weblog's absolute URL is: <b>$url.absoluteSite</b> </br>
</br>
```

2. The entire code of your template should look like the following screenshot (the code you have to change is highlighted):

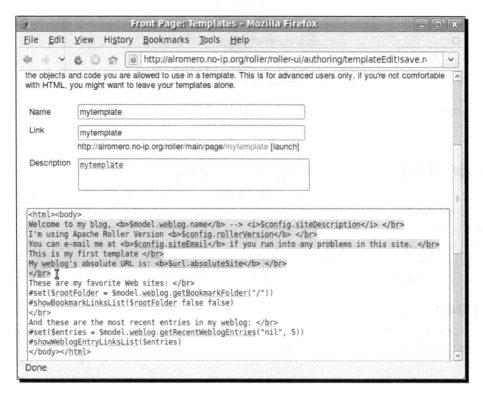

3. Save your changes and click on your template's **[launch]** link to open a new tab in your web browser and see the results:

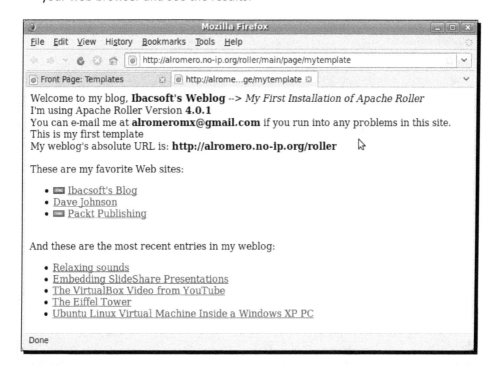

4. Close the results tab if you like, but leave the **Frontpage: Templates** window open for the next exercise.

What just happened?

The following table summarizes the $config object properties you learned to use in the previous exercise, along with their value:

Property	Definition	Value
$config. siteDescription	Shows your site's description.	My First Installation of Apache Roller
$config.rollerVersion	Shows the Apache Roller version used.	4.0.1
$config.siteEmail	Shows the site administrator's e-mail.	alromeromx@gmail.com

You can find all $config parameters under Roller's **Server Admin** tab:

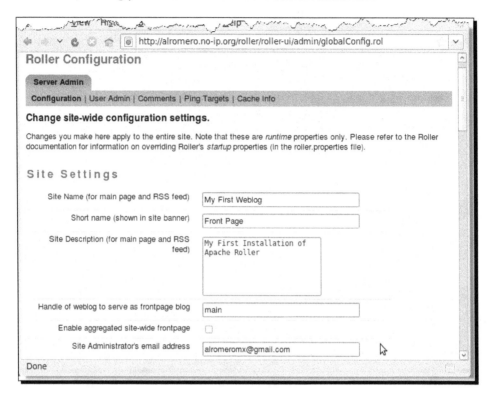

The $model, $category, and $entry objects

These objects are used to access all the data for a specific weblog: weblog entries, categories, comments, among others.

Time for action – properties and methods of the $model model object

The following exercise will show you how to use some properties and methods of the $model object inside your custom template, along with some other data objects such as $weblog, $category, and $entry:

1. Go to your custom template editing page, and replace the last three lines of code above the </body></html> line with the following lines:

    ```
    And these are the 5 most recent entries from each category in my
    weblog: </br>
    <table border="1">
    ```

```
<tr><td><b>Category</b></td><td><b>Entries</b></td></tr>
#foreach ($category in $model.weblog.getWeblogCategory("nil").
weblogCategories)
<tr><td><i>$category.name</i></td>
<td>
#foreach($entry in $model.weblog.getRecentWeblogEntries("$category
.name", 5))
<a href="$entry.permalink">$entry.title</a><br>
#end
</td></tr>
#end
</table>
```

2. The entire code of your template should look like the following screenshot
(the code you have to change is highlighted):

3. Save your changes and click on your template's **[launch]** link to open a new tab in your web browser and see the results:

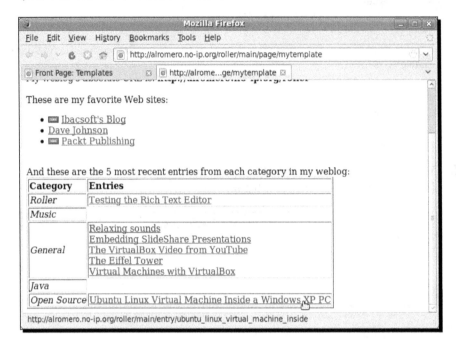

4. Now close the results tab, select all the HTML code from your custom template, and save it in a text file for later use. You can log out from Roller and close your web browser for now.

What just happened?

The following table summarizes the $model, $weblog, $category, and $entry objects' properties that you learned to use in the previous exercise, along with their definition:

Property	Definition
`$model.weblog.getWeblogCategory("nil").weblogCategories`	Gets a list of all the categories within your weblog.
`$category.name`	Displays the name of a category.
`$model.weblog.getRecentWeblogEntries("$category.name", 5))`	Gets the 5 most recent entries from the category defined by `$category.name`.
`$entry.permalink`	Displays the permalink of an entry.
`$entry.title`	Displays the title of an entry.

In this exercise there are also some Velocity instructions involved:

```
#foreach ($category in $model.weblog.getWeblogCategory("nil").
weblogCategories)
<tr><td><i>$category.name</i></td>
<td>
#foreach($entry in $model.weblog.getRecentWeblogEntries("$category.
name", 5))
<a href="$entry.permalink">$entry.title</a><br>
#end
</td></tr>
#end
</table>
```

There are two `foreach` loops, one nested inside the other, to get all of the entries for each one of your weblog's categories. The first `foreach` loop iterates through each category obtained through the `getWeblogCategory` method, and prints the name of each category via the `$category.name` property. The second `foreach` loop iterates through each entry obtained through the `getRecentWeblogEntries` method, and prints the title of each entry via the `$entry.title` property, along with its permalink via the `$entry.permalink` property. The `<a href>` HTML tag converts the entry's permalink into a hyperlink, as shown in step 3's screenshot.

A `foreach` loop is a programming language construct for traversing items or elements in a collection of some kind; in this case, each category of your Roller blog is an item, and all the categories as a whole represent the collection.

The $url and $utils objects

These objects have several properties and methods you can use in your templates to display URLs and format data elements, such as the date and time of publication of an entry in your weblog.

Time for action – properties and methods of the $url and $utils objects

The following exercise will show you how to use some properties and methods of the $url, $utils, $category, and $entry objects inside your custom template:

1. Go to your custom template editing page, and replace the
`<tr><td><i>$category.name</i></td>` line with the following line:

   ```
   <tr><td><i><a href="$url.category($category.path)">$category.
   name</a></i></td>
   ```

2. The following screenshot shows how your code will look like after the change:

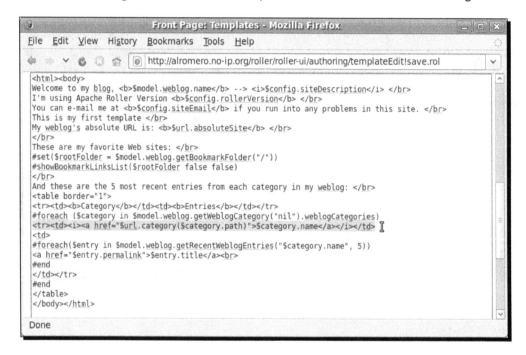

```
Front Page: Templates - Mozilla Firefox

File   Edit   View   History   Bookmarks   Tools   Help

        http://alromero.no-ip.org/roller/roller-ui/authoring/templateEdit!save.rol

<html><body>
Welcome to my blog, <b>$model.weblog.name</b> --> <i>$config.siteDescription</i> </br>
I'm using Apache Roller Version <b>$config.rollerVersion</b> </br>
You can e-mail me at <b>$config.siteEmail</b> if you run into any problems in this site. </br>
This is my first template </br>
My weblog's absolute URL is: <b>$url.absoluteSite</b> </br>
</br>
These are my favorite Web sites: </br>
#set($rootFolder = $model.weblog.getBookmarkFolder("/"))
#showBookmarkLinksList($rootFolder false false)
</br>
And these are the 5 most recent entries from each category in my weblog: </br>
<table border="1">
<tr><td><b>Category</b></td><td><b>Entries</b></td></tr>
#foreach ($category in $model.weblog.getWeblogCategory("nil").weblogCategories)
<tr><td><i><a href="$url.category($category.path)">$category.name</a></i></td>
<td>
#foreach($entry in $model.weblog.getRecentWeblogEntries("$category.name", 5))
<a href="$entry.permalink">$entry.title</a><br>
#end
</td></tr>
#end
</table>
</body></html>

Done
```

3. Save your changes and click on your template's **[launch]** link to open a new tab in your web browser and see the results:

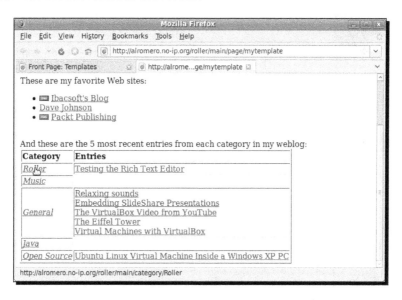

4. If you click on any of the categories, Roller will show you all the posts within the category you chose. For example, if you click on the **General** category, you'll get the following results:

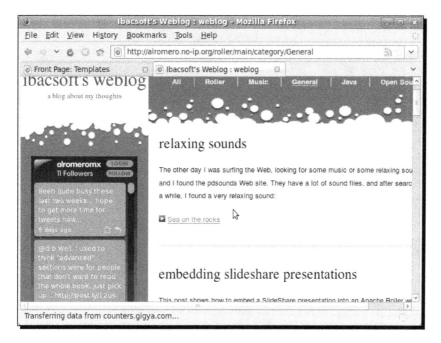

5. Now go back to your custom template's editing page and replace `<a href="$entry.permalink">$entry.title</a><br>` with the following line:

```
<a href="$entry.permalink">$entry.title</a> -> <a href="$url.
editEntry($entry.anchor)"> Edit Entry</a><br>
```

6. The following screenshot shows how your custom template's code will look after changing the previous line:

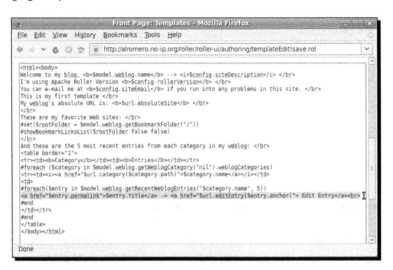

7. Save your changes and click on the **[launch]** link to see how your custom template will look after the changes:

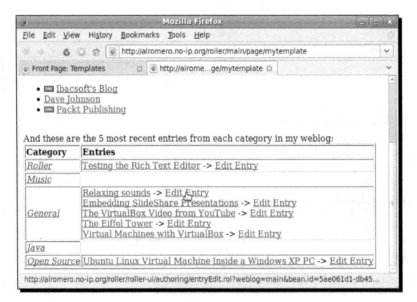

8. Click on any of the **Edit Entry** links and Roller will take you to the editing page for that corresponding entry. The following screenshot shows the edit page for the **Relaxing sounds** entry:

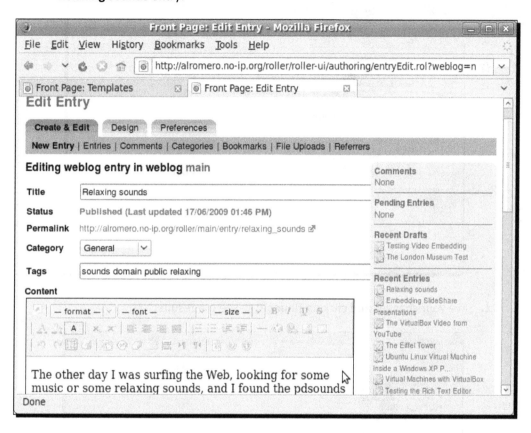

9. Close the **Front Page: Edit Entry** tab and return to your custom template's editing page. Now replace the `<a href="$entry.permalink">$entry. title</a> -> <a href="$url.editEntry($entry.anchor)"> Edit Entry</a><br>` line with the following code:

```
<a href="$entry.permalink">$entry.title</a> -> <a href="$url.
editEntry($entry.anchor)"> Edit Entry</a> --> $entry.pubTime<br>
```

10. The following screenshot shows how your custom template's code will look after changing the previous line:

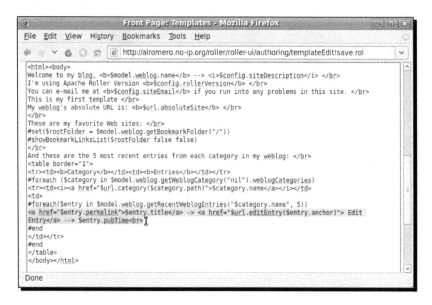

11. Save your changes and click on **[launch]** to see the results:

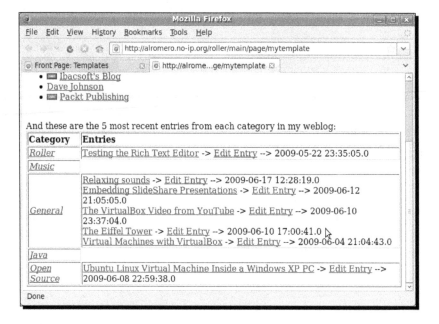

12. As you can see, this last modification to your custom template code shows the creation date and time of each entry. In order to change the date and time format, replace the `<a href="$entry.permalink">$entry.title</a> -> <a href="$url.editEntry($entry.anchor)"> Edit Entry</a> --> $entry.pubTime<br>` line with the following line:

```
<a href="$entry.permalink">$entry.title</a> -> <a href="$url.
editEntry($entry.anchor)"> Edit Entry</a> --> $utils.
formatDate($entry.pubTime, "EEE, d MMM yyyy HH:mm:ss Z")<br>
```

13. Your custom template code should look like this:

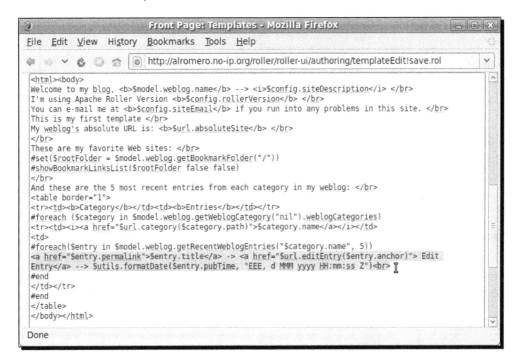

14. Save your changes and click on the **[launch]** link to see the results:

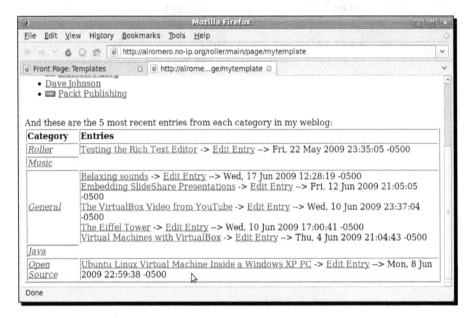

15. You can log out from Roller and close your web browser.

What just happened?

OK, now you've seen some of the things you can do with templates. The following table summarizes all the properties and methods from the `$url` and `$utils` objects you learned to use in the previous exercise:

Property	Definition	Tip
`$category.path`	Contains the absolute path of a category.	Use it with the `$url.category` property to display the URL for a specific category.
`$url.category`	Displays the URL of a specific category from your weblog.	Use it with the `$category.path` property to display the URL for a specific category.
`$entry.anchor`	Contains the anchor that uniquely identifies each entry in your weblog.	Use it with the `$url.editEntry` property to create a URL for editing an entry.

Property	Definition	Tip
`$url.editEntry`	Takes you to the edit page of a specific entry.	Use it with the `$entry.anchor` property to create a URL for editing an entry.
`$entry.pubTime`	Displays the publication timestamp of an entry.	Use it to show the exact date and time of publication of an entry in your weblog.
`$utils.formatDate`	Formats a date object according to the format specified.	Use it with the `$entry.pubTime` property and a date format string in order to change the way of showing the publication date and time of an entry.

These are some of the most used properties and methods from the model and data objects used in Roller to show your weblog's data. In the next section, you'll learn to build a theme from the ground up, using several templates and the properties and methods you saw in the previous exercises, along with some new properties and methods commonly used in Roller themes.

Creating a Roller theme from scratch

Now things are going to get a little rough; just kidding! In Apache Roller, it's very easy to create your own themes, and in this section I'm going to show you how.

> For the following exercises, you'll need to download Chapter 7's support code from the book's website. Extract the `chapter07.zip` file's contents into a directory in your hard disk. For example, I used Ubuntu Linux in the exercises, created a `chapter07` directory inside my `Desktop` directory, and copied the `mytheme` directory inside `Desktop/chapter07`. All the steps in the exercises are based on these assumptions.

Creating a directory for your theme

Every Roller theme has a directory and some required files such as `weblog.vm`, `_day.vm`, and `theme.xml`. The next exercise will show you how to create a directory for your new theme inside Roller's `themes` directory, and how to copy these required files from the support files.

Time for action – creating a directory for your theme

Now, I'll show you all the necessary steps to create your new theme directory inside Roller's `themes` directory in a Linux Ubuntu system, and then copy all the required files. If you're using Windows or any other flavor of Linux, the procedure is very similar:

1. Go to your Roller **themes** directory and create a directory named **mytheme**:

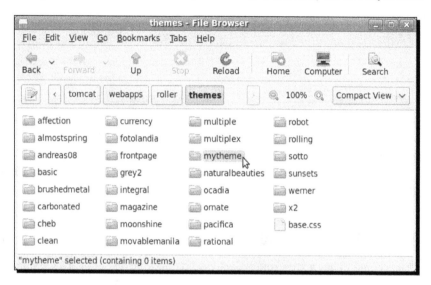

2. Open a terminal window, go to the `themes` subdirectory inside `Desktop/chapter07`, **and type** `sudo cp * /usr/local/tomcat/webapps/roller/themes/mytheme` **to copy all the** `mytheme` files to your Roller installation:

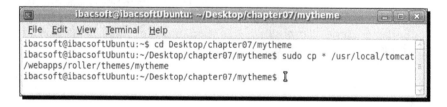

3. In the end, your **mytheme** directory will have four files, as shown in the following screenshot:

4. Now restart Tomcat and wait until it's running again. Then open your web browser, log into Roller, and go to the **Design** tab to see the **Weblog Theme** page:

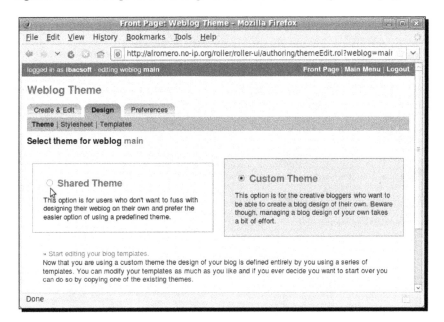

5. Click on the **Shared Theme** option and select **My First Roller Theme** from the drop-down listbox:

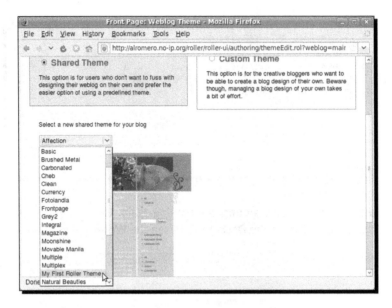

6. Click on the **Update Theme** button to change your current Roller theme, and then click on the **See how your blog will look with this theme** link:

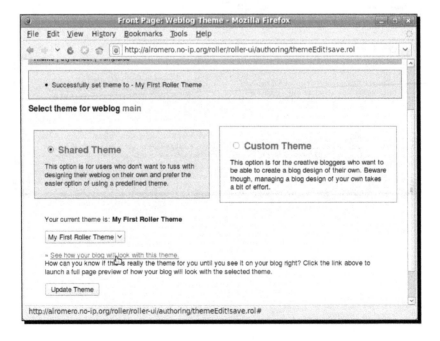

7. Roller will open a new web browser tab to show you a preview of the new theme you selected:

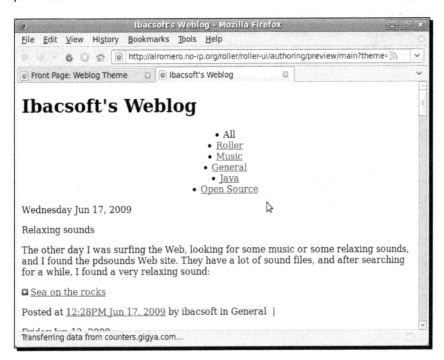

8. Close the preview tab and leave the **Front Page: Weblog Theme** page open for the next exercise.

What just happened?

As you can see from the previous exercise, the `mytheme` theme has a very basic functionality. That's because the CSS stylesheet (`mystylesheet.css`) is empty, so I'm going to show you how to add styles to your headings, links, and all the other elements displayed in your weblog. However, first we need to see a quick introduction to the four files that every Roller theme must have in order to run without any trouble:

File	Definition	Tip
`weblog.vm`	Describes the main page of your weblog.	In this file, you set the structure for your weblog, using macros and elements from Roller and the Velocity template language.
`_day.vm`	Describes how to display one day's worth of entries in your weblog.	Here you can configure how to display each entry's title, content, and comments, for example. You can set the font's color and size of each element, based on the CSS stylesheet definitions.
`mystylesheet.css`	Stylesheet override file that defines the CSS style code used by your weblog.	Here you define all your weblog's styles, such as size and color for headings and fonts used in your posts.
`theme.xml`	Theme definition file that describes each file used in your weblog.	You need to include some basic data about your theme, the stylesheet file, the `weblog` and `_day` templates, and every other file and/or resource used in your weblog.

In the next exercises, you'll learn how to edit these files to change your weblog's visual appearance and suit your needs.

The stylesheet override file

The first thing we need to do in order to change your new theme's visual appearance is edit the stylesheet override file: `mystylesheet.css`. We can do this in two ways: Edit the file directly from the `mytheme` directory inside Roller's `themes` directory, or use Roller's *Custom Theme* feature. If we use the first option, we'll need to restart Tomcat every time we make a modification to `mystylesheet.css`. On the other hand, if we choose the second option, we can edit the stylesheet inside Roller's admin interface and see how our changes affect our weblog's visual appearance immediately, so I'm going to show you how to use the second option.

Time for action – editing the stylesheet override file

It's very easy to edit the stylesheet override file for your custom theme inside Roller, and the next exercise will show you how to do it:

1. Go to the **Front Page: Weblog Theme** tab in your web browser, select the **Custom Theme** option, click on the **I want to copy the templates from an existing theme into my weblog** checkbox, and click on the **Update Theme** button:

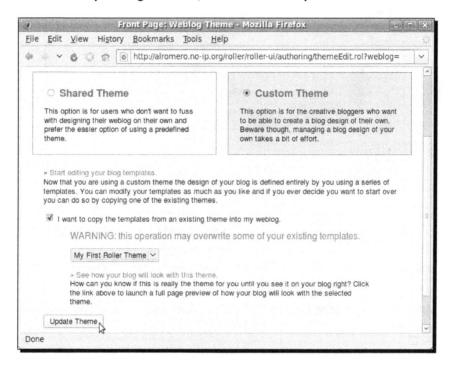

2. Roller will show you the following success message:

3. Now click on the **Templates** link to see a list of the templates you currently have in your custom space:

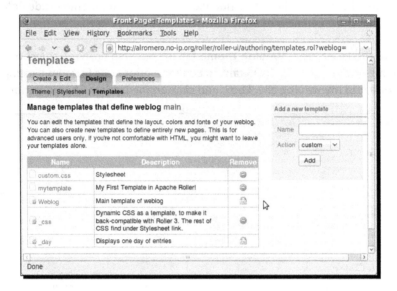

4. Looking at the template list in the previous screenshot, there are some templates from the other custom theme we used in Chapter 6 and we need to remove them now. Click on the **Remove** link of the `custom.css`, `mytemplate`, and `_css` templates to delete them from your custom space, as we won't need them anymore, and they don't belong to `mytheme`.

5. After removing all the unneeded files, there should be only two templates in your list:

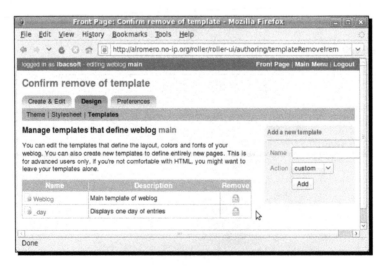

6. Now click on the **Stylesheet** link to see and start editing your `mystylesheet.css` file's code:

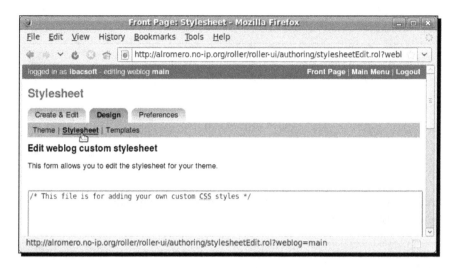

7. As you can see, your custom stylesheet is empty. If you click on the **Front Page** link in Roller's menu bar, you'll see your weblog's current front page:

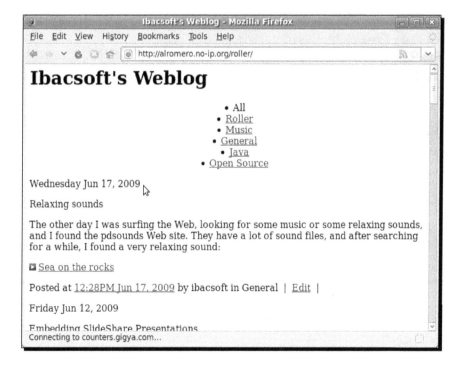

8. Now click on your web browser's **Back** button to return to the stylesheet editing page, and add the following code to your custom stylesheet:

```
div.dayTitle {
    color:brown;
    font-weight:bold;
    font-size:90%;
    text-transform:uppercase;
    border-bottom:1px dotted #666;
}

.entryTitle {
    font-weight: bold;
}
```

9. Your stylesheet should now contain the line beginning with `/*`, along with the code you've just entered:

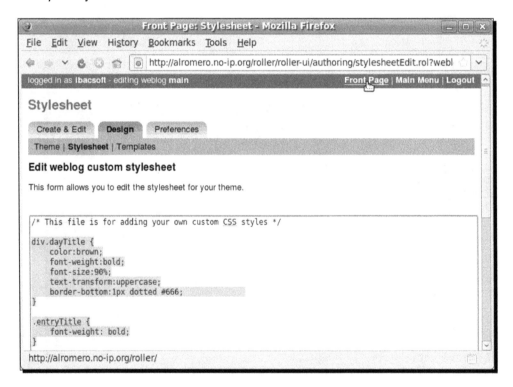

10. Click on the **Save** button to apply the changes to your stylesheet, and then select the **Front Page** link to see how the code you entered affects your weblog's visual appearance:

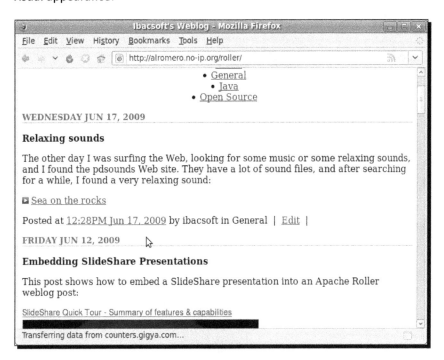

11. If you compare the previous screenshot with the one from step 7, you'll see that the code you entered into the override stylesheet changed the way your weblog displays the *day* and *entry* titles. Now click on the **Back** button of your web browser to return to the stylesheet editing page, and add the following lines of code above the lines you entered in step 8:

```
a {
  text-decoration: none;
}

a:link {
  color: blue;
  font-weight: medium;
}

a:visited {
  color: purple;
  font-weight: medium;
}
```

```
a:hover {
  text-decoration: underline overline;
}

body {
    font-family:"Lucida Grande", lucida, Geneva, Arial,
    sans-serif;
    background:#FFFFCC;
}
```

12. Your stylesheet should now look like this:

13. Click on the **Save** button and then select the **Front Page** link to see your weblog's front page:

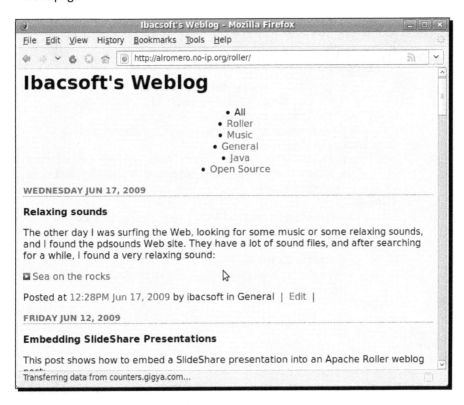

14. Click on the **Back** button to return to your stylesheet editing page.

What just happened?

In the previous exercise, you edited your stylesheet override file (`mystylesheet.css`) to change your weblog's visual appearance. To understand what these code segments do, let's take a look at the _day template's code:

```
<div class="dayBox">
    <div class="dayTitle">
        $utils.formatDate($day, "EEEE MMM dd, yyyy")
    </div>

    #foreach( $entry in $entries )
    <div class="entryBox">
        <p class="entryTitle">$entry.title</p>
        <p class="entryContent">
```

```
                    #if($model.permalink)
                        $entry.displayContent
                    #else
                        $entry.displayContent($url.entry($entry.anchor))
                    #end
                </p>
                <p class="entryInfo">
                    Posted at
                        <a href="$url.entry($entry.anchor)">$utils.formatDate
                        ($entry.pubTime, "hh:mma MMM dd, yyyy")</a>
                    by $entry.creator.userName in <span
                        class="category">$entry.category.name</span>
                          |  
                    #if ($utils.isUserAuthorizedToAuthor($entry.website))
                        <a href="$url.editEntry($entry.anchor)">Edit</a>
                              |  
                    #end
                    #if($entry.commentsStillAllowed || $entry.commentCount >
                        0)
                    #set($link = "$url.comments($entry.anchor)" )
                        <a href="$link"
                            class="commentsLink">Comments [$entry.commentCount]
                            </a>
                    #end
                </p>
            </div>
            #end
        </div>
```

The lines in bold are the ones directly involved with the CSS code you entered in the exercise:

```
<div class="dayTitle">
        $utils.formatDate($day, "EEEE MMM dd, yyyy")
</div>
```

The `div` element represents a "division" or a section in a web page. The only code inside this division is `$utils.formatDate($day, "EEEE MMM dd, yyyy")`. This is a property from the `$utils` object used to show the date and time of each day containing one or more posts in the weblog, in the format specified by the `"EEEE MMM dd, yyyy"` string.

The `class="dayTitle"` code segment indicates that this division will use the styles defined in the `.dayTitle` class from the stylesheet:

```
div.dayTitle {
    color:brown;
    font-weight:bold;
    font-size:90%;
    text-transform:uppercase;
    border-bottom:1px dotted #666;
}
```

This CSS code indicates that every text element inside this division will be shown in brown color, in bold style, with a smaller size (90%) than the other fonts outside the division, and the text will be converted to uppercase. The last CSS element indicates that there will be a one pixel-wide, dotted grey border at the bottom of each text element (#666 is a hexadecimal color code).

All this stuff means that each day in the weblog will be shown like this:

Now, the next line in the _day template:

```
<p class="entryTitle">$entry.title</p>
```

The `<p>` HTML tag indicates a paragraph inside your web page, and `$entry.title` is the only code inside this paragraph. As we saw before, `$entry.title` shows the title of an entry in your weblog. The `class="entryTitle"` element is related to the `.entryTitle` code block in your stylesheet:

```
.entryTitle {
    font-weight: bold;
}
```

This CSS code indicates that all the text inside the paragraph will be shown in bold. In this case, each entry's title of your weblog will be shown in bold:

The rest of the bold lines in the _day template use an `<a>` element, known as an *anchor* in HTML. This element is used to display links in web pages, and is related to all the a elements in the stylesheet:

```
a {
    text-decoration: none;
}

a:link {
    color: blue;
    font-weight: medium;
```

```
}

a:visited {
  color: purple;
  font-weight: medium;
}

a:hover {
  text-decoration: underline overline;
}
```

These elements define how the links in your weblog will be displayed. The first block of code indicates that the links won't have a text decoration (that is, links won't be underlined, as in most web pages), the color of each link will be blue, the font weight will be medium, and the color of visited links will be purple. The last block of code indicates that, if someone positions the mouse cursor over a link, it will be underlined and overlined.

The following screenshot shows what happens when you put your mouse cursor over the date and time hyperlink created with the `<a href="$url.entry($entry.anchor)">$utils.formatDate($entry.pubTime, "hh:mma MMM dd, yyyy")</a>` line in the _day template:

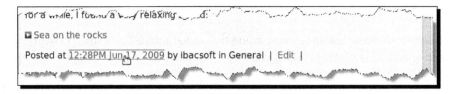

You can see the *underline* and *overline* effects from the `a:hover` CSS element, along with the purple color due to the `a:visited` CSS element.

The `<a href="$url.editEntry($entry.anchor)">Edit</a>  | ` line from the _day template has similar effects:

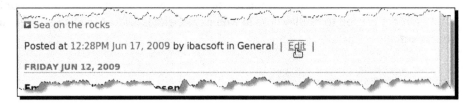

The last block of code we used in the previous exercise is:

```
body {
    font-family:"Lucida Grande", lucida, Geneva, Arial, sans-serif;
    background:#FFFFCC;
}
```

In this case, the body CSS element defines the font used to display your weblog's data. There are several fonts included, to maximize browser compatibility. You can experiment with different fonts and font families to see how your changes affect your weblog's way of displaying data.

The weblog template: Your weblog's main page

Now that we've seen how to edit the `mystylesheet.css` stylesheet override file and how the `_day.vm` template uses CSS styles and Velocity code to display your weblog's data, it's time to see how the `weblog.vm` template works to show your weblog's main page.

Time for action – editing the weblog template

In this exercise, you'll learn how to edit the `weblog.vm` template in your Roller theme, to add a side bar and some other elements:

1. Open your web browser and type `http://yourhostname/roller/ roller-ui/menu.rol` to log into Roller. In my case, the complete URL is `http://alromero.no-ip.org/roller/roller-ui/menu.rol`:

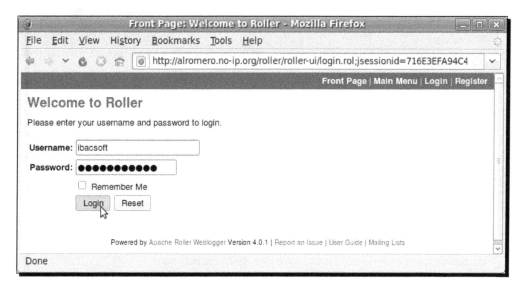

2. Once you're logged in, click on the **Settings** link in your weblog to go to the **Weblog Settings** page:

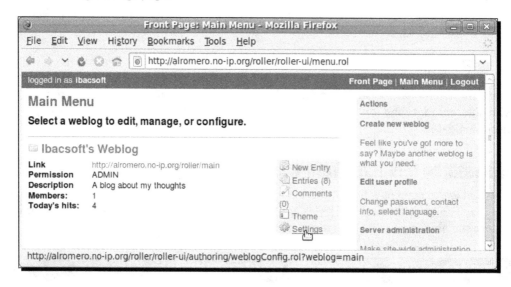

3. Once you're in the **Weblog Settings** page, click on the **Design** tab and then on the **Stylesheet** link to see your custom stylesheet code:

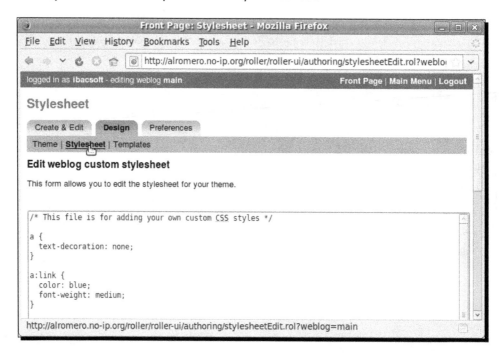

4. Scroll down the stylesheet code window and add the following lines at the end:

```
.rCategory li {
    font-size: 80%;
    display: inline;
    list-style-type: none;
    padding-right: 20px;
}

li.selected {
    font-weight: bold;
}
```

5. Click on the **Save** button and then select the **Front Page** link to see how this code affects your weblog's main page:

6. Now click on your web browser's **Back** button to return to your stylesheet code, and add the following code at the end:

```
.content_wrapper {
    width: 80%;
    float: right;
}

.content {
    padding: 0em 2em 2em 2em;
}

.sidebar_wrapper {
width: 20%;
    float: left;
}
```

7. Click on the **Save** button and then on the **Templates** link to see the list of templates in your theme:

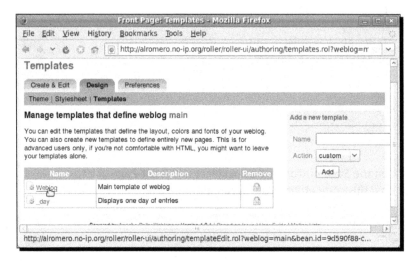

8. Click on the **Weblog** link to edit your `weblog.vm` template code, and add the following lines right before the `</html>` tag:

```
<div class="sidebar_wrapper">
<h2>Search</h2>
    <div class="sidebar">
    #showWeblogSearchForm($model.weblog false)
    </div>
</div>
```

9. Now your `weblog.vm` template code should look like this:

10. Click on the **Save** button and then select the **Front Page** link to see how the code you entered affects your weblog's main page:

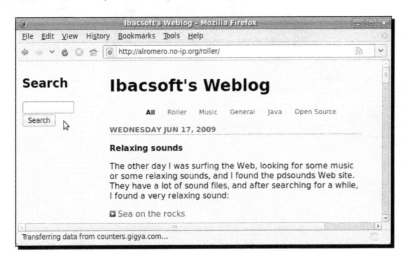

11. Now click on your web browser's **Back** button, and add the following code right before the last `</div>` tag:

```
<h2>Links</h2>
    <div class="sidebar">
    #set($rootFolder = $model.weblog.getBookmarkFolder("/"))
    #showBookmarkLinksList($rootFolder false false)
    </div>

<h2>Navigation</h2>
    <div class="sidebar">
    #showPageMenu($model.weblog)
    #showAuthorMenu(true)
    </div>
```

12. Now your `weblog.vm` template code should look like this:

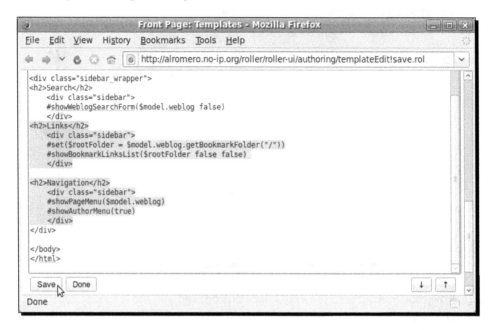

13. Click on the **Save** button, and then on the **Front Page** link to see how the code you entered affects your weblog's main page:

14. Click on your web browser's **Back** button to return to the weblog template editing page, select the **Stylesheet** link to go to your stylesheet code, replace the `width: 80%;` line that's right under `.content_wrapper {` with `width: 79%;` and add the following lines to the `sidebar_wrapper` block of code:

```
font-size: 80%;
border-right: 1px dotted #666;
```

15. The following screenshot shows the line you have to modify, along with the two lines you have to add to the stylesheet file:

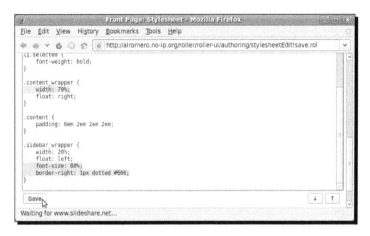

16. Click on the **Save** button and then select the **Front Page** link to see the changes to the stylesheet code reflected in your weblog's main page:

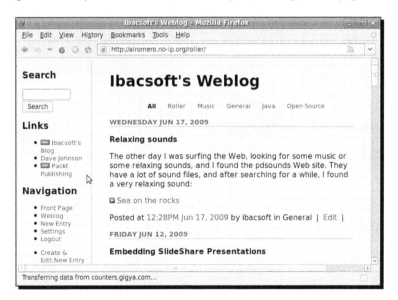

What just happened?

In this exercise, you learned to manipulate some of the CSS styles for your weblog's main page, along with some Velocity properties, methods, and macros used in the `weblog.vm` template of your theme. In step 4, you added two blocks of CSS code to your stylesheet:

```
.rCategory li {
    font-size: 80%;
    display: inline;
    list-style-type: none;
    padding-right: 20px;
}

li.selected {
    font-weight: bold;
}
```

The first block, `.rCategory`, is generated by the `#showWeblogCategoryLinksList` macro, that we used in the following block code, from the `weblog.vm` file:

```
<center>
#set($rootCategory = $model.weblog.getWeblogCategory("nil"))
#showWeblogCategoryLinksList($rootCategory false false)
</center>
```

The `<center>` and `</center>` HTML tags indicate that everything between them must be centered on the page. We already saw how the next two lines work: the first gets a list of categories from your weblog, and the second is a macro that generates the HTML code for displaying that list of categories in your weblog page. Before adding the `.rCategory` and `li.selected` blocks to your stylesheet, the list of categories is displayed as shown in the following screenshot:

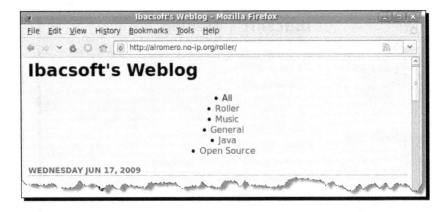

Now let's see what each element inside the `.rCategory` block does:

Element	What it does
`font-size: 80%;`	Reduces the text's font size to an 80% of the original value.
`display: inline;`	The list of categories is displayed inline (no line breaks before or after each category).
`list-style-type: none;`	There's no disc or any other marker shown before each category name.
`padding-right: 20px;`	There's a 20 pixels-wide blank space to the right of each category name.

The second block you added to the stylesheet, `li.selected`, has only one element:

Element	What it does
`font-weight: bold;`	The selected category will show up in bold text. The first time you open your weblog main page, the *All* category name is selected.

After adding the `.rCategory` and `li.selected` blocks to your stylesheet, the list of categories is displayed as shown in the following screenshot:

In step 6, the `.content_wrapper` block of CSS code you added to your stylesheet affects everything between the `<div class="content_wrapper">` element in the `weblog.vm` file, and its corresponding closing tag (`/div`). This block of code sets the width of your weblog's content to occupy only 80% of the whole page (`width: 80%;`) and makes it float to the right (`float: right;`).

The second block of CSS code, `.content`, affects everything between the `<div class="content">` element in the `weblog.vm` file and its corresponding closing tag (`/div`). It creates a blank space between the top, bottom, right, and left borders (`padding: 0em 2em 2em 2em;`). `1em` indicates a space equal to the current font (that is, if the current font size is `12pt`, `1em` = `12pt`, and `2em` = `24pt`. `1pt` is the same as 1/72 inch, for reference purposes).

The third block of CSS code, `.sidebar_wrapper`, affects everything between the `<div class="sidebar_wrapper">` element in `weblog.vm` and its corresponding closing tag (`</div>`). It sets the width of your weblog's sidebar to occupy only 20% of the whole page (`width: 20%;`), and makes it float to the left (`float: left;`).

Now, let's examine the `weblog.vm` template. The block of code you added in step 8 creates a **Search** field in your weblog's left sidebar via the `#showWeblogSearchForm($model.weblog false)` macro, as shown in the screenshot from step 10. The blocks of code that you added in step 11 adds the **Links** and **Navigation** sections to your weblog's left sidebar.

The **Links** section contains a list of bookmarks (blogroll) created with the `#showBookmarkLinksList($rootFolder false false)` macro. The **Navigation** section shows a page navigation menu created with `#showPageMenu($model.weblog)`, which shows a list of all the pages in your weblog, and an authoring menu created with the `#showAuthorMenu(true)` macro, which shows links for editing and configuring your weblog if you're allowed to author it.

In step 14, you modified your `content_wrapper` section `width`, from `80%` to `79%`, in order to allow a one pixel-wide grey border on the `sidebar_wrapper` section (`border-right: 1px dotted #666;`), and reduced this section's font size to 80% (`font-size: 80%;`), in order to make the sidebar elements look less cluttered.

You can see the results of all these code modifications in step 16's screenshot.

Have a go hero – finishing your Roller theme

OK, you have seen some of the most widely used macros, properties, and methods for a Roller theme. I showed you how to use Roller's admin interface to edit your templates and your stylesheet override file, to avoid having to restart Tomcat every time you copy new files to your `mytheme` directory inside Roller's `themes` directory.

Now you need to save all the changes you've made to the stylesheet override file, `mystylesheet.css`, and to the `weblog.vm` file, to a safe location. In this case, you can copy those files back to the `mytheme` directory you extracted from the `chapter07` support file. Use Roller's Stylesheet link to go to your stylesheet, copy all the code in it, and paste it in the `mystylesheet.css` file inside `Desktop/chapter07/mytheme`. Then do the same with the `weblog.vm` file that you modified inside Roller. This is the quickest way to make changes to a theme you're creating and then, when you're satisfied with it, copy all the code from the files inside Roller into a directory on the outside. Then you can compress your theme's directory and even share it with other Roller users!

Oh, and I almost forgot! There are zillions of Roller macros, properties, and methods you can use in your own themes that we didn't cover because of space restrictions. However, you can check out the Roller Template Guide and learn about all of the macros, objects, properties, and methods available. Experimenting is the key to learning, don't forget!

The last thing I want to talk about is the `theme.xml` file. This file must include the override stylesheet, the templates, and resources used in your Roller theme. It uses an XML language syntax, very similar to the HTML code we saw before. Take a look at the `theme.xml` file inside `mytheme` and you'll find the `mystylesheet.css`, `weblog.vm`, and `_day.vm` files we used in this chapter's exercises:

```xml
<?xml version="1.0" encoding="UTF-8"?>
<weblogtheme>
  <id>mytheme</id>
  <name>My First Roller Theme</name>
  <author>Alfonso Romero</author>
  <preview-image path="preview.jpg" />

  <stylesheet>
    <name>MyStylesheet</name>
    <description>Stylesheet Override File</description>
    <link>mystylesheet.css</link>
    <templateLanguage>velocity</templateLanguage>
    <contentsFile>mystylesheet.css</contentsFile>
  </stylesheet>

  <template action="weblog">
    <name>Weblog</name>
    <description>Main template of weblog</description>
    <link>weblog</link>
    <navbar>false</navbar>
    <hidden>true</hidden>
    <templateLanguage>velocity</templateLanguage>
    <contentType>text/html</contentType>
    <contentsFile>weblog.vm</contentsFile>
  </template>

  <template action="custom">
    <name>_day</name>
    <description>Displays one day of entries</description>
    <link>_day</link>
    <navbar>false</navbar>
    <hidden>true</hidden>
    <templateLanguage>velocity</templateLanguage>
    <contentType>text/html</contentType>
    <contentsFile>_day.vm</contentsFile>
  </template>

</weblogtheme>
```

The `<weblogtheme>` XML tag represents the whole weblog theme. Inside this tag, you must include several elements:

- A unique ID for your theme (`id`), that by convention must be the same as your theme's name
- The `name` of your theme
- The name of the `author`
- The `path` of the `preview-image`
- Information about the `stylesheet` override file
- Information about the `weblog` template
- Information about the `_day` template
- Information about any other templates used in your weblog
- Information about resources, such as images

You should take a snapshot of your working theme when you're satisfied with it, so go ahead, and include it in your `mytheme` directory. The snapshot file must be named `preview.jpg`, according to the `theme.xml` file.

If you're using Windows, you can press *Alt + Prt Scr* to capture the active window, then open MS Paint, and press *Ctrl + V* to paste the screenshot on the Paint window, then save the image. If you want to capture the whole screen, press *Prt Scr* without *Alt*.

If you're using Ubuntu Linux, you can also use *Alt + Prt Scr* (or just *Prt Scr* to capture the whole screen) and then paste the screenshot in your favorite paint program, such as the GIMP Image Editor.

In the `chapter07` support file, I also included a directory called `mytheme_final`, where you'll find the `weblog.vm` and `_day.vm` files we saw in the previous exercises, along with the complete `mystylesheet.css` file and a `preview.jpg` image file. You can copy this theme to your Roller installation in the same way you did with the `mytheme` directory, to see the differences between them.

It would be a good idea to include the `mytemplate.vm` file that you created during the first exercises of this chapter in `mytheme`. Just remember to edit the `theme.xml` file and create a `mytemplate.vm` file inside your `mytheme` directory. Don't forget to restart Roller every time you make changes to the `themes` directory!

Now you can take a good look at all the other themes installed in your Roller weblog. Study them carefully, compare them to the `mytheme` templates and CSS stylesheet, and experiment all you can with Roller themes! If you have any questions, don't hesitate to send me an e-mail!

Pop quiz – Roller themes

1. The PR department in your company wants to know how they can include an "About us" page in Roller, so every visitor can see it. What can you do about it?

    a. Create a custom template named `About_us.vm`, copy it to your current Roller theme's directory, include it in the `theme.xml` file, and restart Tomcat so that Roller can recognize the new template.

    b. Use Google to search for a web designer in your area.

    c. Create a separate HTML page and include a hyperlink to it in one of your posts.

2. If you want to change the font used in your weblog posts, you:

    a. Need to change your Roller theme.

    b. Need to edit your CSS stylesheet.

    c. Need to restart Tomcat and MySQL.

3. Where can you add a bookmarks list in your Roller weblog?

    a. In one of your posts.

    b. In the `theme.xml` file of your current theme.

    c. In the `weblog.vm` file of your current theme.

Summary

In this chapter, you learned how to create and edit your first template in Roller, along with some basics about the Velocity Template Language and how to create your first Roller theme from scratch.

Specifically, we covered:

- What is a template, and how to create/edit a custom template with Roller's admin interface

- An introduction to the Velocity Template Language, Roller's model and data objects, and how to use these objects' properties, methods, and macros in a custom template to show data from your weblog

- How to create your first Roller theme from scratch!

- The basics about the `theme.xml`, `weblog.vm`, `_day.vm`, and stylesheet override files used inside a Roller theme

This chapter gave you the basic knowledge to start experimenting with your Roller themes and learn all you can about the Velocity template language and Roller's model and data objects, properties, methods, and macros used to display data from your weblog.

In the next chapter, you'll learn about comments and how they are a vital part of your blog, establishing a solid communication line with your visitors.

8
Comments and Trackbacks

You can have the best graphics, flash animations, and all the latest gadgets installed on your blog, but guess what; If you don't write interesting stuff then readers won't be attracted to your website and they won't leave any comments. That's the real power of having a weblog—you can interact with your visitors via the comments they leave in your posts! You can also build strong commercial and personal relationships this way.

In this chapter, we shall learn:

- ◆ How to manage comments in your weblog
- ◆ How to moderate comments through Apache Roller's administrator interface
- ◆ About spam and all the counter-measures available in Apache Roller
- ◆ About trackbacks and how to use them to interact with other bloggers

 Before getting your hands dirty with this chapter's exercises, make sure to change your Roller weblog's theme to *Basic*, because this is the one I'll use to explain the comments and trackbacks features.

Managing comments

In this section, I'm going to show you how to manage comments inside Roller's administrator interface. The first thing to do is check if your weblog has comments enabled.

Enabling comments in your Roller weblog

When you create a weblog in Roller, comments are disabled, by default. The following exercise will show you how to enable comments in your weblog, via Roller's administrator interface.

Time for action – enabling comments

It's very easy to enable comments in Roller, as you'll see in the next exercise.

1. Open your web browser, log into Roller and click on the **Preferences** tab to go to the **Weblog Settings** page:

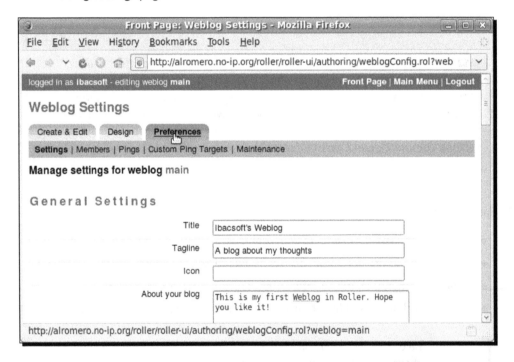

2. Scroll down until you locate the **Comments** section, and make sure the **Allow Comments for your weblog** checkbox is checked:

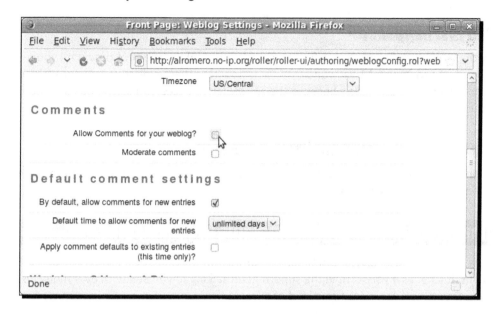

3. Scroll down the page until you find the **Update Weblog Settings** button and click on it. Roller will show the **Saved changes to weblog settings** message inside a green box to confirm your changes. Now click on the **Front Page** link to see your weblog's front page:

4. The **Comments[0]** link indicates that the comments feature is enabled in your weblog, and that there aren't any comments in that particular post.

What just happened?

Now that you have the comments feature enabled, it's only a matter of time until your visitors start raving about how wonderful life is now that they've discovered your weblog. Be sure to respond to all of them, because the key to have a successful blog is being responsive to your readers.

How to leave a comment in your weblog

To manage comments in your Roller weblog, you need to have at least one of them, right? The next exercise will show you how to leave a comment.

Time for action – leaving comments in your weblog

I know it feels weird to leave comments in your own weblog, but don't worry, no one will find out. It's not as if you were in the supermarket talking to yourself with everybody else staring at you, as if you were some kind of a freak!

1. Open your web browser, type your dynamic hostname to visit your Roller weblog's main page (in my case, it's `http://alromero.no-ip.org`) without logging in, and click on the **Comments[0]** link:

2. Roller will take you to the **POST A COMMENT** section for that specific entry. Fill in all the required fields as shown in the following screenshot, just be sure to use your own name and e-mail address instead of mine:

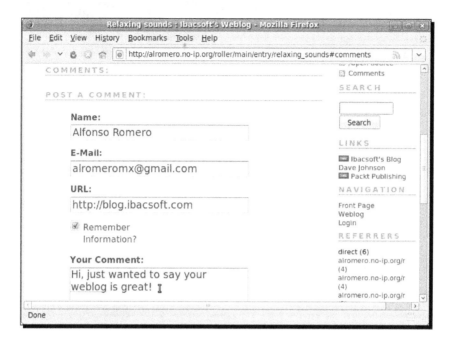

3. Scroll down to the end of the page, answer the math question provided for authentication and click on **Post** to leave your comment:

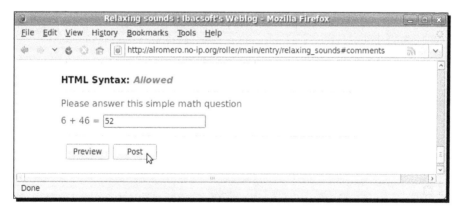

4. Roller will take you back to the entry, showing your comment followed by the **Your comment has been accepted** message:

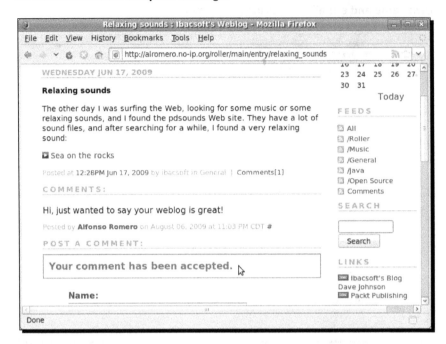

5. Now scroll up to the beginning of the page, and click on the previous post link:

6. Scroll down the page until you locate the **POST A COMMENT** section for that entry. The **Name**, **E-Mail**, and **URL** fields will be already filled in with your personal information:

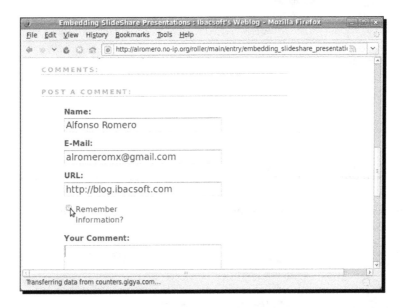

7. Uncheck the **Remember Information?** checkbox to disable it and type your second comment in the **Your Comment** field as shown in the following screenshot:

8. Scroll down to the end of the page, answer the math question and click on **Post** in order to post your comment:

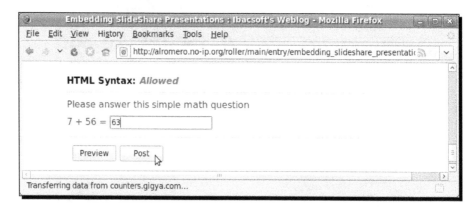

9. Roller will show the **Your comment has been accepted** message, along with the comment you posted:

10. Use the same procedure to post a third comment in the same entry, but this time type **This is my third comment in my weblog** in the **Your Comment** field and use your same personal information in the **Name**, **E-mail**, and **URL** fields.

What just happened?

You can see how easy it will be for your visitors to leave comments, and if they enable the **Remember Information?** checkbox (Roller enables it by default), they won't have to write their name, e-mail, and website information each time they post a comment on your site. Every time they return to your weblog, Roller will remember their personal information, provided they're using the same machine (and have cookies enabled). Now let's see how to manage your weblog's comments.

Deleting unwanted comments in your weblog

Let's practice with Roller's **comment management tool** and the comments you posted in the previous exercise. The following exercises will show you how to delete, moderate, and mark comments as spam. In Roller, it's very easy to delete unwanted comments from your weblog.

Time for action – deleting a comment in your weblog

OK, it's time for you to learn how to use the **Comment Management** page. In this case, we'll see how to delete an unwanted comment from your weblog.

1. Log into your Roller weblog, and click on the **Comments** link from the **New Entry** page:

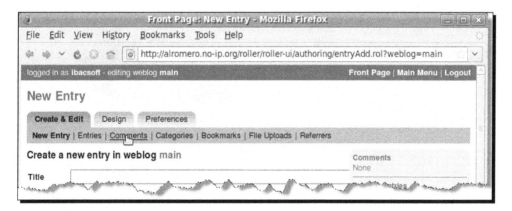

2. Roller will take you to the **Comment Management** page, where you'll see a list of all the comments in your weblog:

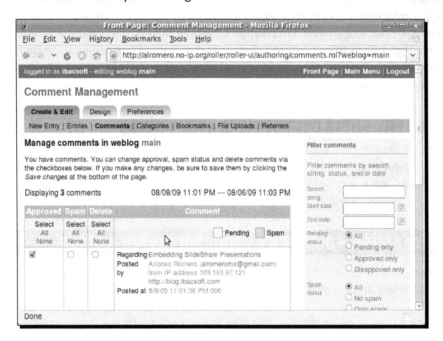

3. Locate the third comment you made (it should be the first one in the list, as it's in a chronological order) and select the **Delete** checkbox to mark it for deletion:

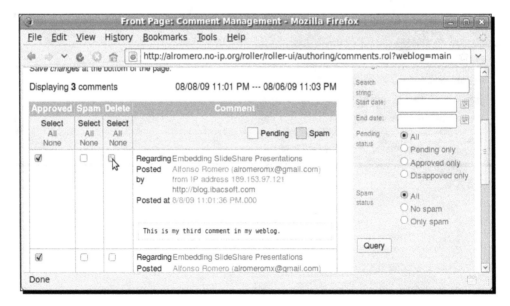

4. Scroll down the page until you locate the **Save changes** button and click on it to delete the marked message. Roller will take you back to the **Manage Comments** page, but this time it will show the **Successfully updated comments** message, along with the updated comments list:

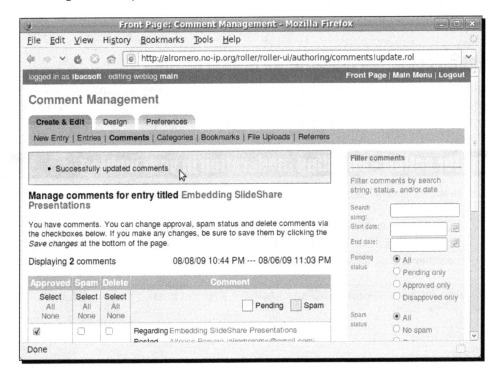

What just happened?

See how easy it is to get rid of unwanted comments. Just go to the **Comment Management** page, select the **Delete** checkbox on any comment that you want to delete, click on the **Save changes** button, and your problem is solved! Over time, you'll end up with a lot of unwanted comments from spammers, hackers, or other malicious people and deleting comments is one good way of defending yourself against them. In the next section, we'll see another way to avoid unwanted comments from showing up in your weblog.

Moderating comments

In an ideal world, people would post comments in your weblog and you wouldn't have to worry about someone leaving obscene or insulting messages, spam, or any other bad stuff like that. Unfortunately, you never know when someone will try to invade your precious blogging space, so it's better to be prepared for it.

Enabling comment moderation in your weblog

Comment moderation is one of the most effective ways of dealing with spammers and obscene comments. The following exercise will show you how to enable the moderation feature to avoid unwanted comments in your weblog.

Time for action – enabling moderation in your weblog

Are you ready for action? Let's learn to defend your weblog space!

1. Log into your Roller weblog, click on the **Preferences** tab to go to your **Weblog Settings** page, scroll down to the **Comments** section and click on the **Moderate comments** checkbox to enable it:

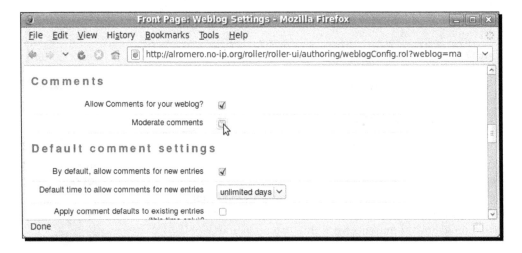

2. Scroll down the page until you locate the **Update Weblog Settings** button and click on it. Now go to your weblog's front page, click on the **Comments[1]** link of the first entry in your weblog, and post a new comment as shown in the following screenshot:

3. Once you answer the math question and click on the **Post** button, Roller will show you the following message, instead of showing your comment:

What just happened?

Once you enable moderation in your weblog, all comments will be marked as pending, until you log in and approve or delete them, as you saw in the previous exercise. The only drawback to moderation is that visitors to your site will see the same message when they leave a comment and nobody will see the comment until you approve it. However, if you keep checking your weblog regularly, there won't be any problems.

Approving comments

Once you have comment moderation enabled, all comments will be marked as pending, until you log into your Roller weblog and decide what to do with them.

Time for action – how to approve and disapprove comments

The following exercise will show you how easy it is to approve and disapprove comments in Roller, thanks to its friendly interface:

1. If you're still logged into Roller, click on the **Create & Edit: Comments** link on the right side of your weblog's main page, under the **NAVIGATION** section as shown in the next screenshot:

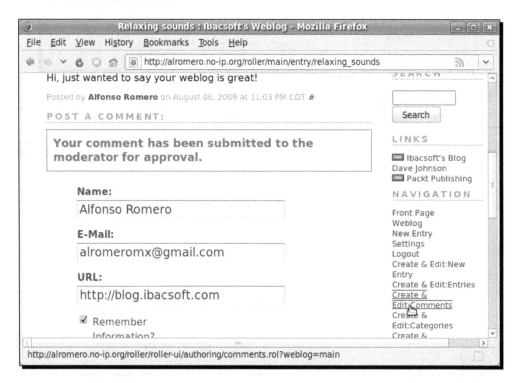

2. The **Comment Management** page will appear. The first comment in the list will be marked as pending (the **Comment** field will be shaded with the same color as the **Pending** box):

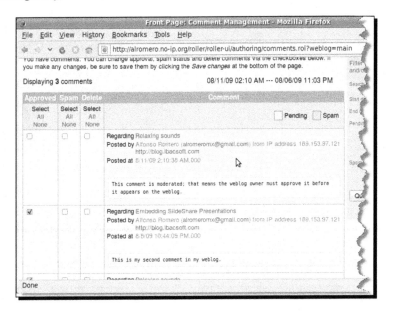

3. Now click on the **Approved** checkbox for that comment, then scroll down the page, and click on the **Save changes** button. Roller will show the **Successfully updated comments** message, and the comment will appear without any shading:

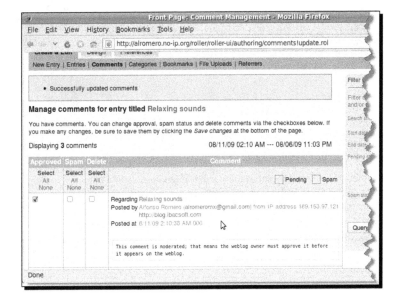

4. To verify that your comment is approved and appears on your weblog, click on the **Relaxing sounds** link in the **Comment** field:

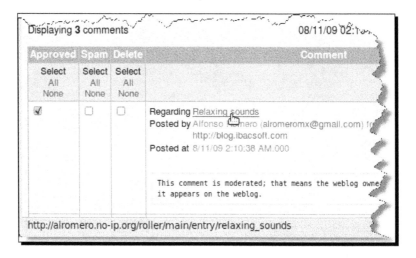

5. The comment you've just approved will show up below the first comment:

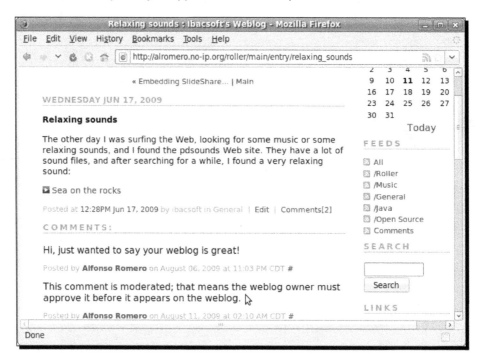

6. Now scroll up the page and click on **Open Source** to see all the entries in this category:

7. Scroll down the first post and click on the **Comments[0]** link to leave a comment. Use the following screenshot as a guide:

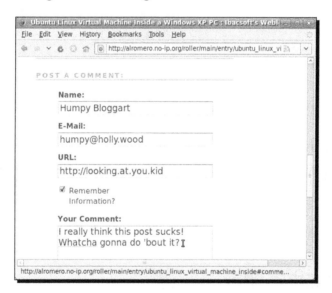

8. Scroll down the page, answer the math question and then click on **Post** to leave your comment on the weblog. Roller will respond with the **Your comment has been submitted to the moderator for approval message**, because moderation is enabled.

9. Go to Roller's **Comment Management** page to see the list of comments (the one you posted before will show up as pending):

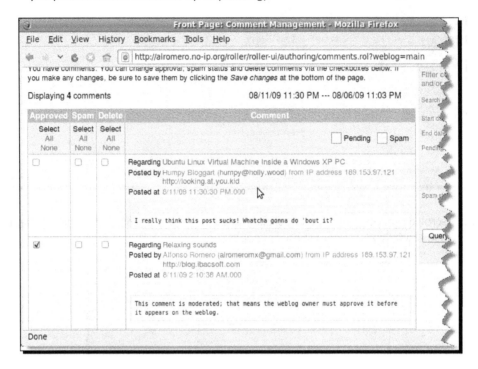

What just happened?

The previous exercise just demonstrated how useful Roller's comment management feature is. You approved the first comment after reading it, and it showed up in your weblog without any problems. However, the second comment was insulting; thanks to Roller's moderation feature, it didn't show up in your weblog, and no one saw it. Now you can decide what to do with it delete it or mark it: as spam, as we'll see in the next section.

Avoiding spam in your weblog

As I already said, one of the biggest problems your weblog can have is spam, but fortunately Roller has several anti-spam features included, as we'll see in the following subsections.

Spam is any unwanted form of communication. Unwanted e-mail was the most common form of spam until now. If you have comments enabled in your blog, any unwanted or aggressive comment from other people can be considered as spam.

Marking comments as spam

The following exercise will show you how to use Roller's **Comment Management** page to mark unwanted comments as spam.

Time for action – marking comments as spam

Spam is bad, but only if you let it infiltrate your weblog's entries. In the following exercise, you'll learn to use a good anti-spam measure to avoid recurring spammers:

1. Log into Roller and go to the **Comment Management** page. The first comment will be marked as pending. Click on that comment's **Spam** checkbox to mark it as spam:

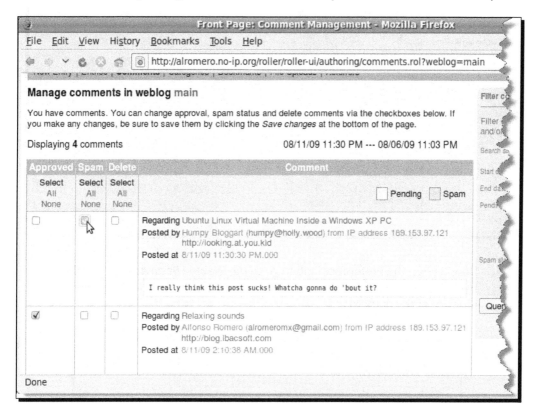

2. Scroll down the page until you locate the **Save changes** button and click on it. Roller will show that comment as spam (the **Comment** field will be shaded with the same color as the **Spam** box):

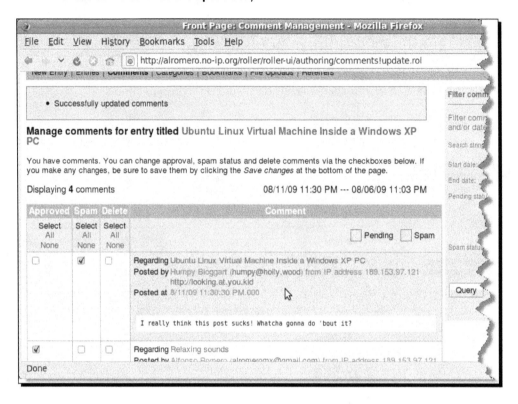

3. Now click on the **Preferences** tab to go to the **Weblog Settings** page, scroll down the page until you locate the **Spam Prevention** section, and then type **Humpy Bloggart** in the blacklist:

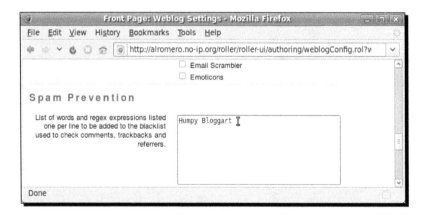

4. Scroll down the page and click on the **Update Weblog Settings** button. Roller will show you the following success message:

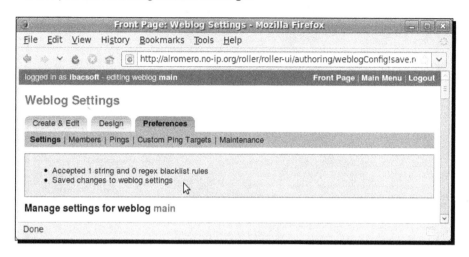

5. Go to your weblog's front page, scroll down the page until you locate the **VirtualBox Video from YouTube** entry, click on the **Comments[0]** link, and type the following information:

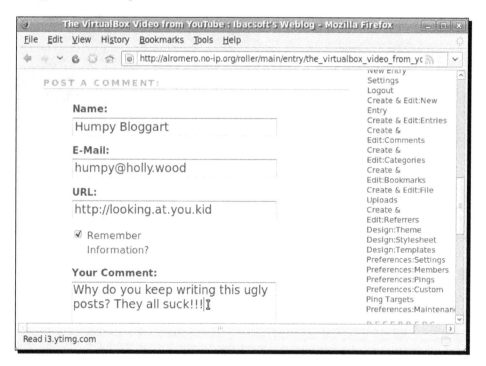

6. Scroll down the page, answer the math question, and click on **Post** to leave your comment. Roller will respond with the following message:

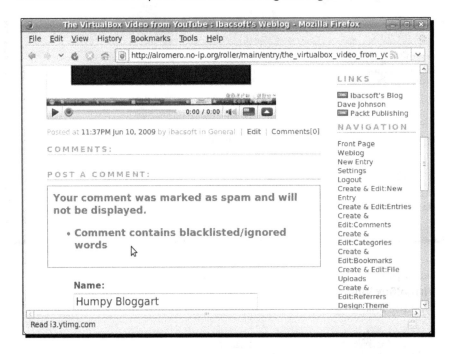

What just happened?

Roller's anti-spam tools are very useful, as you saw in the previous exercise. You can enable moderation in your weblog, review each comment thoroughly as you receive it, and then decide if you want to approve it, delete it, or mark it as spam.

When you mark a comment as spam, you can enter certain keywords in a **blacklist**. This blacklist already contains several thousand words and regular expressions that Roller uses to check incoming comments, trackbacks, and referrers for spam. However, you can add any word you wish, including names and e-mail addresses, as you did in the previous exercise with Humpy Bloggart.

This way, anytime Humpy tries to write an insulting comment in your weblog, Roller will mark it as spam, and then you'll have the chance to review it before deciding to take some further action, such as reporting Humpy to the corresponding authorities.

Have a go hero – using Roller's blacklist effectively

Roller's blacklist includes several thousand words and regular expressions that help in deciding if a comment, link, or trackback has bad or offensive content. However, you can also use it to avoid comments from certain people, block specific IP addresses or domain names, and so on. Actually, there are three blacklists:

◆ **Level 1**: This is a built-in blacklist included in Roller. Only someone with access to Roller's installation directory can change this list.

◆ **Level 2**: This is a site-wide blacklist that only an administrator with global rights can edit. All weblogs created within Roller can use this list.

◆ **Level 3**: Each weblog can use a specific blacklist that can be edited through the weblog settings page.

All incoming comments are checked against these three blacklists. You can try experimenting with levels 2 and 3, by using different names, IP addresses, and hostnames. In the previous exercise (refer step 3), I showed you how to edit the level 3 blacklist through the **Weblog Settings** page of your weblog.

To edit the level 2 list, you need to log into Roller with your administrator account, click on the **Server Administration** link to go to the **Roller Configuration** page, and scroll down to the **Spam Prevention** section.

Using Roller's comment validators

In the previous subsection, we saw how to use the blacklist—one of Roller's comment validation methods. In this subsection, we'll talk about other comment validators included in Roller.

Time for action – Roller's comment validators

There are two comment validators besides the blacklist—the excess links validator and the excess size validator, as we'll see in the following exercise:

1. Go to your weblog's front page, scroll down the page until you locate the **VirtualBox Video from YouTube** entry, and click on the **Comments[0]** link. Use the same values for **Name**, **E-mail**, and **URL** and type the following text in the **Comment** field:

```
Click <a href="http://cell.world">here</a>,
<a href="http://the.best.phones">here</a>,
<a href="http://best.offers">here</a>,
<a href="http://hi.tech.phones">here</a>or
<a href="http://your.phone.is.waiting">here</a>
 to see the best cell phones in the market...
```

2. The following screenshot shows what your comment should look like before posting it to the weblog:

3. Scroll down the page and this time click on the **Preview** button, to see how your comment will look like before posting it:

4. Scroll further down and answer the math question, then click on the **Post** button. Roller will respond with the message as shown in the next screenshot:

5. Now scroll down the page and type the following text in the **Comment** field:

```
I will not write a comment with more than 1000 characters... I
will not write a comment with more than 1000 characters... I will
not write a comment with more than 1000 characters... I will not
write a comment with more than 1000 characters... I will not write
a comment with more than 1000 characters... I will not write a
comment with more than 1000 characters... I will not write a
comment with more than 1000 characters... I will not write a
comment with more than 1000 characters... I will not write a
comment with more than 1000 characters... I will not write a
comment with more than 1000 characters... I will not write a
comment with more than 1000 characters... I will not write a
comment with more than 1000 characters... I will not write a
comment with more than 1000 characters... I will not write a
comment with more than 1000 characters... I will not write a
comment with more than 1000 characters... I will not write a
comment with more than 1000 characters... I will not write a
comment with more than 1000 characters... I will not write a
comment with more than 1000 characters...
```

6. The following screenshot shows what your comment should look like before posting it to the weblog:

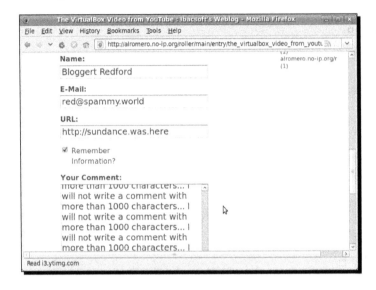

7. Scroll down the page, answer the math question, and click on the **Post** button. Roller will respond with the following message:

What just happened?

The first validator you used in the previous exercise is the **excess links validator**—it makes sure that no one posts a comment with more than three links in your weblog. Spam robots tend to infiltrate the weblogs and try to post comments with a lot of publicity links, but don't worry because this little validator will take care of them for you!

The second validator you used is the **excess size validator**—it makes sure that no one can post a comment with more than 1000 characters. Hey! With "those kinds" of comments, they'd better download Roller and create their own weblog!

 Remember, you can use Roller's level 2 and level 3 blacklists to block links, referrers, and comments on your blog. They will be marked as spam and won't show up.

Trackbacks

Now, it's time to see the real power invested in comments—**trackbacks**. These are basically comments that other bloggers send to your weblog, or vice versa. When you find an interesting post in some other weblog, and that post relates to something you wrote or plan to write in your own weblog, you can write a post about it and send a trackback to that other weblog in the form of a comment. Then, the other weblog's owner will see your trackback and he/she will be aware that you're writing about the same subject! That's how blogs can help an entire community to contribute new ideas and build strong relationships between their members.

Enabling comment notification via e-mail

Before starting to send trackbacks, let me show you how to enable comment notification via e-mail in Roller. This way, you'll be aware of every comment sent to your weblog and take appropriate action as soon as possible.

Time for action – enabling e-mail comment notification in Roller

In the following exercise, you'll see how to enable or disable Roller's comment notification via e-mail. To do that, there's a global setting that affects the entire blog server, and a specific setting for each weblog in Roller:

1. Log into Roller and click on the **Main Menu** link on Roller's menu bar:

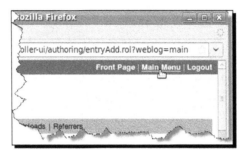

2. On the **Main Menu** page, click on the **Server administration** link, on the lower-right part of the screen:

3. Scroll down the **Roller Configuration** page until you locate the **Comment and Trackback Settings** section, and select the **Email notification of comments?**, **Enable verification of trackback links?**, and **Enable referrer linkback extraction?** checkboxes to enable them, as shown in the following screenshot:

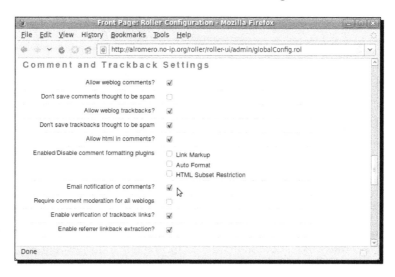

4. Scroll down to the end of the page and click on the **Save** button to apply the changes you made to the **Comment and Trackback Settings** section. Click on the **Main Menu** link again, and then click on your weblog's **Settings** link:

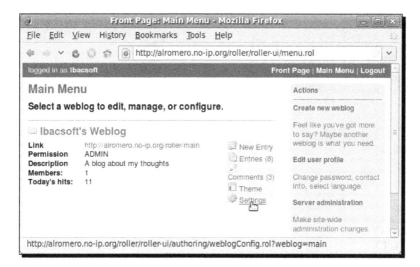

5. Scroll down the **Weblog Settings** page until you locate the **Comments** section and select the **Email notification of comments?** checkbox option to enable it:

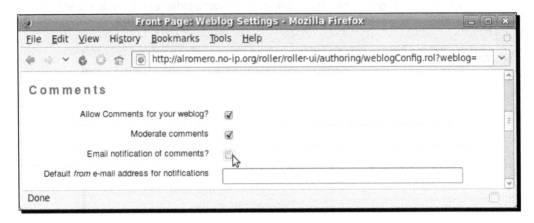

6. Scroll down the page until you locate the **Update Weblog Settings** button and click on it. Now go to your weblog's front page, scroll down to the end of the page, and click on the **Comments[0]** link from the first post in your weblog:

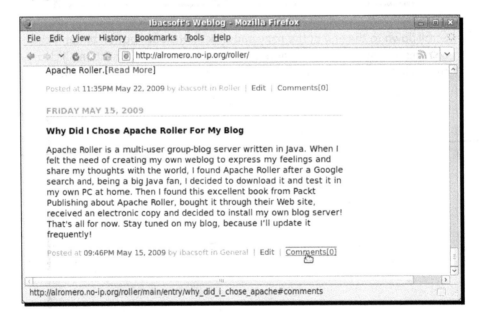

7. Use the following screenshot as a guide to write your comment:

8. Scroll down the page, answer the math question, and click on the **Post** button to post your comment. Now check your e-mail account (the one you used during Roller's installation process) to see if you received an e-mail notification regarding the new comment in your weblog:

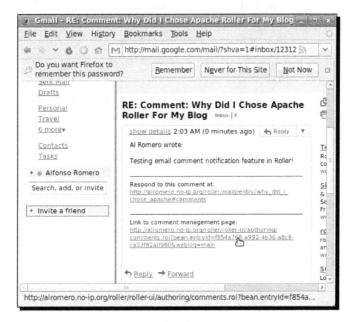

9. Click on the **Link to comment management page** (shown in previous screenshot) you received in the e-mail notification. This link takes you to your Roller weblog's administrator interface as shown in the following screenshot:

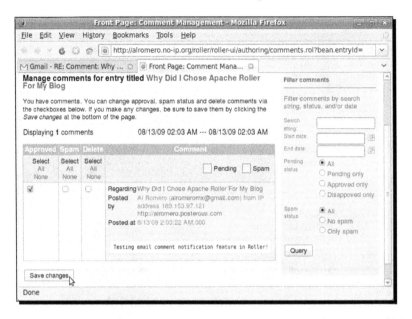

10. From this page you can approve, delete, or mark the comment you received as spam. In this case, select the **Approved** checkbox and click on **Save changes** to approve the comment and display it in your entry:

What just happened?

Roller's e-mail comment notification lets you stay informed of any comments posted by visitors on your weblog. Each e-mail you receive includes, the text of the comment along with a link to the entry in which the comment was posted and another link to the comment management page, as you saw in step 8 of the previous exercise.

To enable comment notification via e-mail, you need to modify two settings—Roller's global e-mail notification option in the **Comments and Trackbacks** section of the **Roller Configuration** page, and weblog's e-mail notification option in the **Comments** section of the **Weblog Settings** page, as we saw in steps 3 and 5, respectively.

In step 3, you enabled two additional options—**Enable verification of trackback links** and **Enable referrer linkback extraction**. I definitely recommend you that enable these options, because they allow Roller to validate trackbacks and avoid spam, making sure that trackbacks contain a link to your weblog, and not to another website.

Sending a trackback from your weblog

Suppose you're reading an interesting post about your favorite music in Harry's blog, and you decide to write a post in your Roller weblog to express your opinion about Harry's post. If you just go and write a post in your own weblog, Harry won't even notice it. However, if you create a post and then send a trackback to Harry's blog, he'll be aware of you and your weblog. You can use this same procedure whenever you want someone to know that you share the same interests as his/hers!

The `http://ibacsoft.no-ip.org` URL that I'm going to use in the following exercise is not a real blog; I created it just to show you how to send trackbacks to other Roller blogs, but you'll need to replace that URL with a real working one, such as `http://www.rollerweblogger.org` or `http://blog.ibacsoft.com`, or any other blog with the trackbacks feature.

Time for action – sending trackbacks

The following exercise will show you how to send a trackback from your Roller weblog to another Roller blog:

1. Log into Roller and go to the **New Entry** page to write a new post. Type **Testing trackbacks in Roller** in the **Title** field and **I'm using this post to test the trackbacks feature in Roller!** in the **Content** field, as shown in the following screenshot:

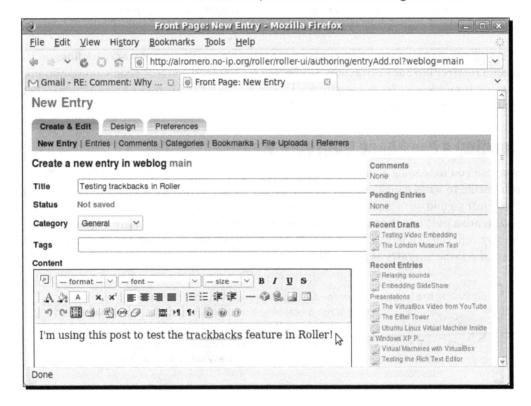

2. Scroll down the page and click on the **Post to Weblog** button to post the new entry in your weblog. Open a new tab in your web browser and go to the blog where you want to leave the trackback (in this exercise, I'll use `http://ibacsoft.no-ip.org/roller` for demonstration purposes), as shown in the following screenshot:

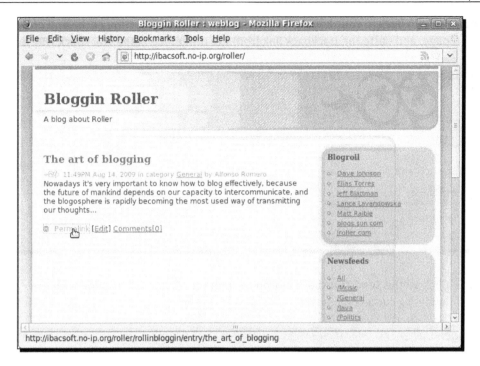

3. Right-click on the **Permalink** (or on the title, **The art of blogging**) and select the **Copy Link Location** option from the pop-up menu, as shown in the following screenshot:

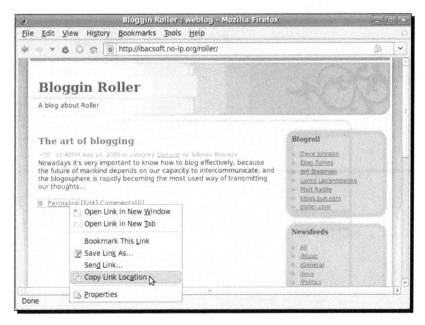

4. Now go back to your Roller entry, locate the **Trackback** section at the end of the page, and paste the trackback link from the other blog in the **Trackback URL** field:

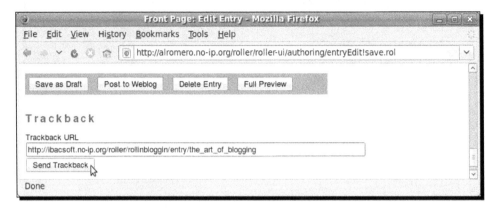

5. Click on the **Send Trackback** button to continue. Roller will respond with the following success message:

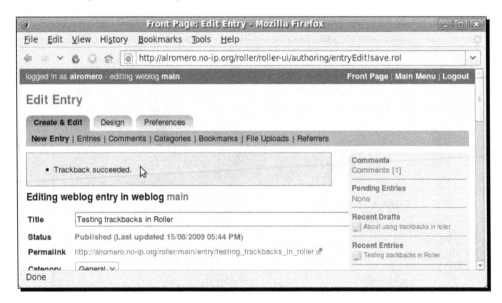

6. Now go to `http://ibacsoft.no-ip.org/roller` and take a look at the
Comments section in the post you sent the trackback to (**The art of blogging**):

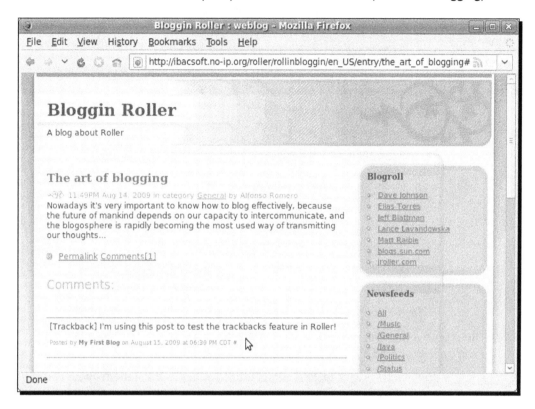

7. Your trackback will show up with the **[Trackback]** word before the text you
wrote, and if someone clicks on the **My First Blog** link, they'll be taken to
your weblog.

What just happened?

Trackbacks are one good way of interacting with other bloggers, as you saw in the previous
exercise. The process is relatively simple—copy the link of the post you want to send the
trackback to, create a new entry in your blog to talk about that other blog's post, and then
send the trackback. This is global interaction at its purest form!

One word of advice though—not all blogs support trackbacks. I know it's sad, but not
everyone has seen the light and uses Roller. Just kidding!

There are a lot of blog servers (such as WordPress, Movable Type, Blogger, Roller, Drupal, and so on), and not everybody uses the same standards. However, you can simulate trackbacks, in case some blog doesn't allow them; simply leave a comment with a link to your own post. When someone sees that comment (including the blog owner) and clicks on that link, they'll be taken to your weblog!

Pop quiz – comments and trackbacks

1. In a weblog, comments can be used to:

    a. Meet new people.

    b. Enhance collaboration between developers in an open source community blog.

    c. Leave spam.

2. What's the secret to a successful blog?

    a. Creating a lot of posts with interesting information.

    b. Buying the most expensive computer to install Roller and host your own weblog.

    c. Paying thousands of dollars for online advertising.

3. Your boss wants to know how you can use trackbacks to promote the new can opener offered by your company. What can you do?

    a. Send a trackback to your competitor's weblog and tell them about your new products.

    b. Send an obscene comment to your competitor's sales department blog.

    c. Search for blogs with can openers product reviews and send trackbacks to those blogs, to make them aware of your new product.

4. The IT department boss wants to know how to deal with spam. What would be the best option?

    a. Enable comment moderation.

    b. Don't accept comments in the company's weblog.

    c. Get a good antivirus.

5. Why is it good to enable comment notification via e-mail in your Roller weblog?

    a. Because Roller answers all comments automatically for you.

    b. Because you can reduce incoming spam in your weblog.

    c. Because you can be aware that someone is leaving a comment in your weblog via your e-mail client.

Have a go hero – blog and social media blending

Now that you have learned all the basics about comments and trackbacks, it's time to start "blending in". Go out and search for blogs related to your interests, start leaving comments and trackbacks, and don't forget to write posts about it too. Remember, the key to a successful blog is creativity!

You can also explore several options related to comments that we didn't cover in this chapter, such as the Akismet.com spam prevention service and the **Akismet validator**. There is also a Roller property called **comment throttling**, that's used to prevent someone from posting too many comments too quickly.

Summary

Whew! I thought this chapter was going to be shorter than the others, but the truth is: comments are an essential part of weblogs, and there are a lot of things to discuss about them.

Specifically, we covered:

- How to use Roller's comment management tools to approve, disapprove, and delete comments
- How to moderate comments in Roller using comment management tools
- How to avoid spam and use all the anti-spam tools available in Roller
- How to use trackbacks to interact with other bloggers

Now that you're an expert on comments (well, at least an expert on *managing* comments in Roller), the next chapter which will be available on our website (`//www.packtpub.com/files/9508-Chapter-9-Advanced-Topics.pdf`) will teach you about some advanced topics such as Atom and RSS feeds, how to manage several weblogs and several users in Roller, how to use aggregators and pings, and so on.

Pop Quiz Answers

Chapter 1

Weblogs and newsfeeds

1	2	3	4	5
c	d	c	c	b

Chapter 2

Installing Roller on Windows

1	2	3	4
b	c	b	c

Chapter 3

Installing Roller on Linux

1	2	3	4
b	c	b	c

Chapter 4

Working with Roller

1	2	3	4	5
b	a	c	c	b

Chapter 5

Images, sounds, and videos

1	2	3
b	a	b

Chapter 6

Editing themes and promoting your weblog

1	2	3
b	b	a

Chapter 7

Roller themes

1	2	3
a	b	c

Chapter 8

Comments and trackbacks

1	2	3	4	5
b	a	c	a	c

Index

K

key values, security.xml file
  changing 124, 125

L

Linux environment
  checking 90
localhost 41, 93

M

macro
  about 276
  showWeblogEntryLinksList macro 279
mod_jk connector, Roller installation on Linux
  installing 128, 129
  installing, steps 128-135
mod_jk connector, Roller installation on Windows
  about 77
  installing 77
  installing, steps 79-84
MySQL database server, Roller installation on Linux
  installing, steps 102-104
MySQL database server, Roller installation on Windows
  about 48
  Dedicated MySQL Server Machine option 56
  Developer Machine option 56
  installing 48-55
  Server Machine option 56
MySQL JDBC driver, Roller installation on Linux
  downloading 111-114
  installing 111-114
MySQL JDBC driver, Roller installation on Windows
  about 63
  installing 63

N

newsfeed
  about 25
  Atom format 25
  Bloglines, using 30-34

  features 24
  readers, using 30
  review questions 34, 35
  RSS format 25
  subscribing 26, 28, 29
  Technorati, diagrammatic representation 24
  using, for blog promotion 25-29
No-IP.com account
  opening 250-255
  update client. installing 255

P

Port 25 19
properties, Roller installation on Linux
  context.xml file 121
  roller-custom.properties file, creating 120
  security.xml file 123
properties, Roller installation on Windows
  Context.xml file 71
  roller-custom.properties file, creating 70
  security.xml file 73

R

required files, Roller installation on Linux
  JAF API 108
  JavaMail API 105
  MySQL JDBC driver 111
required files, Roller installation on Windows
  JAF API 59
  JavaMail API 57
  MySQL JDBC driver 62
Rich Text Editor, weblog
  Create & Edit tab 173
  Toggle HTML Source button 174
  Update Weblog Settings button 173
  using 172-175
Roller. *See* **Apache Roller**
Roller, installation on Linux
  Context configuration file 119
  properties 119
  sudo command 121
Roller, installation on Windows
  Apache web server 38
  Windows environment, checking 38

U

user, Apache Roller
creating 140-144

V

validators 15
Velocity template language
$config object model 280
$model.weblog.name 275
$url.absoluteSite element 275
data objects 279
macro, using 276-278
model 279
video streaming 214

W

web categories, Apache Roller
blog category, defining 153-156
Image field 157
non-empty categories, deleting 157
weblog
basic concepts 8
files, uploading 184
Google Maps, including in posts 208
promoting, on Delicious 250
promoting, on Digg 250
promoting, on StumbleUpon 250
promoting, on Technorati 250
SlideShare presentations, including in posts 218
spam, avoiding 340
use 8
versus CMS 23
YouTube, including in posts 214
weblog, Apache Roller
creating 140-144
weblog, enhancing
basic settings, adjusting 158-161
bookmark, creating 162
bookmark, editing 162
Rich Text Editor, using 172
Summary field 175
weblog, use
experiences, sharing with other 19
other website, commenting on 12-16

professional activities, Microsoft employee
blogs 16-18
professional activities, promoting 16
Technorati website 9
thoughts, expressing 9, 10
weblog handle, Apache Roller
adjusting 144-147
weblog promotion
Digg It button, adding 261-264
dynamic DNS service account, getting 250-253
on Delicious 250
on Digg 250
on StumbleUpon 250
on Technorati 250
web port (80) 255-261
weblog template, Roller theme
.rCategory block 316
<weblogtheme> XML tag 320
editing 309-316
finishing off 318-320
li.selected block 317
weblog theme
additional themes 230
Brushed Metal and Basic themes, difference
between 227-229
default themes 230
difference between, exploring 227
Frontpage theme 229
Roller theme, choosing 224-227
Windows environment
Apache Roller, downloading 57
checking 38
JDK, installing 42

X

Xinha option 173
XML icon 170

Y

YouTube videos
bandwidth 214
exploring 218
including, in posts 214-217
uploading, difference 214

Thank you for buying
Apache Roller 4.0: Beginner's Guide

Packt Open Source Project Royalties

When we sell a book written on an Open Source project, we pay a royalty directly to that project. Therefore by purchasing Apache Roller 4.0: Beginner's Guide, Packt will have given some of the money received to the Apache Software Foundation project.

In the long term, we see ourselves and you—customers and readers of our books—as part of the Open Source ecosystem, providing sustainable revenue for the projects we publish on. Our aim at Packt is to establish publishing royalties as an essential part of the service and support a business model that sustains Open Source.

If you're working with an Open Source project that you would like us to publish on, and subsequently pay royalties to, please get in touch with us.

Writing for Packt

We welcome all inquiries from people who are interested in authoring. Book proposals should be sent to author@packtpub.com. If your book idea is still at an early stage and you would like to discuss it first before writing a formal book proposal, contact us; one of our commissioning editors will get in touch with you.

We're not just looking for published authors; if you have strong technical skills but no writing experience, our experienced editors can help you develop a writing career, or simply get some additional reward for your expertise.

About Packt Publishing

Packt, pronounced 'packed', published its first book "Mastering phpMyAdmin for Effective MySQL Management" in April 2004 and subsequently continued to specialize in publishing highly focused books on specific technologies and solutions.

Our books and publications share the experiences of your fellow IT professionals in adapting and customizing today's systems, applications, and frameworks. Our solution-based books give you the knowledge and power to customize the software and technologies you're using to get the job done. Packt books are more specific and less general than the IT books you have seen in the past. Our unique business model allows us to bring you more focused information, giving you more of what you need to know, and less of what you don't.

Packt is a modern, yet unique publishing company, which focuses on producing quality, cutting-edge books for communities of developers, administrators, and newbies alike. For more information, please visit our website: www.PacktPub.com.

Java EE 5 Development with NetBeans 6

ISBN: 978-1-847195-46-3   Paperback: 400 pages

Develop professional enterprise Java EE applications quickly and easily with this popular IDE

1. Use features of the popular NetBeans IDE to improve Java EE development

2. Careful instructions and screenshots lead you through the options available

3. Covers the major Java EE APIs such as JSF, EJB 3 and JPA, and how to work with them in NetBeans

4. Covers the NetBeans Visual Web designer in detail

Learning Jakarta Struts 1.2: A concise and practical tutorial

ISBN: 1-904811-54-X   Paperback: 220 pages

A step-by-step introduction to building Struts web applications for Java developers

1. Learn to build Struts applications right away

2. Build an ecommerce store step-by-step using Struts

3. Well-structured and logical progression through the essentials

Please check **www.PacktPub.com** for information on our titles

Apache Struts 2 Web Application Development

ISBN: 978-1-847193-39-1   Paperback: 384 pages

A beginner's guide for Java developers

1. Design, develop, test, and deploy your web applications using Struts 2 framework

2. No prior knowledge of JavaScript and CSS is required

3. Apply the best of agile development techniques and TDD techniques

4. Step-by-step instructions and careful explanations with lots of code examples

Blogger: Beyond the Basics

ISBN: 978-1-847193-17-9   Paperback: 356 pages

Customize and promote your blog with original templates, analytics, advertising, and SEO

1. Customize your Blogger templates

2. Grow your blog into a professional, feature-rich site

3. Add social bookmarks to your blog

4. Optimize your blog with SEO

5. Integrate analytics and advertising with your Blogger blog

6. # Concise, clear, and easy to follow; rich with examples

Please check **www.PacktPub.com** for information on our titles

Mahara 1.2 E-Portfolios: Beginner's Guide

ISBN: 978-1-847199-06-5   Paperback: 240 pages

Create and host educational and professional e-portfolios and personalized learning communities

1. Create, customize, and maintain an impressive personal digital portfolio with a simple point-and-click interface

2. Set customized access to share your text files, images, and videos with your family, friends, and others

3. Create online learning communities and social networks through groups, blogs, and forums

4. A step-by-step approach that takes you through examples with ample screenshots and clear explanations

Drupal: Creating Blogs, Forums, Portals, and Community Websites

ISBN: 978-1-904811-80-0   Paperback: 284 pages

How to setup, configure and customise this powerful PHP/MySQL based Open Source CMS

1. Install, configure, administer, maintain and extend Drupal

2. Control access with users, roles and permissions

3. Structure your content using Drupal's powerful CMS features

4. Includes coverage of release 4.7

Please check **www.PacktPub.com** for information on our titles

PUBLISHING

WordPress MU 2.8: Beginner's Guide

ISBN: 978-1-847196-54-5   Paperback: 268 pages

Build your own blog network with unlimited users and blogs, forums, photo galleries, and more!

1. Design, develop, secure, and optimize a blog network with a single installation of WordPress

2. Add unlimited users and blogs, and give different permissions on different blogs

3. Add social networking features to your blogs using BuddyPress

4. Create a bbPress forum for your users to communicate with each other

WordPress 2.7 Complete

ISBN: 978-1-847196-56-9   Paperback: 296 pages

Create your own complete blog or web site from scratch with WordPress

1. Everything you need to set up your own feature-rich WordPress blog or web site

2. Clear and practical explanations of all aspects of WordPress

3. In-depth coverage of installation, themes, syndication, and podcasting

4. Explore WordPress as a fully functioning content management system

5. Concise, clear, and easy to follow; rich with examples

Please check **www.PacktPub.com** for information on our titles

www.ingramcontent.com/pod-product-compliance
Lightning Source LLC
Chambersburg PA
CBHW062044050326
40690CB00016B/2984